Little Girl in the Wall

Donna Casasanta
and
Debbie Brooks

NEWMAN SPRINGS PUBLISHING
320 Broad Street
Red Bank, NJ 07701

First originally published by Newman Springs Publishing 2019

ISBN 978-1-64531-073-0 (Paperback)
ISBN 978-1-64531-072-3 (Digital)

Printed in the United States of America

Contents

Chapter 1

I was born a bastard in the mountains of West Virginia. How do I know? Because I had been called an unwanted bastard most of my childhood. I remember listening to my aunts talk about my natural mother and father and the events surrounding my birth. Marie didn't want me, and my real father sure as hell didn't want me because they were committing adultery. Earl, her husband at the time, was a womanizer and a drunk and left her in the fall of 1938 to pursue his dream of being a musician. Marie had to take care of herself and what children she did keep. I was told that my natural father was an Italian who worked in the coal mines with seven children of his own.

My Aunt Laurie once told me that while Marie was in labor with me, she told her family, "If you know anyone who wants this little bastard, please let me know, and I'll name it after them." From the time I was born, I was passed from one aunt and uncle to the next until I was eight years old.

When I was three weeks old, Marie visited one of her sisters and asked her to baby sit while she went shopping. Only thing is, she never came back for me. Looking back on it now, the best thing she ever did for me was give me away.

I was passed from one aunt and uncle to the next—never staying more than a few weeks or months at the most. I was often hungry; wearing dirty, ragged clothes; playing outside in the dirt with whatever I could find laying around. At about four years old, I wound up with my Aunt Laurie and Uncle Lewis. Aunt Laurie bore a striking resemblance to Aunt Bea on *The Andy Griffith Show*, and Uncle Lewis was a tall, skinny man. He always wore an old hat, and his teeth were tobacco stained, and his breath always smelled of stale liquor. But the worst thing about him was his temper.

I remember being terrified of Uncle Lewis, especially when he had been drinking. I tried to stay out of his way because whenever he saw me, he smacked me or pushed me out of the way. Whenever he came home drunk, Aunt Laurie tried to hide me from him because whenever his glassy red eyes fell on me, he started screaming and slapping me around, complaining what a useless piece of shit I was, and I was just another mouth to feed. He told Aunt Laurie that he was going to throw me in the river and let me drown, so he wouldn't have to feed me anymore.

One hot summer evening when my uncle came home drunk and was swearing and kicking furniture over, Aunt Laurie took me upstairs and pulled the dresser out from the wall. There was a huge black hole in the wall just big enough for a four-year-old to fit in. She kept whispering, "Be quiet and don't squirm around, so he can't hear you."

"Please don't put me in here, Aunt Laurie! Please!" I begged. Tears were rolling down my face, and I felt my entire body shaking. I was terrified of being put in that hole, and no one would ever find me.

Aunt Laurie started crying also, and she held me tight before she pushed me inside the hole. "I don't want to have to do this, honey, but you know what will happen if he finds you," she warned.

I crouched down and sat with my knees up to my chin and whimpered as she pushed the dresser in front of the hole. She kept whispering, "Shhhh…or he'll hear you."

It was so black that I couldn't see my hand in front of my face, and I heard scratching inside the wall. I was terrified, and I wanted to scream for Aunt Laurie to let me out. Suddenly, I heard crashing downstairs and my uncle hollering, but I couldn't make out what he was saying. Something smashed against the wall, and I heard him stomping up the stairs. I was so petrified that I urinated on myself, and I held my breath and crouched down lower in the wall to try and make myself invisible.

Later, I found out that it was an empty whisky bottle that was thrown against the wall in the stairwell. I stayed in that stinking black hole for what seemed like hours. He must have fallen asleep, given up, or passed out. A few minutes later, everything was quiet. The screeching of the dresser being pushed away from the hole brought some light in, and I saw Aunt Laurie's hand as she held my hand and pulled me out of the hole. I grabbed her around the waist and sobbed against her bulky stomach. She soothed me for a few minutes and took one look at the mess I had made. She shook her head, cleaned me up, and put me to bed. That routine went on for a while.

Sometimes, my mind wanders back to those times when Aunt Laurie hid me in the wall. I was so terrified. I wasn't sure what scared me the most, my uncle finding me or spending hours alone in the dark. In the summer time, it was so hot in that hole that I was soaked in sweat and panting for air. Occasionally, she snuck a glass of ice water up to me or ice wrapped in a hand towel. Once, when she came to get me, she said I was unconscious, and she carried me out to the creek and dunked my whole body in the water to cool me off until I regained consciousness.

I remember begging her, "Please don't put me in that hole!" I was so afraid of the mice or rats or whatever it was I heard scratching around inside those walls. "I can hear things moving around inside there."

"I don't want to have to do this, Donna. But if I don't, you know what he will do to you!" she scolded.

After I was in the hole, and she pushed the dresser back in front of it, I began to cry silently. Sitting there in the dark, I began to wonder what I had done that was so bad to make my real mother and father give me away. I cried and promised myself that when I got married and had children that I would love my kids no matter what and never give them away

One autumn day, Uncle Clyde and Aunt Ester came visiting with my half sister Phyllis whom they were raising. Phyllis was a couple of years younger than me, and Marie had her after she got back with Earl. It was nice playing with another little girl. All I had ever known were brothers or boy cousins. We had fun playing with her dolls and pretending that we were moms and taking care of our children. When Uncle Clyde and Aunt Ester got ready to leave, we were on the front porch playing.

"Come on, Phyllis, It's time to go home," Uncle Clyde said in his booming voice.

Phyllis looked up at him with her huge green eyes and said, "Can Donna come home with us?"

Uncle Clyde shook his head. "No. She lives here."

"Please!" Phyllis begged. She jumped up and grabbed his hand. "Please, let Donna come live with us! She's fun for me to play with."

Uncle Clyde looked down at me and his brown eyes softened. Both of my aunts came out on the porch then, and Aunt Ester asked, "What's going on?"

"Can Donnie come stay with us?" Phyllis asked again.

"I don't know…"

I looked down on the rotten wooden porch. My dark dresses hiding my face, I whispered, "I'll be good." I would have said or done anything to get away from my current circumstances.

When I glanced up, Uncle Clyde was looking at Aunt Ester, and she nodded ever so slightly. Phyllis jumped up and down and yelled, "Yay, yay, yay!" Then she grabbed my hand and pulled me up the stairs saying, "Let's go get your things!"

It didn't take long to stuff what few clothes I had into a brown paper bag. I remembered taking one last look around at that tiny little room that was my bedroom. I told myself then that I was never coming back, and if I ever got off that mountain in West Virginia, it would never see me again.

It was a turning point in my life when I went to live with Uncle Clyde and Aunt Ester. She was very good to me and Uncle Clyde worked in the coal mines. He must have made a decent living because Phyllis and I always had a nice home to live in, nice clothes to wear, and plenty to eat. Uncle Clyde always kept a nice car or truck, and he took us on trips to visit different places around the countryside, and sometimes we went to different states to visit other relatives. I remember staring out the window as we drove out of the mountains and wishing that I never had to come back. I dreamed of the day when I could leave that place forever.

Drinking must come with the territory of being a coal miner. It seems that all the women just put up with it. Every time Uncle Clyde started drinking, Aunt Ester took Phyllis and me down the hill to visit with her mother whenever he drank too much.

When I was about seven, Uncle Clyde would whip me for the least little thing and let Phyllis get away with murder! I think it was because she looked more like him, and I reminded him that I was just another mouth to feed—like a dog. Whenever I tried to sneak extra food or hide from her, Phyllis always got me into trouble. She was lazy, and I had to do her chores to keep from getting into trouble. One of our jobs was to carry in the coal and wood for the fireplace every evening. Phyllis would always whine and complain about it, and I wound up doing it by myself.

One afternoon, we were playing with some neighbor kids, and I loaned my coat to one of the little girls who was cold. I certainly knew what it felt like to be cold and hungry, and I felt sorry for her. Just as soon as we got home, Phyllis ran into the kitchen and hollered, "Donna gave her coat away!"

"That's alright," replied Aunt Ester as she patted me on the back.

Uncle Clyde whipped his belt off with a snap and yelled, "I don't work myself to death to give the neighbor kids free coats!"

As the belt sliced into my backside, I tried not to cry and told myself that I would get even with Phyllis.

A few days later, Aunt Ester's sister came over to babysit us while she and Uncle Clyde went shopping. I went out to play, and Phyllis followed me. I decided it was time to get even. Pretending to go to the bathroom, I went into the outhouse. Phyllis followed me in. I grabbed her by the neck and stuffed her head inside the toilet hole.

"If you ever tell on me again, I'm going to drop you in there! Got it?" I shrieked. I was so furious I was shaking, and all I could see was red.

She never squealed on me again, but she didn't stop whining and complaining. I figured, why complain about it? Someone has to do it. Might as well be me. Once it's done, you don't have to think about it anymore. I'm still that way today, and I still can't stand a lazy, grumbling person.

Besides the occasional drinking spats that Uncle Clyde had from time to time, I had a reasonably happy life there. I hated the coal mines. It was so dirty. All the houses were on hills, and there was no grass in anybody's yards because there was too much coal dust for the grass to grow. It was always dark and gloomy, and everyone shuffled around with their head hung down. It was a depressing life, and it went on like that for a few years.

When I was eight years old, Uncle Clyde decided to visit his brother Cecil. My Uncle Cecil and Aunt Edna lived on a farm in Ohio and were taking care of three of my half brothers. I was so excited! I couldn't wait to see my brothers! I kept jumping around in the back seat and asking, "How much longer? How much longer?" I believe that was one of the happiest moments in my life as I watched the mountains fade further into the distance.

As soon as we pulled up in the yard, my brother Jack ran out the front door yelling, "Donna! Donna!" I jumped out of the car, and we hugged for a long time. It was so good to see my brother again. Aunt Edna walked out on the front porch wiping her hands on her apron. She had blonde hair pulled back into a bun and kind, sparkling blue eyes. She was tall with an hour glass figure. At one glance, you could tell that she took care of herself.

A tall man strolled out behind her and placed his huge hand on her shoulder and his dark brown eyes sparkled as he watched us piling out of the car. He ran one of his hands through his dark wavy hair that was slightly salt and peppered, and I smelled pipe tobacco that wafted through the air to my nostrils. It smelled clean and woodsy. He took the pipe out of his mouth and motioned for us to come up the stairs. "You all come in and rest. You must be exhausted," he said. "I'll help you with your bags and Edna can show you your room."

"Come on, Donna," Jack said, "I'll show you around." He grabbed my hand and dragged me around to the back of the house.

My three brothers, Jack, Bill, and Augie and Phyllis and I played hide-and-seek; run sheep run; red light, green light; and every other game we could think of that whole weekend. We ran and played and wore ourselves out. Phyllis had a hard time keeping up with us because she was the youngest. I felt bad for her, but not too much as I was enjoying myself being just a kid.

The weekend went by so fast that the next thing I knew it was time to go home, and Aunt Ester began packing. "Can I stay here?" I asked quietly. I did not want to go back with them. It was nice there on the farm. The place was so clean and sweet smelling, and Aunt Edna and Uncle Cecil were so nice.

"No. You have to come home with us," she told me as she finished packing our belongings. "Here," she told me as she handed me a huge bag of clothes, "run this out to Uncle Clyde."

I carried the bundle out to the car where Uncle Clyde was arranging things in the trunk, "Can I stay here?" I whispered.

"Get in the car with Phyllis," he yelled at me. Then he dismissed me with a wave of his hand and stuck his head back in the trunk and fumbled around. I did as I was told and got in the car.

A few minutes later as he was saying his goodbyes to Aunt Edna and Uncle Cecil, I snuck out of the car and dashed into the woods as fast as my little legs would carry me. Jack saw me from the window take off and ran out and found me, and he hid me in a hollow tree. I heard everyone calling me, but I refused to come out. I had made up my mind that I was not going back to that mountain and those coal mines. That part of my life was over!

Everyone stopped looking for me about dusk because Uncle Clyde had to be in the mines the next day. Later Jack told me that Uncle Cecil said if they found me, they would send me home. When I heard Uncle Clyde's car start up, I slipped out of the tree and peeked out from behind some bushes. I watched the car turn onto the road from the long driveway and headed out of sight.

Jack whispered, "Donna? Are you in there?"

"Yes," I whispered back and climbed out of the bushes. Jack took my hand, and we walked slowly up the hill to the big house.

Uncle Cecil and Aunt Edna were sitting at the kitchen table sipping coffee. "There you are, young lady. What have you got to say for yourself?" Uncle Cecil asked.

I sniffed and asked quietly, "Can I come live with you?"

My aunt and uncle exchanged glances and Uncle Cecil said quietly, "We'll have to talk it over."

For the next couple of days, I did my best to make them want to keep me. I kept my room clean. I helped my aunt in the kitchen prepare the meals and clean up afterward. After a day or two, my Aunt Edna told me, "Your Uncle and I have talked it over, and if you really want to, you can stay with us for a while."

I grabbed her around her tiny waist and tears poured down my cheeks as I whispered over and over, "Thank you. Thank you. Thank you." Then I sniffed and said, "I'll be a good girl. You'll see. I'll make you happy you took me in."

She gently pushed me away and whispered, "I know you will, Donna."

Uncle Cecil walked in with my three brothers and said, "I guess you told her."

Aunt Edna looked up at him and smiled.

Jack grabbed me in a bear hug. "Woo-hoo! Welcome home, sis!"

Home. That was a word I could finally believe in.

Chapter 2

Aunt Edna was a wonderful cook and a great housekeeper. She had never had children, but now they had three of my brothers and me to take care of. The four of us got along well. It was wonderful having three brothers to look after me when I went to school to protect me from any bullies who called me names.

I was so happy with Uncle Cecil and Aunt Edna. He didn't drink like all my other uncles, and he was always so kind and happy. Even after a hard day working in the fields, he came home and spent time with us or helped us with our evening chores. Aunt Edna made all our clothes, and we always had clean sheets on our beds and good food to eat. I think it was hard for her to hold us and tell us that she loved us. She showed her affection by caring for us.

One afternoon, I was in the kitchen with my aunt helping her make biscuits. I looked up at her and whispered, "Can I call you Mom?"

Her blue eyes glistened with tears and she looked down at me and smiled. "Of course, you can, honey." From that time on I called her Mom, and my uncle Dad.

They had a hundred and eighty acre farm in rural Ohio, and we raised almost everything we ate. We had apple and peach trees, corn, beans, carrots, tomatoes. You name it, and we had it. One of my jobs was to hold the cow's tail while Mom milked it. Jack and I had to slop pigs. Whew! Did that stink. I hated it. I tried breathing through my mouth to keep from inhaling that pungent odor. My brothers worked in the fields during harvesting time and chopped wood for the stove.

As I look back on it now, I realize that Mom and Dad did all they could for each one of us. I found out later that they had taken in Bill when he was only six months old. When they first took me and Jack in, we were so under nourished that we had rickets and our tonsils were eaten up with infection. The doctor commented that it was surprising that the infection hadn't killed us yet because we were swallowing the infection every time we drank or ate anything.

I remember Jack and I used to sneak out to the apple trees and eat green apples before they were ripe and eat as many as we could until our stomachs ached and were bulging. "You've been in the apples again, haven't you!" Mom scolded when we came in the kitchen door holding our mid sections and moaning. I am still not sure why we kept eating those apples. We knew what would happen. Yep. You guessed it—a big ole dose of castor oil.

Once, when Jack saw the spoon full of that stuff headed toward him, he moaned, "Can't I just crawl over in the corner and die!"

Despite my stomach ache, I couldn't help but giggle.

Holding our noses helped a little as it went down. Poor Jack spit for an hour afterward. Once, he missed the trash can and spit on Mom's dress. His eyes got big as saucers and his head shot up to see if she was mad. I was suddenly terrified for him, remembering what my other aunts and uncles were like. But Mom just smiled and said, "Well, mister, I think you have a dress to wash."

We both sighed in relief.

Because of all the extra food we had from canning and growing fresh fruits and vegetables, Mom and Dad opened a small store. We carried dry goods, fresh and canned fruits and vegetables, and even some homemade candy.

Mom and Dad always told us, "If you take anything from the store, write it down in the book under the counter. That way, we can keep track of everything." Being the sweet, angelic kids that Jack and I were (yeah, right!), we took a candy bar each, but instead of writing down our names, we wrote down Bill and Augie. Then we laughed and skipped out of the store, merrily chomping down on the chocolate.

One spring day, we were all out in the fields helping Dad plant corn and beans. Every now and then, Dad hollered, "Break!" and Mom went to the house to get us something to eat.

As soon as Dad yelled, "Break," Jack, Augie, Bill, and I made a mad dash for the creek where the clean, fresh spring water came down from the mountain. The boys could run faster than I could and were splashing around in the water by the time I got there. I leaned over to take a drink of water and a snake raised its head, and its little tongue slid in and out of its mouth. I was so scared that I must have turned white. It felt like my heart was going to jump right out of my chest. I yelled, "Snake!"

The boys stopped splashing around and looked at me. "There's no snake!" Augie admonished me.

But there was a snake, and I saw him. I thought he was Satan himself; it scared me so bad. I could hardly sleep for days. I was about eight or nine at the time.

One afternoon, I was playing down by the creek, and it was getting dusky out. Mom was calling us to come in for dinner. Bill and Jack were hiding up in a tree with a pair of suspenders. Just as I passed under the tree, Jack threw them around my neck because he knew I was terrified of snakes and screamed, "Snake! Snake! Snake!"

I screamed at the top of my lungs and fell to the ground, rolling around, trying to throw that thing off me, screaming the whole time. I could imagine this horrible huge slimy thing biting me and twisting its ugly body around my neck.

Dad charged down the hill with a hoe in his hand with Mom hot on his heels. Dad took one look at me screaming and rolling around on the ground wrestling with a pair of suspenders, and he looked up. He heard Jack and Bill laughing hysterically in the tree. He grabbed the suspenders and threw them to the ground, and he picked me up in his arms. I clung to him for life, and he whispered soothingly, "It's okay, Donna. It was just a pair of suspenders. Bill and Jack were playing a trick on you. Shhhh…hush now."

When his words finally sunk in, I furiously glared up at the boys. "I'll get even, you'll see!" I screamed at them.

The boys had to do my chores for a week, but as far as I was concerned, that wasn't near enough punishment.

Every night Mom boiled water on the stove for our baths. She poured the hot water into a huge metal tub and kept boiling water and pouring it into the tub until she had the tub half full. Next, she poured cold water from the sink into the tub to cool it off for bathing. Being the sweet little girl that I am, Mom let me take my bath first. After she washed my hair, she asked me to finish washing myself, and then she left me alone. Just to get even for the snake incident, right before I stepped out of the tub, I urinated in the water because I knew the boys went in next.

Jack glared suspiciously at me when I came from behind the sheet smiling angelically, humming a little tune. "She peed in the water!" Jack accused.

Mom turned to look down at me with her hands on her slender hips and asked, "You didn't do that, did you, Donna?"

"Of course not!" I declared. My huge eyes wide in shock that my brother could accuse me of something so horrible! I was a good actress even back then.

"See, Jack. Now get in the water and take your bath," Mom ordered.

Jack stormed behind the bedsheet and flung his clothes as missiles at me. As soon as he splashed down in the water, he hollered, "Ew! Gross!"

I snickered. Mom glanced suspiciously down at me.

As the boys got a little older, Mom and Dad let them build a fire outside and heat the water in the tub and then carry the tub inside. Jack confessed to me many years later that they all urinated in the water before they carried it in. Many people have always told me what beautiful skin I have. I guess I can thank my brothers for that.

One night, when we were all visiting Dad's mother, who was full-blooded Cherokee. It was the same grandmother that Jack and I stayed with when I was younger. She was about ninety years old, and she already had her casket made, and it was in a barn loft. We were playing hide-and-seek with our cousins who were visiting her at the same time. I noticed a hollow log, and I leaped into it to hide.

A few minutes later, something began to sting me. When I looked down, there were yellow jackets all over me. I bolted out of that log like a bullet. There were bites all over me—my eyelids, face, nose, arms, legs. I took off screaming toward the adults. Grandma calmed me down and mixed up some white stuff and spread it all over my bites. It helped the stinging, and I was back in the game.

We found everyone but Jack. He was sneaky like me, and he could hide exceptionally well. We looked everywhere, and we still couldn't find him. We decided to look in the barn one more time. We ruffled through the hay stack and looked in all the stalls—not a bit of evidence of where he could be. We climbed the ladder to the hayloft calling his name. We're all tired and mad because we couldn't find him.

"You win!" we called out. "We give up!" Suddenly, the coffin lid squeaked as it began to rise. We screamed and scrambled down the latter to get out of there! Augie flew down the latter so fast, he left a smoke trail. I was so afraid that I jumped out the hay loft. It's a miracle I didn't break my legs. Then we heard Jack laughing.

Grandma wobbled into the barn and said, "If you scratch my coffin, I goin' to take this here can," and she held up a snuff can, "and hit you upside the head with it!" Jack was afraid of her, and he jumped out the coffin.

After dinner, Dad built a bonfire out back. Just as I stepped off the porch to the step below, something bit me at the back of my ankle. I screamed, and everyone came running to see what was wrong. A snake had bit me. It was too dark to tell if it was poisonous or not, and the snake had slithered off.

"Hold her still, Cecil," Grandma instructed my dad. She pulled her knife out of the sheath she always kept on her belt and made an X. She placed her weathered old lips on the back of my ankle and began to suck the poison out and spit it on the ground.

"Lands sake," she said, "the devil is after you. You must be going to do something great in life for the Lord because the old evil one is trying to stop you."

I never forgot those words.

One day, a letter came from our paternal mother, Marie. I was about nine years old. The letter told Mom and Dad that she wanted us back. Marie said in the letter that I could babysit her youngest baby, Freddie, and my brothers could get jobs and help Earl pay the bills.

Mom and Dad sat us all down at the kitchen table and read us the letter. After reading it out loud to us, my Mom glanced at each one us and said softly, "It's up to you. If you want to stay with us, we would love to have you. But if you want to go and live with your real mother, we won't stop you."

We all looked around at each other wondering what the other one was thinking. I knew I didn't want to go anywhere else. I had found home, and I was staying. I began shaking my head, "I'm not going," I said matter-of-factly. Dad patted my hand and grinned. Mom looked relieved.

"I'm staying too," Bill said.

Jack said, "I'm going."

"Me too," chimed in Augie.

"Jack, no!" I cried. "You can't! She gave us away! She didn't care about us! Why do you want to go back to her now?"

He shrugged his shoulders and said, "I just wanna see her."

"Oh, Jack!" I wailed and ran upstairs to my room and slammed my door. I could not believe that my family was being split up again.

A week later, all five of us were standing at the bus stop. Jack and Augie had their clothes neatly folded in old suitcases beside them. Every few minutes, I stole glances over at them, and my heart ached that my brothers were leaving me. I felt as though I were being abandoned all over again. I loved my two brothers despite their pranks and picking on me. I held my dad's hand, terrified that he was going to put me on that bus too. And I knew that no matter how much I loved my brothers, I was not going to leave the one stable and loving home that I had ever had.

We had already said our goodbyes, and there was nothing else to say. When the bus pulled up, Dad helped them get on with their suitcases. Jack glanced down at me from the window and waved, but I didn't wave back. I looked down at the ground and tried not to cry. But I felt the waves of disappointment and loneliness grip me, and I began to cry. I wailed for the loss of my brothers. My dad picked me up in his arms and held me tightly. I could tell he tried not to cry as well.

Mom sniffed and dabbed at her eyes and said, "Well, let's go home."

Now it was just Bill and me.

After Jack and Augie had left the farm, Bill and I had a lot more chores. We also had more food, clothes, and toys. We were doing okay and were happy living on the farm with our new mom and dad.

I heard later that Jack got into trouble and spent some time in jail when he was sixteen. Augie joined the service and later confessed that the army was the only thing that kept him out of trouble.

Growing up with Mom and Dad was some of the best times of my life. Mom made most of our clothes, and she made me pretty dresses and a nice winter coat. It was the first time in my life that I had underwear, slips, and a nightgown. Always stylish, she bought me hats and gloves to wear to church. I had a nice soft bed in a room all to myself. Yes, I was very happy there.

They took us to church, and I loved my Sunday-school teacher. Her name was Miss Connolly. She was probably about sixty-five with gray hair and a wide smile with sparkling blue eyes. Her husband had died a few years earlier, and she took a real interest in her Sunday-school class. She was a wonderful teacher, and she taught us all about Jesus and how powerful God is in our life if we will just welcome Him in. I never forgot that, and I never forgot her. She always made me feel special. When I was eleven years old, I went forward on Sunday and gave my life to Jesus and repented of my sins. I tried very hard to be a good girl.

After I gave my life to God, we had an old-fashioned baptism. There was a creek that ran down beside the old country church house. When the preacher put me under the water and he said, "I baptize this child in the name of the Father, of the Son, and of the Holy Ghost," he is holding me under the water the whole time, and I was running out of breath. Before the preacher could pull me up out of the water, a hand came out of nowhere. The robe that hung down to the wrist was whiter than snow, and it glowed a brilliant white. I knew that Jesus was there, and it was his hand that pulled me up out of the water. No one else saw him because I asked. Everyone told me that I was caught up in the experience of being saved, but I knew better. And He has had His hand on my life ever since.

I enjoyed school, and I made good grades. When I lived with Aunt Laurie, I used to eat lunch by myself because I didn't want any of the kids to see what I had to eat. And they played games; I was always the last one chosen. But living with my new parents, Mom always made me a great lunch. And she kept my hair combed and fashioned it in the latest style. With my new clothes and my new look, most of the kids didn't know who I was when I went back to school in the fall. There was a 360-degree turnaround in me. I was a poor little beggar girl who turned into a princess, and sometimes I felt like a princess too. The girls who used to laugh at me and make fun of me suddenly wanted to be my friends.

Like every other little girl, I began to grow and fill out. At age eleven, I was a little embarrassed by my chest beginning to push against my blouses and dresses. They weren't huge yet, but I did start to fill out a little sooner than other girls. I noticed boys taking a second look at me at school.

One afternoon, a couple of weeks after my thirteenth birthday, Mom and Aunt Pauline, who was my stepmom's sister, were going into town, and I didn't want to go. The few times I did go with them, they walked for hours and looked in store windows but didn't buy anything. Bill did not want to go either. Mom agreed, but we had to stay home and not go in the woods. We had just eaten lunch, and I told Mom that I would stay and do the dishes.

While I cleaned up the kitchen, Bill sat in the living room listening to the radio. Just as I turned around with the dishes in my hands, I saw a man that I had never seen before watching me through the screen door. He was tall. I noticed that his head was only a few inches from the top of the doorframe. And he was big. He grinned at me, and his teeth were yellowed and stained from tobacco juice. He rubbed the stubble on his jaw.

"Hey," he said, "who are you?"

"I belong here," I told him. "Who are you?"

Bill heard the conversation and said, "Uncle Leman."

"Hey, how have you been, boy?" Uncle Leman asked. "Do you want to see my new car?"

Bill jumped up and rushed outside. I could hear them talking and laughing through the kitchen window. I was relieved and continued to wash the dishes. While I was standing at the sink in front of the kitchen window, I heard the car start up and pull out of the driveway. I thought he must have taken Bill for a ride in his new car, and I didn't think too much of it.

Suddenly, I heard the screen door open behind me, and I whirled around.

Uncle Leman smiled at me and took a step toward me.

"Where's Bill?" I asked.

"I let him take my new car for a spin," he said as he pointed his thumb behind him. His eyes roamed slowly up and down my body. "You know, you are a pretty little thing," he continued. "How old are you now?"

"Thirteen," I squeaked and turned around to the sink where the dishes waited.

"You look more like fourteen or fifteen," he said hoarsely. "You know you're going to make some lucky man a nice little filly one of these days."

I felt like I had to get out of there. I didn't like what he said or the way he said it. I knew our collie, Lady, was outside somewhere, and she was a good guard dog. I started toward the kitchen screen door, intending to walk around him and go outside. Suddenly, he grabbed me and carried me to the back bedroom. I screamed and kicked as I beat him with my little fists. I scratched and bit, trying everything I could to make him let me go. I even tried to stick my thumbs in his eyes.

When he reached the bedroom, he threw me on the bed and fell on top of me and began tearing my clothes off. He held me down with one arm and fumbled around with his belt and zipper with the other. I screamed until I was hoarse. Our collie outside was barking and growling as she scratched at the door trying to get in. She knew something was wrong.

"Shut up, bitch," he growled through clenched teeth and slapped me across the mouth. I tasted blood as it squirted into my mouth.

Suddenly, I remembered what my Sunday school teacher had said: "No matter what might be happening in your life, call on Jesus, and He will help you. It says so in His word. He will not let you down."

I started praying then. I asked Jesus to help me, and I told Him how much I loved Him and believed in Him. "I trust in you. Help me, Lord Jesus. Please help me!" Suddenly, I felt this inner strength, and I began kicking and squirming even harder. I felt a pressure on the inside of my thigh, and I began to feel sick. Suddenly, I threw up all over him and myself. I bit his ear, and he howled and grabbed his bloody ear. As soon as he turned me loose with one hand, I reached over and grabbed the lamp on the night stand, and I smashed it against his head with all my strength, praying and calling on Jesus the whole time. I know that Jesus gave me the strength to fight this man off.

He jumped up, holding the side of his head and ran out of the house, leaving a trail of blood behind him. I must have cut him deep based on all the blood that dripped throughout the house. I sat there stunned for a few minutes, and then when the realization hit me—what I had just gone through—I cried. I'm not sure how long I sat there crying. I cried until I heard a car in the driveway. I looked out the window and Leman was dropping Bill off, and he pulled out of the driveway before I could get outside and tell my brother what he had tried to do to me.

Bill heard me crying in the back bedroom, and I heard him running up the stairs. He took one look at the broken lamp and my torn clothes and exclaimed, "What happened, sis?"

"He...he...he...," I stammered, "t...t...tried to d...do something nasty to me!" I cried.

"Leave everything just the way it is. Don't clean up anything," he told me. "I'll go find Mom and Dad. If he comes back, hide and don't let him find you. Lock all the doors till we get back!" Then Bill shot out the door like a rocket.

Dad rushed home, and Mom ran down to the neighbor's house and called the police. The police came out and took pictures of the bedroom and of the bruises on my body where he had tried to hold me down. I even had bruises on my throat and my face where he slapped me. Then I had to tell them the whole ugly story all over again. The police told Mom and Dad that I had to go to a doctor to be examined that same day. After the examination, the doctor had determined that he had not raped me but had caused some damage to my hymen. Mom and Dad swore out a warrant for his arrest.

My stepparents were very proud of the way I stood up to my attacker.

Later in life, when I got married, the attempted rape came back to haunt me.

Chapter 3

Bill and I had a good life with Mom and Dad. We had a nice home and lots of good food to eat. Mom was a wonderful cook. As I think back on it now, I believe that's where I get my talent for cooking. Although I was not her blood child, I find that I have a lot of her mannerisms. I did appreciate everything that my stepparents did for me as well as my brothers.

I used to go down to the creek by myself and pretend that I was married and had children of my own. I pretended to cook and take care of my house. I often placed big rocks around (as big as I could carry) and pretend that they were my sofa, chairs, stove, and refrigerator.

One afternoon, I asked my dad, "Can I take the old pig house we don't use anymore and make a pretend playhouse?"

"You don't have to do that, Donna," he told me. "I'll build you one as soon as I get time."

"No, Dad. You don't have to do that. Please let me try."

"Okay, go ahead and try, but don't be disappointed if you can't."

"Oh, I won't."

I got busy that afternoon raking all the pig crap and muck out of the little building. I worked as hard as I could for two weeks. Mom gave me some old material for me to use, and I made some curtains for the open windows. I found an old piece of lumber Dad had stored in the barn rafters, and Bill helped me make a pretend stove, sofa, chair, and refrigerator. He even helped me paint them. He never told me so, but I think he felt guilty for leaving me alone with Leman while he drove the new car. I never blamed my brother for what happened to me; he had no idea what Leman was capable of.

Finally, I had my little playhouse done with curtains and pre-tend appliances and furniture. Mom gave me some old throw rugs for the floor and some old dishes. I loved my little playhouse, and I spent hours in it pretending to be grown-up with a husband and children. That was all I ever wanted—to have kids of my own to love and take care of.

I loved the outdoors also. In the summer time when school was out and all my chores were done, I stayed outside or in my play-house, and I wouldn't be back for hours. I remember Mom calling and calling for me to come in. Once, when Mom was having a hard time to get me to come inside, Dad hollered, "Donna! You better come in! It's getting dark out and bad things happen after it gets dark!"

That was all I needed to hear. I was on my way up the backstairs as fast as my legs would carry me in about five minutes. From that time on, I came in as soon as the sun started to go down.

We were a happy family. I remember all of us sitting around the fireplace in the evening with Dad smoking his pipe and telling us stories. Sometimes, Mom told us a few of her stories as a little girl growing up, but Dad's stories were a lot more interesting. Bill and I never confessed that we enjoyed Dad's tales more because we didn't want to hurt her feelings.

Once, I told a lie on my brother. I blamed him for something that I had done. Mom suspected me all along and finally got me to tell the truth. "You know what happens when we get caught in a lie, don't you?" she asked me.

"Yes," I replied.

"Now, go find me a switch."

I felt so disgusted with myself for lying that I picked out a nice thick one and brought it into the kitchen where Mom was waiting. She took the switch I had picked out and looked at me and asked, "Donna, what do you want me to do with this? Do you want me to whip you or kill you?" Then she did something that really surprised me—she laughed.

I was terrified that she was going to send me away for being bad, and she was laughing.

When she finished laughing, she wiped tears from her eyes and said, "Okay. I'm going to let you off this time, but I had better never catch you lying again."

"Yes, Ma'am," I replied with relief.

"You know God is watching all the time. He sees and hears everything we do and say. So, when you pray tonight before you go to sleep, ask for His forgiveness."

"Okay," and I hugged and kissed her on the cheek. "I love you," I whispered.

"I love you too," she replied softly and stroked my hair.

As I got older, my face began to lose the childishness and soften into womanhood. My eyes were pools of dark mystery, and my hair was long strands of molten ebony. My skin was flawless and smooth

As I got older, so did Dad, and it was getting harder and harder for him to plow the fields, plant, and harvest. He began having chest pains, and the doctor told him he couldn't keep going on the way he was going. One night after supper, Mom and Dad sat Bill and me down and told us they were going to put the farm up for sale. Bill and I were delighted because we were tired of farmwork and were excited to move into town. Bill was eighteen and about to graduate from school; I was fourteen and excited to be moving into town.

It took Dad a couple of months to sell the farm, getting a real good deal. Dad went into Columbus, Ohio, looking for work while Mom, Bill, and I stayed home and began packing. It took Dad a few weeks, but he found a good job at Allied and Company. They manufactured parts for airlines and submarines. They also made parts for GE, Western Electric, and Frigidaire. Dad made good money and moved up fast in the company. Within ten years, Dad became the vice president for that district. Bill went to work for the railroads. It was a little harder for Mom to adjust to city life because she missed the farm.

One summer, after I had turned fourteen, I got a job babysitting for the Alburn family, one of the neighbors. One of the kids was one year old and the other one was five. I cleaned the house, did the laundry, and prepared some meals for twelve dollars a week. It made me feel all grown-up.

One night, we were all going to the church social at the local church we had joined after moving to the city. I sneaked into my mom and dad's room and took a tube of lipstick from her dresser. She had plenty, and I didn't think that she would miss just one. I usually sat in the back of the church with the rest of the preteens. The preacher was on fire that night. He was preaching hellfire and brimstone! Suddenly, Mom craned her head back and gave me "the look." She had noticed the pink lipstick. My stomach lurched, and I knew I was in big trouble.

The next autumn, I was fifteen but looked more like eighteen. My dark eyes and olive skin accentuated my long black hair. My chest had grown to where I now wore a 38C bra. I didn't hang around with the kids my age because they were too immature for me. Mom was working as a cosmetologist, and I was taking care of the house, washing the laundry, and cooking supper every night except Sundays—Mom and I prepared the Sunday meal together.

One afternoon, Mom and Dad announced that we were going to have a family reunion the following weekend. We spent several days cooking and preparing food to take with us, such as potato salad, macaroni salad, deviled eggs, homemade cakes, pies, and of course, Mom's fried chicken, which was store-bought, and all we had to do was fry it. Thank goodness!

On Saturday morning, we loaded the car with all our goodies, anticipating what everyone else would bring. I wore a bright yellow dress that showed off my black hair and olive skin. All the way over to the lake, Mom kept reminding me, "Please don't mess your dress up, Donna. Please be careful and don't spill anything on it or get it dirty. It will be hard to clean."

"Yes, Ma'am. Yes, Ma'am," I kept telling her.

Dad drove us out to a nearby lake where you could swim or take your boat out—if you had one. Most of the relatives who came were on Mom's side of the family, but a few of the Clouse family came as well. Uncle Eugene was Mom's brother, and he was married to a Clouse, and she invited her relatives. I had heard that Uncle Eugene was a tobacco farmer and had five kids. Three of them were around my age, and two of them were a few years older than I was.

My cousins ran up to me very excited to see me even though I had only met them a few times before growing up. One of the boys flashed a bright smile and exclaimed, "Uncle Harold is coming too! He'll be here in a few minutes. He just came back from the Korean war!"

"Let's play croquet!" one of the boys said, and we set up the game and started playing. After that, we pitched horseshoes. I tried to be mindful of the yellow dress and not get it dirty.

My cousin Carmen and I eventually got tired of the game, and we wandered over to a huge tree that fortified some shade by the riverbank and sat down talking. A softball game was starting, and she jumped up and ran over to play. I knew I couldn't play in my yellow dress, and I tossed my black hair behind my back and watched them pick sides.

Suddenly, I heard a very sweet masculine voice, which spoke very softly as though he were speaking to a doe afraid to scare her off. "I was sitting over their watching you and wandered why you're not in the game."

I turned around, and I stared at him. He had the most beautiful smile with huge dimples on each side of his face. He was wearing his green army fatigues, which accentuated his beautiful hazel eyes that twinkled. His copper red hair shone like a new penny in the sunlight, and I thought to myself, *Wow!*

He asked, "Cat got your tongue? Well, my name is Harold. What's your name?"

"Donna," I replied shyly.

He sat down, and we stared at the river together for a few minutes. "How about we go over there and get in the game?" he asked.

I thought for a split second, *Mom is going to kill me if I get this dress dirty.* Then I said, "Okay."

We sauntered over to the field where the kids were playing softball and asked if we could join. We were put on opposite teams, and his team made Harold pitcher. When it was my time to come up to bat, he said, "I have never had the pleasure of striking out such a beautiful girl as you are, sweetie."

"I have eleven brothers altogether, so take your best shot!" I parried back at him.

He grinned and pitched the ball. I slammed that ball with all the strength I had in my 112 pounds and sent it screaming out of the park.

"Oh," he said, "pretty and competitive."

"You got it, buster," I replied confidently.

It was getting warm out, and Harold took his jacket off and was only wearing his green army T-shirt. I laughed as he was taking off his jacket and said, "What are we playing? Softball or strip poker?" I couldn't help but notice the curly red hairs peeping over the top of his shirt. I tried to avert my eyes because I knew it wasn't proper for a lady to stare, but I just couldn't help myself. I was like a moth drawn to a flame.

In the end, my team beat his team, and I was delighted. It was lunch time, so we all sat down to eat and then someone mentioned, "Let's play some more softball."

We played two more games. Everyone was sweating and dirty and my cousin Carmen said, "Hey, let's go swimming!"

"I know a great place!" Harold exclaimed. "There's an old rope tied to a tree, and we can swing out over the river and fall into the water. Everyone just stared at him, wondering where such a place was.

"It's just a little ways down from here," Harold said

Carmen ran to our parents and got permission for all of us to go with Harold to go swimming. A bunch of us piled into his 1953 Chevrolet Bel-Air convertible—I loved that car. Harold drove us to Uncle Eugene's, and we changed into swimsuits and took off for the river.

One by one, we lined up to swing out on the grapevine and splash into the middle of the river. When it was my turn, I told Harold, "I'm not a very good swimmer."

"Don't worry about it. I'll catch you." Then he grabbed the rope and swung out over the river and gave the old Tarzan yell and splashed into the water. He came up and shook the water out of his head like I dog and grinned up at me. "Come on! I'll catch you. I Promise!"

A little frightened, I reached for the rope. I took one more look at him, and I swung out and let go and fell straight into his arms.

His eyes twinkled down at me, and then he let me go, and we swam together for the embankment to get back in line.

We splashed and played and swung out on the rope for hours. We noticed that the air was getting a little cooler, and the sun was beginning to go down. "I have to get back. Mom is going to have a fit!" I exclaimed.

When we got back to the picnic, it was dusk. Everyone was cleaning up the mess and packing the cars to go home. Carmen sweetly asked my mother if I could stay for the rest of the week, and they could drive me home the following weekend.

Mom said, "Donna, you can't stay. You don't have any clothes to wear."

My heart stopped beating in my chest. *Oh, no,* I thought because I wanted to see Harold again, and I was afraid I would never see him again.

"It's okay," Carmen remarked. "She can wear some of mine and Pam's. We have plenty."

I smiled at Carmen in relief.

Mom finally relented and said I could stay for a few days. I think she gave in because she knew that I never went out, and I went to church every Sunday, plus I had a babysitting job and helped Mom with the shopping, cooking, cleaning, and so on.

As Dad pulled out with Mom and Bill, Harold said to Aunt Edna, "I'll drive the kids home." She nodded, preoccupied with getting all their things back in the car.

We all piled in Harold's car again, and he took off. He drove faster this time, taking the curves hard that I slammed against his side. Every time, he looked down at me with those twinkling hazel eyes and smile. As soon as we got to Carmen's house, we ran upstairs and took off our swim suits and put on shorts and shirts.

When we were all sitting in the living room, Harold said, "Hey, how about I take everyone who can fit in my car to the drive-in movie tonight?"

Next thing I knew we were all looking through the paper on the living room floor to see what was playing. We finally settled on *Moby Dick*, which I had wanted to see for a long time, but Mom didn't approve because it had bad language in it. Boy, did I feel grown-up! I was going to see a movie that was off-limits to me before. *Hey, Mom, I thought, look at me now!* I knew she would beat me half to death if she knew. *Oh, well,* I thought and shrugged my shoulders.

Harold, Carmen, and I were in the front seat. I was sitting beside Harold, of course. And Ronnie, Paulette, Anna, and Jimmy were in the back seat. Ronnie had a crush on me, but he was my age. I wasn't interested. I wanted a man, not a little boy. I needed someone who could take care of me.

Harold drove very slow on the way home. I think he was afraid for the day to end. When he pulled up into Uncle Eugene's drive, everyone but Harold and I piled out of the car and rushed into the house to tell the grown-ups about the movie we just saw. We sat in the driveway with the top down talking for a long time. He told me a little about his time in the army and a little bit about his family. Uncle Eugene kept coming out on the front porch, looking at his watch, and then going back inside. A little while later, Aunt Edna came to the door and said, "Harold, that's jailbait, you know."

"Gosh," he replied, "we're just talking, sis. Can I go to jail sitting in your driveway with the top down and just talking?"

Harold and I both could tell that there was a spark between us, and so did everyone else. He looked down at me after Aunt Edna went back inside in a huff and said softly, "I have never known anyone as beautiful as you. I didn't know women like you even existed in the real world." Then he turned on his radio, and we sat there, quietly listening to the music. I was trying very hard to be grown-up.

Finally, Uncle Eugene came to the door and said, "Okay, Donna. I have to ask you to come in. It's twelve o'clock. Harold, you go on home now, and if you want to come back out tomorrow and see us"—he emphasized us—"you can."

We touched hands, and he got out and came around to my door and opened it for me and walked me to the front door. "Goodnight," he whispered. And he handed me a note.

I stood in the doorway and waved at him as he pulled out of the driveway. He hollered, "I'll see you tomorrow, Sweet Thing!" and he grinned and waved back, gunning his car as he left. I watched as he drove away—his bright red hair shining in the moonlight—until his tail lights disappeared around a curve. There was something about him that drew me like a magnet. I didn't know what it was, but it felt wonderful, and yet it made me sad at the same time. I hurried upstairs and went into the bathroom to read his note in privacy. It read,

Sweet Thing, here's my phone number. Give me about 30 minutes to get home, then call me.

I hurried up and took my shower and put some nightclothes on. I was so tired that I was afraid of falling asleep. Harold knew he couldn't call Uncle Eugene's house because he didn't want to wake everyone up. He told me later that he drove like a bat out of hell to get home because he wanted to be there when I called. He had to drive from Winchester, Kentucky, to Lexington.

I kept watching the clock on the wall. Every second seemed like minutes. Finally, when I knew thirty minutes had passed, I called his number. He answered on the first ring. I could tell his voice was trembling, "Oh, thank God!" he whispered. "I was terrified you wouldn't call. I've been pacing the floor for the last five minutes." And I heard him sigh on the other end. "You know, Donna, you're a very special lady. You stole my heart the minute I laid eyes on you. You are a goddess in my eyes."

"Oh, Harold," I giggled. "You're funny."

"I'm not kidding."

Suddenly, I heard Uncle Eugene clear his throat behind me and say, "Donna, should I guess who you're talking to." I glanced behind me, and he raised his left eye brow at me. "I guess it's Harold."

"Yes, Uncle Eugene," I replied and lowered my head.

"You know, Donna, he's too old for you."

"We're just talking."

Uncle Eugene shook his head and walked away grumbling. "Just a few more minutes."

Harold said, "You know, I prayed to God while I was overseas serving my country, to send me a great girl I could love and who could love me. But I didn't know He cared so much about me that

He dropped an angel out of heaven into my lap." Harold was such a romantic.

Suddenly I heard a woman's voice in the background, "Who are you talking to at this hour? It's 1:30 in the morning! Are you talking to that little girl your sister told me about?"

Harold sighed, "Yeah, Mom,"

"You'd better be careful," she warned. "Her family is going to blow up when they find out!"

"Go back to bed, Mom. I can handle it."

"Okay, son, so long as you know. You are an adult, so I can't tell you what to do."

She must have left the room then. Harold asked, "Are you still there?"

"Y…y…yes," I stammered. It seemed so natural for us to be together. It was as though I had known him for years, and yet I had only met him that day. I was excited and afraid all at once.

"You know, Sweet Thing, I don't know what's going on, but I feel like you were meant to be in my life." His voice was so husky, it made me shiver despite the warm night.

"I know. I feel so comfortable talking to you and being with you," I confided.

"Same here, My Sweet. I'll come over early in the morning, and maybe we can help Eugene hang tobacco together. I promised him last week that I could help him."

"What's that?"

He chuckled on the other end, "Listen, Sweet Thing, just wear a long-sleeve shirt and blue jeans because that tobacco can harm your arms and legs as you handle it. And pin that beautiful hair up."

"Okay."

"I'll get all the other kids to help us. I'll promise them another movie at the drive-in or take them to the hamburger joint."

"You know, Harold, I didn't bring any clothes with me because I didn't know I was going to wind up in Kentucky."

"Well, the girls will have something you can wear. They work in the fields all the time."

"Okay."

"I don't want to hang up, Donna, but we have to get some sleep, or we won't be worth a hoot tomorrow. Okay, Sweet Thing?"

"Yes," I agreed with him, "but I don't want to hang up."

"I don't want to say goodbye, but we have to."

"Okay. Goodnight."

"Maybe we should say good morning instead," and he chuckled again.

I loved to hear him laugh. It was such a deep, throaty sound—almost musical. And then we hung up. I don't think I slept more than an hour the rest of the night. I dozed off once or twice, but only for a short while. I laid there in bed beside Carmen and watched the hands on the clock slowly turn. I couldn't wait to see him again. My whole life I had always been unwanted and unloved. No one had ever made feel so special and accepted as Harold did. He made me feel as though I was worth something and not just a bastard to be kicked around.

Uncle Eugene was up early, but Aunt Edna was not a morning person, and she and the girls were still sleeping. I was up early, rummaging around in the closet, looking for some long pants and a long-sleeve shirt to wear. None of the girls' shirts that I tried on buttoned up because my breasts were bigger than theirs. I rolled my eyes and groaned inwardly. I hated not looking normal. Later in life, I realized that I was blessed with such a bosom. I finally found some jeans and a shirt that belonged to Ronnie folded neatly in the washroom.

At exactly seven a.m., Harold pulled into the drive. I was watching for him from the upstairs bedroom window. As soon as he wheeled in the driveway, I stepped back from the window because I didn't want him to see me waiting for him. Uncle Eugene sat on the porch, smoking a pipe. I knew he was down there because the sweet smell of his pipe tobacco wafted up to Carmen's room.

"Good morning, Gene," I heard Harold's sweet voice.

"Good morning, Son. Are you here to get started on the tobacco with me or to see you know who?" Uncle Eugene asked him.

"How about both? You know, mix business with pleasure?" Harold teased.

"Sounds like an outstandin' idea to me."

"How about I start some breakfast for everyone?" Harold offered.

"Everyone?"

"Sure."

Harold must have gone into the kitchen because I could hear him slamming a pan down on the stove and the refrigerator open, then the sizzling of bacon. I heard Uncle Eugene stomp up the stairs to wake everyone up. I met him halfway down the stairs. "Well now, Little Princess. You always get up early?" he asked.

"Yes," I replied as I walked on down the steps. I saw him from the corner of my eye shake his head as he continued up the steps. I hung around the corner of the kitchen watching Harold fix break-fast. He was wearing washed-out jeans with a blue checked shirt and a T-shirt underneath. His shirt was unbuttoned, and I could see his chest hair sticking out from the top of the T-shirt. I had this funny feeling in the lower pit of my stomach, and I didn't know what it meant. For some reason, I had this wild urge to run up and grab him and hold him tight, and I could not understand why. I stood there fascinated as I watched him.

He turned around with a pan of biscuits in his hand and said, "Oh! My Sweet Thing is an early riser! That's good, 'cause so am I." And he winked at me.

He said, "My Sweet Thing," I thought to myself. "My Sweet Thing!" It pleased me all the way down to my toes. I started to tingle all over—even in the roots of my hair.

I smiled and asked, "Is there anything I can do?"

He smiled that dimply smile I came to love so much and said softly, "I have a lot of plans for you, My Sweet Thing," and then he winked at me again. My stomach lurched. "But for now," he contin-ued, "how about setting the table."

"Okay. That'll work." I walked over to the cabinet and stood on my tippy toes and reached into the kitchen cabinet to get the dishes out. Harold reached into the cabinet at the same time to get a big bowl for the fried potatoes, and our hands touched. We both stood still for a few seconds, and I glanced up to look into his beautiful hazel eyes.

His eyes glanced down at my lips, and ever so quietly he whispered, "I want to kiss that delectable mouth of yours so bad my stomach hurts."

I licked my lips nervously but before I could reply, we heard Uncle Eugene stomp back down the stairs. I quickly turned away from Harold and tried to calm my shaking hands. After a few seconds, I turned back around and reached up and got the dishes out and began setting the table while Harold put the steaming potatoes in the bowl. They smelled delicious, and my stomach growled.

As we stood at the stove pouring the gravy in the bowls and taking the biscuits out of the oven, Uncle Eugene had disappeared out on the porch. Harold leaned over and whispered, "I want to kiss you, but I'm afraid I won't be able to stop." We both laughed nervously as all the other kids pounded down the stairs.

Ronnie bounced into the kitchen and took one look at me and exclaimed, "Wow! My jeans look a lot better on you than on me! And I must say you *really* know how to fill out a shirt!"

I must have blushed because he grinned and continued, "When you take them off, don't put them in the dirty clothes. I'm goin' to frame them and hang them over my bed!" Then he pretended to twist a fake mustache on the ends and rake me up and down. Everyone laughed but Harold. From the corner of my eye, I noticed that he was not amused.

After breakfast, Uncle Eugene complimented the cook. "Great breakfast, Harold! Where did you learn to cook like this?" he inquired.

"Well, Eugene, you don't go in the army for nothin', and all that KP duty taught me plenty." Then Harold sat back in his chair and said confidently, "I can make it on my own if I wanted to. But I'm going to find me some filly and settle down and have a few kids or so and pray that they all look like their mommy, whoever that might be." Then he looked over at me and gave me that great big smile of his.

"Sounds like you gotta plan," Uncle Eugene commented. "Have you sowed all your wild oats already?"

"Yeah, and then some."

I felt my face grow hot again.

While everyone pitched in and cleaned up the kitchen and put the dishes away, Uncle Eugene hooked the horse up to the flatbed. Carmen and Paulette started showing me how to pack a lunch and make some water and iced tea to take with us along with some blankets to set the food on. Together, we loaded up the flatbed, and Ronnie threw on some folding chairs and a baseball, bat, and gloves.

"What did you bring those for?" I asked.

"'Cause sometimes when we get the flatbed full, Dad takes it back down the hill and puts the tobacco in the barn and brings it back, and we fill 'er back up again. While he's gone, we play ball."

"Oh," I replied.

Although cutting down tobacco and placing it on the flatbed was not easy work by any means, it was wonderful because I got to work shoulder to shoulder with a very nice guy. We got one flatbed loaded, and Uncle Eugene headed down the hill with it. There was a huge picnic table that Uncle Eugene had built a long time ago, and we all sat down and had something to drink and a snack. Then we started a ball game. When it was Harold's turn to bat, he hit it as hard as he could and sent it flying into the woods. Everyone went running out into the woods to find it.

As soon as they took off running, he grabbed my hand and said, "Come on!" and pulled me behind some trees. "Okay, we've waited long enough to be alone. May I kiss you?"

"Yes," I replied nervously.

He put his arms around me and held me tenderly. Slowly he lowered his head, and our lips softly met. "Oh my gosh!" he exclaimed. "Do you feel what I feel?"

"I don't know what you're feeling," I told him.

Suddenly he let me go and ran toward the mountain spring and splashed into it. There was a waterfall about eight feet high, and he stood under it and let the water splash all over him.

"What are you doing?" I asked.

"Cooling off, My Love. Cooling off," came his quick reply. I felt my face grow hot as it must have turned a bright red.

I heard running footsteps, and when I looked behind me, Carmen, Ronnie, Paulette, Jimmy, and Phyllis came crashing out of the woods with the ball. "Hey, what're you doing, Uncle Harold?" Ronnie asked.

"Just cooling off," he replied and grinned at me.

"That looks like fun!" and Ronnie joined him. Next thing I know, we're all standing under the waterfall *cooling off*.

Uncle Eugene came back with the flatbed and noticed us under the waterfall. He sauntered over and stood under for a few minutes also. It was a warm day (in more ways than one).

I had to go to the bathroom, and I asked Carmen, "What do you do when you have to, you know, go?"

She handed me some toilet paper that was in a paper bag of the flatbed and said, "Pick a tree."

I looked at her in shock. "No!"

"I'll go with you, and we'll watch for each other."

We slowly made our way out into the trees looking for a good spot. When the boys saw us leave with the toilet paper, they knew to stay away. When we came back out, Harold asked, "Everything come out okay?"

I cocked my head to one side sort of puzzled. He just grinned, and we went back to work cutting tobacco and loading the flatbed.

"One more load should do it!" Uncle Eugene called as he started back down the hill with the second load. As soon as he left, we started to play again. The other kids started to fuss at Harold for knocking the ball over the hill every time it was his turn to bat.

Ronnie told him, "One more time, Uncle Harold, and you're out of the game!"

Harold just laughed. We kept playing until Uncle Eugene came back, and we continued cutting and loading tobacco again.

When we finished the last load and headed for the house, it was about six o'clock. Aunt Edna had a big supper waiting for us when we came home. It was extremely warm in the house because back in 1956, houses just didn't have air-conditioning. We decided to eat under the shade tree in the yard. After we finished eating, Harold asked Aunt Edna, "Is it okay if I take whoever wants to go to the movies?"

"I don't know… What do you think, Eugene?"

"They all worked really hard today. I think they deserve a treat," he replied.

We jumped up and helped clean the mess up, and Carmen and I took a shower while the boys ran down to the creek and washed up. Carmen gave me some white shorts and a pink T-shirt to wear. I pinned my hair up, and Harold jumped in the shower and changed into some old clothes that belonged to Uncle Eugene. The drive-in was playing *The Searcher* with John Wayne.

After the movie had started, Harold asked me, "Do you want to go over there and swing on the swings, Sweet Thing?"

"Sure," I replied.

He took my hand, and we strolled slowly over to the swing set. We could still see the other kids in the car, and they could see us, but now we could talk without everyone hearing everything we said. We exchanged our addresses because we wanted to write to each other after I went back home. By the time the movie was over, we walked back to the car, and everyone was sound asleep.

We got back in the car, and he slowly drove us home. We said very little to each other on the ride back. After a few minutes, he reached over and took my hand, and he held it all the way home. As soon as we pulled up, all the kids jumped out of the car and went inside and straight to bed.

Harold said, "I'm going to try and talk my Eugene and Edna into letting me take you to the Frostie hamburger place for a while, okay?"

I nodded shyly.

"Stay here in the car, and I'll be right back," he said as he jumped out of the car and ran inside the house.

I could hear Aunt Edna getting louder and louder, and finally she came to the front door and waved me into the house. Harold was still trying to convince her to let me go. Finally, she said, "Okay, Harold. But I'm telling you right now, you had better have her back in two hours! And I mean it!"

"I'm not going to run away with her. We just enjoy each other's company."

"Okay. You got two hours starting now. And you know you're putting me in the middle with her family."

"I know," he answered sheepishly. "I'll treat her with the utmost respect."

He pulled the car very carefully out of the driveway because he knew they were watching and drove slowly down the road. Just as we got out of sight he said, "Let me synchronize my watch," and he fiddled around with his watch for a minute. Then he reached over. "May I kiss you now?"

I nodded again.

He pulled his car over the side of the road and scooted closer to me. The kiss was soft and tender. I felt him tremble, and he jumped out of the car and began walking away from the car. Then he turned around and walked back to the car and turned around walking away again.

"What are you doing?" I asked.

"Just thinking," and he continued to walk.

After a few minutes, he got back in the car, and he drove to the Frostie Root Beer stand. Because the small restaurant had curb service, we didn't have to get out of the car. We ordered root beers because both of us were too nervous to eat anything. At least that's how I felt. We quietly stared out the windshield and sipped on our root beers for several minutes. Finally, he broke the silence and said, "You know, Sweet Thing, I don't have nothin' to offer you, but I think I'm in love with you already."

"I don't know if I love you, Harold, but I do know I enjoy being with you. And when I am not with you, I feel all alone in the world again. And then I'm with you again, and everything seems right with the world again," I confided and looked up at him.

He sucked in his breath and continued, "Well, like I said, I don't have anything to offer you but myself. But I'll do everything I can to make your life comfortable, and I *do* know I love you."

I felt the tears welling in my eyes, and I sobbed, "That means I'll have to quit school and move away from Mom and Dad. I don't know if I'm ready for that."

He placed his hands on each side of my face and brushed away a tear with one of his thumbs and said softly, "I'll wait for you as long as you want me to." He smiled and continued, "Donna, I'm asking you to be my wife," and he paused and added, "when you're ready."

I couldn't believe that someone as wonderful as this man wanted me—*me*, a bastard from nowhere who was nothin' but a piece of crap, which is what I was told my entire life—to be his wife. I cried harder and was speechless. After a few minutes, I nodded and wiped at my tears with the back of my sleeve.

He grinned and hugged me tight, kissing me on the top of my head to calm me down. A few minutes later, he glanced at his watch and sighed, "I have to get you back, or Edna will kill me."

We drove back to my aunt and uncle's in silence. I think we were both busy digesting what we had just discussed. Harold walked me slowly to the door and said good night. Aunt Edna and Uncle Eugene were waiting on me when I walked in the door. I heard Harold's car start up and pull out of the driveway.

Uncle Eugene cleared his throat and said, "He's too old for you, Donna. You have to call this thing off."

"Harold is a very good, loving, and gentle man, Donna," Aunt Edna chimed in, "but you are still a little girl. Please don't hurt him or yourself. Call this off, please."

I plopped down on a chair in the living room and hung my head and confessed, "I'm confused, Aunt Edna. I don't know what to do. I think I care for your Harold very much, but I don't know if it's love I feel. I only know that when he is not around, I am thinking of him. And when he is around, I feel like I belong with him, and everything is going to be alright."

I shrugged my shoulders and continued, "I do know that when I marry, I want a man like him."

I glanced up at them and whispered, "His gentleness, his sense of humor, and his sweet disposition…I just…I don't know," and I flung my hands up in the air.

Aunt Edna began shaking her head, and her red curls bounced around softly. "You know, Donna, I'm going to have to call your parents and tell them."

I jerked my head up and begged, "Please don't do that, Aunt Edna. Please!"

41

"I'm sorry to have to do that, but if it was Carmen falling for a man eight years older than her, I'd want to know. So I hope you understand."

I lowered my head and nodded slowly as the tears started to roll down again. I knew all hell was about to break loose at home.

The next morning, Aunt Edna called Mom and told her about Harold and me. Mom must have told Aunt Edna she wanted to speak to me because Aunt Edna handed me the phone. I cleared my throat and tried to say as normally as possible, "Hi, Mom, what'd you want?"

"You know what I want, young lady!" she scolded. "You stay away from that Clouse boy!"

"But—"

"And we'll be there sometime tomorrow to pick you up!"

"Mom, we're just talking to each other."

"I don't care! You stay at Eugene and Edna's house, and don't you dare go anywhere with him alone!"

I sighed heavily because I knew there was no reasoning with her when she was in a rampage. "Okay, Mom."

I said good night to my aunt and uncle and slowly made my way up the stairs.

I waited until they were both asleep, and then I crept quietly back downstairs and called Harold's number. He answered the phone, and I could tell he was nervous. He said, "Hi. I'm glad you called."

I briefly told him what happened.

"My mom and dad are really upset too. They keep telling me that you're too young for me and to stay away from you." He snorted, "as if I could do that!"

I laughed tearfully and said, "Aunt Edna called my mom and dad, and they're coming after me tomorrow."

"Yeah, I figured that." Then he told me very quietly, "I really love you, Donna, and I want to spend the rest of my life with you. And I think you love me too."

I shrugged my shoulders even though he couldn't see me and replied, "But I don't know what love is. All I do know is that I care for you very much."

"Well, how about if I come over early in the morning, and we can be together till they get down here to get you?" he asked.

"Okay."

I heard his mother in the background say a little loudly, "Son, you'd better leave that pretty little thing alone. She can get you into a lot of trouble."

"Mom, I can't get her pregnant on the phone! Leave me alone!"

I couldn't help but laugh.

"Go ahead and laugh," he told me. "I'm already in a lot of trouble with my family and yours. But I know that someday you're going to be mine."

The next day, we spent all day with my cousins swimming, talking, and playing ball. We knew our time was short together, and Aunt Edna refused to let us be alone. About five o'clock that evening, Aunt Pauline and Uncle Warren pulled into the drive to take me home because Mom and Dad couldn't get off from work in such a short time. I was excited to see them because I could talk to Aunt Pauline without her getting judgmental and losing her temper.

When they first came in, Harold was there beside me holding my hand. Aunt Edna introduced them to Harold, and Harold said, "I want you to know that we have only been talking, and most of the time the other kids were with us. We were hardly ever alone. Nothing has happened, and nothing will happen until we are properly married." And he gave my hand a gentle squeeze and continued, "And you can tell her parents that."

Uncle Warren nodded, and then we sat down together and socialized for a while. Aunt Edna fixed dinner, and we sat down at the dinner table with the rest of my cousins and ate. Uncle Warren looked over across the table at Harold and said, "We'll be leaving in the morning to take her back home."

"I understand," Harold replied. "I'll be writing and calling Donna, and I hope her parents will allow her to do the same."

After dinner was cleaned up, the adults went into the living room to talk, and I'm sure Harold and I were the subject of their conversation. The rest of us sat on the back porch and talked for a while. Someone suggested a bonfire, and before I knew it, we're roasting wieners and marshmallows over the fire. Several hours later, Aunt Edna called us to come in for the evening. Harold kissed my cheek and whispered in my ear, "It's going to be okay, Sweet Thing."

I watched him get in his car and back out of the driveway. We waved at one another, and I watched his car until it disappeared around the curve. Tears were dripping down my cheeks as I turned around to go back inside. I felt empty and lonely when I was not with him.

The next morning, Harold was there bright and early, wearing his jeans and a white T-shirt and stood by his car with his hands in his front pockets. Uncle Warren was putting our things in his new Pontiac. I walked up to Harold, and he took my hands in his and kissed me on the cheek and whispered, "Don't worry. I'll be calling you as soon as you get home." Then he flashed me that brilliant smile of his.

I watched him from the back window as we pulled out of the driveway. I craned my head around as best I could to keep him in sight until I could no longer see him. Then I slumped down in the back seat and fought the tears that welled just inside my eyes, threatening to spill out and pour down my cheeks.

Both Aunt Pauline and Uncle Warren were quiet and didn't preach to me about how we weren't right for each other. About noon, we stopped for something to eat, and Aunt Pauline said, "Donna, you can be so much more than just a wife and mother. I will say that everything I have heard about Harold has all been good. Everyone speaks very highly of him. His family is afraid you will hurt him because you are too young to know what you really want out life."

I started to shake my head.

She reached across the table and touched my hand, "I know you think you do. Trust me, you don't. When we are your age, we think we know everything. But in time, you will find out that you don't know everything."

When we finally got home, Mom and Dad were waiting on me—and were not very happy, I might add. Mom said, "Donna, there is so much more in life for you than being just a housewife and having a bunch of kids tied to your apron strings. Everything we have heard about Harold is very favorable, but, honey, he is *eight* years older than you!" She made a point of emphasizing the eight.

I sat quietly in the living room and let her continue her tirade.

"He has sewn his wild oats and is ready to settle down, but you haven't."

I slung my raven hair behind my back and said quietly, "You know, Mom and Dad, I just want to go to my room, take a nice hot shower, put on my clothes, and lay down and think about this. Okay?"

"Sure, go ahead," Mom replied. She glanced over at Dad, who shrugged his shoulders.

I had taken my shower and was lying on the bed when the phone rang. Mom opened my bedroom door and said in exasperation, "It's him."

I jumped off the bed and dashed down to the hallway by the stairs to the phone, and we started talking. I laid across the steps upside down with the phone plastered to my ear. A while later, Mom and Dad made their way up the stairs to go to bed. Mom said, "I hope that boy has plenty of money to talk this long on the phone."

She paused on the steps and looked down at me and asked, "By the way, what do you two talk about it?"

I smiled and said, "This and that and the other." I heard Harold chuckle on the other end.

"Come on, Honey, leave them alone," Dad admonished her.

We continued to talk for a little while longer. Then Harold said, "She's right. I better hang up. It's going to cost me my whole pay check for this call." We said our good nights and hung up.

I had a hard time going to sleep because all I could do was think about him—the man who told me I had stolen his heart. I must have finally fell asleep because Mom woke me the next morning. I had to babysit the Alburn kids that day.

Dad dropped me off on his way to work and said he would pick me up on his way home. As soon as Mr. and Mrs. Alburn had left for work, I called Harold and gave him the Alburn's phone number.

"I was afraid your parents had talked you out of being with me," he confessed.

"Not a chance, Big Guy."

"Big Guy? How did you come up with that?" he asked me curiously. "I'm just an average size guy. I'm not tall and not short. Just average."

"I don't look at a person's size. I look deep inside to their heart. And you have a great big one," I told him.

He chuckled on the other end. "Hey, I sent a package to your parents."

"You did? What?"

"Don't say anything to them and see if they say anything to you about it."

"Okay." It appeared he wasn't going to tell me what was in the package he sent, so I didn't pressure him about it.

"Let me know, okay?"

"Okay."

"I have to get to work, so I can buy you a ring."

"That's not important to me."

"I want the whole world to know that you're mine, and I don't want any guys cutting into my territory," he replied.

"You don't have to worry about that. All the boys my age are airheads and still play with cap guns," I said as grown-up as I could.

He laughed and then said a little seriously, "And you should probably still be playing with dolls too."

"But I'm glad you are older than me. That's what attracted me to you," I told him matter-of-factly.

"What attracted me were those eyes of yours. They should be labeled dangerous. A man could get lost in them forever, did you know that?"

I snorted, "You're just saying that."

"No, I mean that with all my heart. I love you, Sweet Thing. I have to go. I'll call you at home tonight."

"Okay, Big Guy."

We hung up.

He called me every night for the next few nights. On Thursday night when he called me, he asked me, "Did your Mom and Dad get the gift I sent?"

"I don't know. They haven't said anything about it."

He was quiet for a few seconds, "Well, okay. Let me know if you find out. I bought you a ring, and I want to bring it to you this weekend."

I sucked my breath in. I couldn't believe it. Someone loved me enough to buy me a ring! "But, how are you going to give it to me this weekend? I'm supposed to go with the Alburns to Lake Buckeye for the weekend."

"When are you leaving?"

"Saturday morning. I'm supposed to spend the night Friday. We can leave early Saturday morning."

"Okay, I'll come by Friday night. What time do they go to bed?"

"Anywhere between ten and ten thirty."

"After they go to sleep, walk up the street, and I'll meet you there and give you the ring."

"Okay." I was so excited. Everything was happening so fast.

We hung.

That Wednesday evening, during dinner, Mom said, "We got a package today from Harold."

"Oh?" I replied a little nervously. "What was it?"

"It was two records and a letter."

My head darted up from my plate of food, and I asked as innocently as I could, "Really?"

"Yes. The letter said, '*Mr. and Mrs. Allen, please listen to these records because this is how I feel about your daughter. I will never hurt her or desert her. You must believe me, Harold.*'"

"What were the records?" I asked.

"One was *Oh Donna* and the other one was *Georgia On My Mind.*"

I think it must have softened their hearts a little toward Harold. But I wasn't sure. It was hard to read my parents.

When Harold called me the next morning, I said, "They got your package."

"What did they say?" he asked anxiously.

"Nothing, really. But they weren't mad, and that's a start."

"Okay. Don't forget. I'll be there Friday night. Can you see the street from the bedroom window at the Alburns?"

"Yes," I replied a little nervously.

"Okay. Keep a look out after ten o'clock for me because the way I got it figured, I should be there sometime between ten thirty and eleven. When you see my car go down the street real slow, you sneak out and come down the street, and I'll give you the ring, and then you can slip back into the house."

"Okay, Harold."

I was so nervous that I didn't eat much. My hands trembled every time I picked anything up or sat it down. I noticed Mom watching curiously, but she didn't say anything.

Friday night finally came, and after I went to bed, I kept watching the light under Mr. and Mrs. Alburn's bedroom door, waiting for it to go out. Finally, about ten twenty, the light went out, and I crouched down by the bedroom window in the kids' room and waited for Harold's car to go by. About ten minutes later, I saw his car drive by very slowly, and he was watching the house.

Looking back on it now, I should have waited a little longer, but I was so excited to see him. Every minute of waiting seemed like hours. I couldn't wait any longer. There was a man outside who had professed his love to me, waiting to give me a ring and steal a kiss or two.

I thought for sure the Alburns were asleep and snuck out of the bedroom barefoot, holding my shoes in one of my hands. The steps were old and some of them creaked when you stepped on them. I tried to step on the side of the steps to keep from making any noise. I felt like James Bond sneaking around in the night, and I giggled nervously. I clamped may free hand over my mouth to squelch the giggling, and I tried to calm my beating heart.

Finally, I made it down the stairs, making only a little noise, and to the front door. As carefully as I could, I unlocked the door, took the chains off, and pulled the door open as carefully as I could. The screen door made a little screeching sound as I opened it, and I cringed and glanced behind my back. No lights came on...yet. They didn't have any air-conditioning, and all the windows were open to catch any breezes to keep the house cooler. I was terrified that they had heard me open the door.

Finally, I was on the front porch. I put my shoes on and started running down the street toward the direction I saw Harold's car go. Harold had parked under a streetlight, and he was waiting for me. He jumped out of the car, but I saw panic deep in their depths. I flew into his arms, but he shoved me behind him. I heard running footsteps, and I peeked around Harold and saw Mr. Alburn pointing a German Luger at us wearing his pajamas.

"Hey, bud," Harold said sternly. "Don't point that gun at her. You got that?"

"Yeah, I got it," Mr. Alburn replied. "Just what are you planning on doing with this minor?"

"I brought her an engagement ring. I'm going to give it to her, talk for a few minutes, and then I was going to go on my way," Harold confidently replied.

"I don't think so. I think you were going to kidnap her and run across the state line somewhere and get married."

"No. That's not all what we had planned."

"We planned just what Harold told you," I interjected.

Mr. Alburn looked down at me and noticed the protective arm Harold had around me and said, "Well, come on back to the house with me, and I'll call your Mom and Dad. They told me something like this might happen."

The three of us walked back up the street to the house with Mr. Alburn holding a gun on Harold the whole time even after we got to the house, and we were sitting in the living room waiting on Mom and Dad. Dad arrived a few minutes later and took the scene in— Mr. Alburn holding a gun on Harold who was sitting in one chair and me across the room in another.

"I don't think that's necessary," Dad told Mr. Alburn. "Put the gun away."

I was crying, and Harold was trying to comfort me from across the room.

"Come on," Dad said. "We have to go home and talk this over with your Mom."

Then he turned to Harold and said, "You follow us, Harold."

"Yes, sir. But first I want you to know that I was just bringing her an engagement ring, and that was all. But this man," Harold was pointing at Mr. Alburn, "thought I planned to run away with your daughter. Don't think I didn't' think of that, 'cause I did. But I was going to do whatever Donna wanted. I was just going to give her a ring and let her think about it a few more weeks."

"Okay, son. I believe you, but we have to go talk it over with her mother."

When we got home, Mom was up and had a pot of coffee on waiting on us. We all sat down at the kitchen table. "Harold, do you want some coffee?" Mom asked politely.

"Well, yes. Thank you. I will have a long drive ahead of me."

Mom got up to make him a cup and Harold continued, "I want to tell you Mr. and Mrs. Allen, I love your daughter. I have treated her with nothing but respect, and I will continue to do so. I can wait as long as it takes Donna to make up her mind. I've told Donna that she can finish school if she wants. That's fine. I'll wait for her. Or if you want me to wait until she's twenty-one. That's fine too. She's worth waiting for." Then he turned those hazel eyes on me, and he smiled. I melted right there in that chair.

"Well, thanks for the records," Mom replied. "We were quite sure you had made up your mind about her."

She turned to me and asked, "The question is, how does Donna feel about the situation?"

"I want to marry him now, Mom," I replied without any hesitation. I wanted to have a home of my own and a husband and children to take care of. I wanted to make sure that they got everything in life that I never had.

Mom took a sip of her coffee and seemed to be contemplating. "Okay, let me tell you this, Harold," and she turned back to him. "You come back next Friday, and I'll go with you to get the marriage license. But if they ask me how old she is, I will not lie. Understand?"

"I understand."

He gave me the ring and said good night and said, "I'll see you Friday, Sweetie."

I watched until he was out of sight, and then I came back inside. My heart was breaking. I cared for him very much, but I also loved my Mom and Dad. They were the first people in my life who loved me and gave me a stable home. They respected me and loved me as a human being, and I loved and respected them. They gave me everything I ever needed or wanted. My whole life was about to change—again.

Chapter 4

The next morning, I told Mom that I didn't want to go with the Alburns that weekend, and she called them for me. She also told them that I would be there on Monday and through the week, but I might not be back the following week if I got married. That was one of the longest weeks of my life. I tried to keep busy, but my mind kept drifting back to Harold.

Friday finally came, and Harold was at the house at 6:00 a.m. I had packed my suitcase the night before, and Mom had packed a few things, and we drove to Southshore, Kentucky, which was 180 miles from Columbus. Mom's sister, Sylvia, lived there. As soon as we arrived, Aunt Sylvia asked, "You know, Donna, the whole world is in front of you. Are you sure you want to do this?"

I sighed. It was the same old question. "Yes, I'm sure," I replied.

"Okay, honey. You have my support, and I will help you in any way I can."

Mom stayed at Aunt Sylvia's while I went with Harold to Franklin County to get our license. Harold wore his uniform, and I wore a white dress and high heels with my hair up to make me look taller and a little older. The man at the license office took one look at me and raised his eyebrow and asked, "She's eighteen. Is that right, son?"

"Yes, sir," Harold replied.

He shrugged and wrote out the license and handed it to us. Then he told us where to go to get our blood test, and after the blood test we had to bring it back to him. We got the blood test, gave the certificate to the man at the courthouse, and he stamped the license. Now we could get married. The man at the courthouse told Harold,

"Well, soldier, you have a great little gal here. You better treat her right and congratulations." Then he smiled at us.

All we needed now were two witnesses. We drove back to Aunt Sylvia's to pick them up, but Aunt Sylvia couldn't go because she had two small children. We drove Mom over to Aunt Laurie's, who didn't live far from Aunt Sylvia, and we went in search of a preacher to marry us. We went to the First Baptist Church, and the pastor was there, and he married us. Harold was still wearing his uniform, and I wore the white dress with rhinestones along the bodice and the white shoes. Mom found me a blue hankie, and Aunt Laurie loaned me her wedding ring. Mom bought me a corsage—so now I had something old, something new, something borrowed, and something blue. I was ready to plunge into the future with so many twists and turns I could never imagine.

We stood before the pastor and said our vows. We were both nervous. Harold's palms were sweaty. Finally, the pastor pronounced us man and wife. He softly kissed me, and his eyes glowed as he looked down at me. "You're mine," he whispered and grinned that beautiful dimply grin of his.

Mom hugged him and kissed me, and Aunt Laurie hugged us both and kissed us on the cheeks. Harold turned around to give the pastor some money and the pastor bent down on the desk to fill out the marriage certificate. "Do you mind," he said. "It's number 13. I can tear it up and get another one."

Harold looked at it and said to me, "I'm not superstitious. Are you, Honey?"

"No," I replied nervously. But so many times after that day I wished I had said yes.

But God had a plan for us—long before we ever met.

We got back in the car, and Mom and Aunt Laurie had some rice in their purses, and they threw it on us. We all laughed. Harold drove Aunt Laurie home, and then he drove Mom back to Aunt Sylvia's. She planned on spending the night with her sister, and then Dad drove back the next day to pick her up.

We changed clothes and freshened up, and Aunt Sylvia served us cake and coffee. It was about 6:00 p.m. when we said our goodbyes and thanked everyone. After we had driven for a few miles, Harold pulled over to the side of the road and took me in his arms and said ever so softly with his eyes shining brightly at me, "You're mine. All mine." And he kissed me tenderly. "I don't know what I have done to deserve you, but whatever it was, 'Thank you, God.'" He smiled at me. "Let's put the top down, Baby, and get all the fresh air we can. We have about three hundred miles to drive."

Harold took all the back roads because he loved the countryside and driving down country roads. I was just happy to be with him. Several hours later, we arrived in Frankfurt, Kentucky, and he said, "It's getting late, and I'm tired. Let's stop for the night, and I'll finish driving into Lexington tomorrow. Okay?"

"Okay," I replied a little nervously.

He pulled into the parking lot of very nice hotel. I had never spent the night in a hotel before. We strolled into the lobby holding hands. The older gentleman at the front desk peered at him over his glasses and asked, "Is this your wife, sir?"

"She is," Harold proudly replied.

"Do you have a marriage certificate?"

"Marriage certificate?" Harold asked in faked bewilderment. "What's that?"

I poked him in the arm and exclaimed, "Harold!" My face turned every shade of red you could think of.

Harold chuckled and pulled it out of his uniform pocket. "Watch it, mister. The ink is still wet."

We were given a nice room on the third floor. Harold sat our suitcases on the bed and said, "Honey, I'm going downstairs and get us some ice and sodas."

"Okay." I was glad to have a few minutes alone. I took the pins out of my hair and shook the long tresses out and let it cascade down my back. I slipped into my light blue baby-doll pajamas and sat down and brushed my hair one hundred times, just like I did every night.

Harold came in a little bit later and stopped dead in his tracks as he stared at me. He had bought four different kinds of sodas and some cheese and crackers. He cleared his throat and placed the sodas, cups, and so forth on the table. Then he poured a little bit each of the Dr. Pepper, Coke, Cherry Coke, and root beer into a cup of ice and handed it to me. Then he made another one just like it. He held his up and said, "Now, we can say we had mixed drinks on our wedding night!"

I giggled, "You're so crazy, Harold."

"Yeah, I know. But isn't that great, my Little Sweetie Pie?" Then he jumped on the bed and patted the space beside him. I slowly walked over and sat on the edge. He took me by the hand. "I know you've never been with a man before, and I'll only do want you want me to. You say stop at any time, and I promise I'll stop. By the way, do you know anything about a man and wife's intimate relationship?"

"A little, I guess," I confided nervously and shrugged my shoulders averting my eyes.

He put his arms around me and said so softly, I had to strain to hear what he was saying, "You do something to me that no one else could ever do. You know that, don't you?"

"No," I replied a little breathlessly.

"Okay. We'll leave that alone for now." Then he got up and went into the bathroom. I could hear him bumping around in the bathroom, and a few minutes later he came back out wearing his under shorts and T-shirt. I started laughing and pointing at all the red hair on his legs. He glanced down at himself and asked, "Why are you laughing, Babe?"

"You have red hair on your legs!" and I kept on giggling.

"Didn't you notice that when we went swimming a few weeks ago?"

"I guess I didn't," and I slapped my hand over my mouth to keep from giggling.

He shrugged and turned on the TV. "What do you want to watch?"

"I'd rather listen to music," I told him honestly.

He turned off the TV and turned on the radio beside the bed on the nightstand. The radio started blaring out Big Band music. He glanced down at me and asked, "Do you like this kind of music?"

"Yeah."

"That's strange," he commented. "That music was before both of our time. Most of it, anyway."

"Yeah, I know."

Harold turned the light out, and we lay in the dark and listened to the music for a few minutes. Suddenly, he asked me, "You wanna dance?"

"I can't dance."

"Wanna bet?" He pulled me up out of bed and into his arms, and we started jigger bugging. Then a slow song came on, and he pulled me close to him, and we fit together like a hand in a glove. It felt almost natural to me. It was so nice not having to worry about being caught. Harold was a great dancer. Another fast number came on, and we started dancing fast again.

A few minutes later, I fell on the bed and exclaimed, "I have to stop!"

He shrugged his shoulders and pretended to dance with someone else. "I'm not as old as you think!" he exclaimed. "You puttered out on me."

I laughed and said, "I'll show you!" Before I could get up off the bed, the phone rang. It was the hotel lobby asking us to please turn down the music. We did. And we lay there laughing together. Then we started kissing. A few minutes later I heard him whisper breathlessly, "If I hurt you, just say so, and I'll stop."

We continued kissing and he slipped my pajamas off. He took one look at my body in the moonlight, and I heard him suck his breath in. Then he pulled off his T-shirt and kicked his undershorts off. He pulled me close to his body, and our naked bodies met. He was patient and very gentle with me. I felt something build up deep inside, but at the time I didn't know what it was. Our kisses became more passionate. "Are you sure you want me to go on?" he asked.

"Yes, I think so," came my breathless reply.

"Are you sure, Honey?" he asked me again. "We can wait until you're older."

"No. It's okay," I reassured him. I knew there was something more to experience, and I thought I was ready. The radio continued to play softly, and he was kissing my neck and moving lower to my chest.

"Are you sure?" he asked one more time.

"Yes. Yes. Go ahead."

I felt a stinging and ripping sensation. The pain made me think of that man who tried to rape me. I screamed, "Get off me! Get off me! I hate you! I want to go home!"

I looked at his stricken face and immediately wanted to take the words back, but all I could do was cry. He jumped up and turned the radio off and slipped a towel around his waist and covered me up with the sheets. As I lay there sobbing unable to stop, Harold kept whispering over and over, "Honey, I'm sorry. I'm sorry. I didn't mean to hurt you. It only hurts like this the first time, that's all. I won't touch you again until you're ready. I promise."

I started to calm down, and I said through the tears, "There's something I have to tell you."

"Whenever you're ready, Babe. Here, let me pour you a soda, okay?" He poured me a root beer and handed it to me. "You can tell me anything. It's not going to change the way I feel for you, and I'll always love you. I'll wait as long as it takes before we try to make love again."

"Harold," I began between sobs, "someone tried to rape me when I was eleven years old."

Harold's jaw dropped open in disbelief—not that he didn't believe me but that someone would try to do such a thing to an eleven-year-old girl.

"I had to fight him off to protect myself," I sniffed. I took a sip of the root beer. "It was only by the grace of God that I was able to stop him."

He held me tenderly and whispered hoarsely, "Oh, baby. Oh, baby. I'm so sorry. I love you, Donna. That will never change how I feel about you."

We lay there the rest of the night. He held me in his arms and kissed my forehead and rubbed my arms. I completely gave him my heart that night. I knew then that Harold was my protector, and he always took care of me. I knew that Harold was a blessing from God. Only God could know what kind of man it would take to break down the wall of mistrust that I had placed around myself while growing up as a little girl. Mom and Dad had chipped some of the concrete away from my heart, but Harold had destroyed it.

A little while later when I was getting nice and sleepy, he asked, "Do you know who this person is and where is?"

"Yes. He was arrested and me and some other women testified against him, and he's serving life in jail."

Daylight had started to peek through the drapes, and I could see tears in Harold's beautiful hazel eyes, and he had a hurt expression on his face. "Honey," he began, "I can't even begin to imagine what you must have gone through. But I am here for you now and always." Then he kissed me tenderly. "I'll go to my grave making it up to you. We're paid up until 11:00 a.m., but I think we'll get an early start, so we can get home and go apartment hunting."

A worried expression crossed his face and he looked down at me and asked, "Are you mad at me?"

"Why?"

"You know, you said you hated me last night, and you wanted to go home. Do you still hate me and want to go home?"

I smiled and touched his unshaven cheek tenderly. "I know. I'm sorry. I didn't know what I was feeling last night. I was scared and confused. Please forgive me."

He took my hand and held it to his lips, "You are always forgiven. Always. Nothing on this earth could steal my love from you, Donna. You will always be my, Sweet Thing."

"I love you, Harold," I whispered. And his face beamed.

We got to his house early, and his mother ran out the front door and pulled us both into her huge arms at the same time and hugged us. Behind her stood a small older gentleman wearing an old suit and hat with tobacco juice on his chin, grinning. "Let go, Mommy," he scolded. "Let's me get a hug in, will ya?" But she didn't let go. She just kept hugging and kissing our cheeks. I was beginning to suffocate in her loving embrace.

"We've got a big family party fixed up for you this evening at Eugene and Edna's," she exclaimed with twinkling blue eyes.

"Okay, Mommy," Harold gasped, "but you have to let go of us so we can breathe!"

She let us go and Poppie, Harold's dad, hugged and congratulated us. He was half her size, but I still felt welcomed.

As soon as we stepped into the modest older home, which I found out later didn't have a bathroom but an outhouse out back, Harold asked all business as he set our cases down, "Do you have the paper, Mommy?"

"Yes, and I circled some apartments for rent I thought you might like," she beamed.

Harold glanced quickly through the paper and made a few calls. After looking at several apartments, we began to get discouraged because they were either too small, too dirty, bad neighborhood, etc. We finally found a one-bedroom apartment, fully furnished that a widow was advertising for rent that was upstairs with a private entrance. We called her, and she said we could come right over to see it.

The lady—her name was Leona—was very sweet. She had lost her husband a few months earlier and needed to rent out the upstairs, or she was going to lose her home. Harold told her we would take it, and he paid her the deposit and first month's rent. All we had to buy were a few dishes, pots and pans, towels, and linens.

We drove back to his parents' house and packed up his few belongings—some records, a radio, record player, clothes, and things. All we had of any value was each other and his car.

"Now, don't forget. We're having a big dinner at Edna's tonight," his mother reminded us.

Harold groaned, "Mom, do I have to?"

"Yes, you do. And then we'll leave you and your pretty wife alone for a little while, anyway." She grinned that grin that so much looked like Harold's and laughed. Her blue eyes twinkling.

We drove the three miles back to the apartment and unloaded our belongings, dumping them wherever we found a spot. "Don't worry about it," I told him. "I'll straighten it up tomorrow while you're at work." We freshened up because we had been on the run all day, and I dressed in my pedal pushers, a nice blouse, and a pair of sandals. Harold put on his famous jeans and white T-shirt that I came to love him in. I glanced around at our little apartment and sighed because I really wanted to stay and start setting up housekeeping, but at the same time I didn't want to disappoint his family. We left our little apartment to go to Uncle Eugene and Aunt Edna's for the big shindig.

When we pulled in the driveway, Harold's eyes lit up and my jaw dropped down to my chest. My mouth must have been a big O because I could not believe my eyes! They had strung a huge sign across the front of the house that read in giant hand-printed letters, "Welcome to the Clouse Family, Donna! Congratulations, Harold!"

Suddenly, the front door burst open and what appeared to be an army ran toward us; but instead of carrying guns, they carried all kinds of food and wedding gifts. Harold's entire family had shown up to welcome us home. His three sisters and their families and all of his brothers (Harold was the youngest of thirteen children) and their families. I really liked his sister Mildred; she was a lot like Harold. And of course, Mommy and Poppie Clouse came running as best they could up to the car. I found out later that there were also some close friends of the family that had come as well. Even some people from the First Baptist Church that his mom and dad went to were there. There were people from mommies carrying newborns to older people sitting in rocking chairs, all smiling and all happy, and all ages in between. There were children running around all over the place laughing, with mother's scolding them for getting into the food too early. Later that evening, I saw a jug being passed around the men.

Harold's best friend, "Peevine," and his wife were there. His name was Harold also and practically lived at the Clouses' growing up. When he was little, he used to go outside and instead of going up to the outhouse, he peed on Mommy's flower vines on the porch. So Mrs. Clouse started calling him Peevine, and the name stuck. I couldn't bring myself to call him that. His wife, Lil, just called him Harold. Peevine was extremely tall, towering over any of the Clouse men, with sandy hair and green eyes. Lil was nice and very pretty; she was also tall, but not as tall as Peevine, with long brown hair and striking blue eyes. She was expecting her first child. We became best friends overnight.

I had never had so many hugs and kisses at one time in my entire life! There appeared to be at least one hundred people on that tobacco farm that evening. My heart ached for the love I felt pouring out of each and every one of my new family members. Instead of being a lonely girl hidden in a wall to keep from being beaten, I was now a young married woman with a new family who were the epitome of love and affection.

When it came time to open the gifts, we were truly overwhelmed by their thoughtfulness. We received sheets, blankets, silverware, glasses, pots and pans, dishes, towels, washcloths, a coffee pot, mixer, toaster, lamps—Mommy (Harold's mother) must have tipped everyone off.

Some of the boys brought their instruments, and they set up a dance floor on the driveway and started playing and singing. Those who wanted to dance got up and danced. Harold was a wonderful dancer. He was so attentive and made sure that his family didn't overwhelm me too much.

Boy, did we eat! There were all kinds of food there. They roasted a hog, fixed fried chicken, four or five different kinds of potato salads. There was even a sweet potato salad, which I had never had before; it was delicious. We had baked beans, coleslaw, and all kinds of cakes, puddings, pies. I could go on and on.

There were children playing all over the place, and I enjoyed watching them. Harold confessed to me later that some of the men were passing around homemade moonshine. It was a dry county back then.

Finally, about two in the morning, the party started breaking up, and some of the family and friends began to leave. We were exhausted, but we thanked everyone for the wonderful gifts they brought. I took down everyone's names to send them thank you cards later. Harold sauntered over to his mom and dad, with his arm around me and said, "Mommy and Poppie, we have to go. I have to be on the job in the morning at 7:00 a.m." Harold worked as a machinist at an ice cream factory in Lexington. Everyone hugged and kissed us all over again. We said our goodbyes and left with all our gifts stuffed in the car to where there was barely room for us and drove back to Lexington.

We finally got back to the apartment around 3:00 a.m. Harold took one look at the circles under my eyes and said, "We'll unload the car tomorrow."

I didn't argue. "Okay."

We were so tired, we could hardly climb the stairs, but we went up them as quietly as we could to keep from waking the landlady, Leona, and her daughter, Ariana. We washed up and passed out holding each other in our arms. The alarm clock went off what seemed like fifteen minutes later. Harold jumped up, showered, and leaned over and kissed me.

He lingered over me for a moment and whispered softly, "I usually come home for lunch."

I had no idea what to fix for my new husband. We hadn't known each other long enough to learn likes and dislikes. "What do you want for lunch?"

"Just you, Babe," he murmured, hazel eyes sparkling hotly. "Just you."

I felt my hot face redden, and he laughed and dashed down the stairs.

I yawned and stretched and buried my head under the covers. It had been a busy last few days, and I was exhausted. I went back to sleep. When I woke up and glanced at the clock, it was 10:30. I had never slept that late in my entire life! Harold told me that he usually came home around 12:15 for lunch. I hurried up and showered and fixed my hair. We hadn't had time to go to the grocery store yet, so there was no food in the apartment to fix him any lunch. I felt a pang of guilt when Harold came home with a bag of hamburgers and French fries and two soft drinks.

"We'll go out tonight and get some groceries in the house," he said between mouthfuls of his cheeseburger.

"Okay." (I said okay a lot back then. I was young and didn't have a lot to say. I was a newlywed and figured Harold was older and wiser and knew a lot more than I did.)

After we ate, I started cleaning up the kitchen table. Harold peeked around the corner at me and said softly, "Come here."

I dropped the wrapper in the trash and strolled over to the bed where he was standing. He laughed and grabbed me and threw me on the bed and said with fake menace and twisting his pretend mustache on the ends, "I'll take my desert now." My eyes must have grown as big as saucers and my jaw dropped down onto my chest and he laughed. "Second thought, I'll take a rain check." He kissed me tenderly and sighed. "I'll see you tonight." Then he dashed through the screen door and pounded down the steps.

"Wait!" I hollered down to him. "Let's get the stuff out of the car, and I'll bring it up while you're at work!"

"That's a splendid idea!" he exclaimed.

We both worked as fast as we could to get the car unloaded because we didn't want him to be late getting back to work. He knew the guys at work would give him a ribbing for being late from lunch—being a newlywed and all.

After the car was unloaded, we looked at all the new house gifts lying on the steps and at the bottom of the steps. He whistled and asked, "Are you sure you can handle all this by yourself?"

"Sure!" I responded with enthusiasm. "It'll give me something to do all afternoon while you're at work."

"Okay," he replied with trepidation, "but if you see it's too much for you, just leave it and I'll get it when I come home."

"Okay, but don't worry. I can handle it. You'll see." I smiled and tossed my long black hair behind my neck.

He kissed me again and went back to work. Before I had a chance to carry our new gifts up the stairs to our little apartment, Ariana stuck her head out their screen door and asked sweetly, "Can I help you?" She had big blue eyes with blond hair and was about my height and very thin.

"Sure," I shrugged. "If you want to."

It took Ariana and me about twenty minutes to carry everything upstairs. She glanced around at all the new boxes and asked, "Did you buy all of this?"

"No," I smiled. "They had an old-fashioned bell ringing for us last night."

She cocked her blonde head to one side and asked, "What's that?"

"That's when friends and neighbors and family members of the bride and groom get together and bring gifts and food and play music. We danced and ate for hours. I met all his friends and family. None of my people were there because they all lived too far away. Harold had a lot of friends and family," I told her as we started to open boxes and unwrap everything. "I think he missed his calling. Harold is great to be around. Everyone who ever meets him, loves him. He is a wonderful husband, friend, employee, coworker, uncle, brother. I could go on and on. He charmed my mom and dad. I don't think he has ever met anyone who didn't like him on the spot. He's always so easy to be around." I enjoyed talking about Harold to someone—it just felt right.

A little while later, we were standing knee deep in boxes and wrapping paper. I took one look around. "I don't think we'll have to buy anything except food for a while." I thanked Ariana, and she went back downstairs to her home.

We had two of some things from different people, and I set all those things together on the table. Harold and I could decide which ones to keep and which ones to take back to the store. Some of the gifts had the sales receipt left on them, and we could return the gift if we needed to.

Harold came home from work a little early, and we went grocery shopping to get some things for a week. He was surprised when he came home. I had everything put away, cleaned up the apartment, and had another shower. He came in carrying a table top nineteen-inch black-and-white TV.

"Where did you get that?" I asked.

"My boss asked me if had one, and I said, 'No, not yet,' and he told me there was one in the back office and we were welcome to it."

"It's kind of ugly," I told him, "but with a little polish and a plant on top, will do wonders!"

He put the TV on a table in the living room and plugged it in. All we got was static when he turned it on. "I didn't realize we had to have rabbit ears," he mumbled.

I pictured a rabbit sitting on top of the TV with its ears sticking up in the air. "A what?" I giggled.

He laughed. "Boy, you really are rich! I love your innocence."

I felt my face turn red because that comment made me feel a little childish.

We sat at the kitchen table looking over all the gifts that we had two of trying to decide which ones to keep. "Well," Harold began, "these folks cared enough about us to buy us a gift, so how about we choose the one we want to use now, and I'll put the other one in the closet. And when one breaks down, we have a backup. How's that sound?"

I nodded and agreed. "That sounds like a good plan to me."

"And," he continued in that southern drawl of his, "if we get desperate, we can hock one." He laughed with those big dimples creasing the side of his mouth.

"Hock? What's that?" I asked, my innocence showing again.

"I'll explain if we ever get that desperate."

There was one box we hadn't opened yet from his mom and dad. She had already given us a homemade quilt, which I loved. We opened the box together, and inside was a baby blanket and a baby bib that said "First Born" on it. It was soft and trimmed in blue, yellow, green, and a little pink. I stared at it in awe. "Well, we know what Mom and Dad want from us now." Harold commented.

"What do you mean, Honey?" I asked.

He laughed again and grabbed me, and we both fell backward on the floor. He made sure that I fell on top of him to keep me from getting hurt. "A sweet, chubby baby! That's what!" and he kissed me. "Are you up to the task, Mrs. Clouse?"

Harold was the first person to call me "Mrs. Clouse," and it hit me all at once. I was no longer Donna Allen. I was a married woman. I looked down into my husband's hazel eyes that sparkled hotly for me, and I smiled a long seductive smile. He sucked his breath in as I leaned down and kissed him with all the passion a fifteen-year-old can. He groaned and kissed me hotly. He rolled me over and was lying on top of me, and he continued to kiss me.

A heat welled up deep inside of me, and I wanted my body to be absorbed by his body. I felt like I couldn't get enough of him. He kissed my neck and I shivered. He moaned in response and whispered hotly, "Do you want me, Baby?"

"Yes," I replied urgently. "Yes."

Very gently, he began removing my clothes. I closed my eyes, and I felt my breasts being exposed to the hot air. He groaned and said, "Oh my God. You're so beautiful."

I didn't know what was happening to me, but I reveled in the feeling, and I wanted more. Harold slipped my shorts and panties off, kissing me the whole time, moving from my neck, to my lips, my cheeks, my eyes, and breasts.

"Are you sure, Honey?" he whispered in my ear as he nibbled on my ear lobe. I could tell he was afraid that I would stop him. He kissed my breasts, and my nipples hardened. It felt wonderful, and I didn't want him to stop—not ever.

"I love all of you, Donna," he told me hotly, and his lips moved down my right leg to my toes and then over to my other toes and up that leg to my shoulders and neck again.

"Are you sure, Baby?" he asked again. "We can go lay down on the bed if you're uncomfortable."

"No, no, no," I told him. "Now. Here now, please," I begged. I was afraid to lose that wonderful feeling of bliss I was experiencing.

We had scooted across the floor while we were kissing, and we were lying halfway between the bathroom and kitchen. When we realized where we were, we laughed. He looked down at me and his eyes kindled. He kissed me hotly once more and then he slowly penetrated me.

"Oh!" was all I could say. It hurt and felt good all at the same time. It was something that I had never ever experienced before.

Harold stopped, afraid that he had hurt me and began to withdraw. I grabbed him around his buttocks and pulled him closer. He groaned and began moving gently. I wanted him, but it also hurt some. I felt this need to make him happy. I felt the old fear of that time that man tried to rape me well up inside of me, but Harold's groan of pleasure blocked it out.

He whispered, "Baby. Oh, Baby," and he kissed my breasts and neck and lips; it seemed all at once as he moved inside of me. "Oh, Donna. You're mine. You're really mine. At last. At last! Till death do us part. I will never let you go." And then I felt him explode inside of me.

I felt the tears well up inside of me and began to cry. He tasted my tears as they rolled down my cheeks and the side of my neck. He stopped. I felt his body tremble, and he asked shakily, "Why are you crying, Sweet Heart? Did I hurt you?"

I was overwhelmed with emotion that someone finally loved me, and I could only shake my head.

"You are a part of me," he said, "and I'm a part of you. That's how God intended it for married couples, Honey. We are not doing anything wrong. This is part of love between a man and wife." He smiled tenderly. "Now you are a woman, Sweet Thing." He laughed. "But I've got one question for you?"

"Wh…what's that?" I stammered, wiping the tears off my face. He started kissing and caressing me again.

"Can we use the bed next time?"

I suddenly started laughing. I laughed so hard that the tears started pouring again, and I snorted.

Harold looked down and exclaimed in mock dismay, "Now look what you've done. You hurt little Freddie's feelings, and he shrunk up on me!"

We lay there laughing with each other for a long time. After that time, whenever our eyes strayed to that spot between the bathroom and kitchen, we always grinned at each other. I felt a warm stickiness between my legs. When I glanced down, I had started to bleed. We got in the shower together and washed each other.

"I love your hair," he told me as he picked up the black strands and smelled it. "It smells like heaven."

We continued to caress each other, and he asked, "Do we have to go to the store? I could just live off you. How about you, Honey?"

"It doesn't matter to me," I told him. "Whatever you want."

He looked down at me hotly, "I want you."

"Me too," I replied, and we continued to hold and kiss each other.

"You know, Sweet Thing, I could die of a heart attack in here with you right now 'cause I'm older than you. In fact," he continued, "I'm an old man compared to you. But let's go for it anyway. What d'ya think?"

"Yeah, yeah," was all I could get out. It really hurt this time in the shower, but it felt wonderful also. I didn't let him know I was getting sore.

Because we had used up all the hot water, it began to run cold. We laughed when "little Freddie" disappeared again. "You see what you did to my treasure?" he asked.

I laughed until my stomach hurt. He reached up and turned off the water, and we continued to stand there laughing at each other. We stepped out of the shower and wrapped towels around ourselves and lay down on the bed because we were too tired to get dressed. Harold turned on the radio, and we listened to some music for a while.

A few minutes later, Harold said, "I have to go pee. I hope I can find little Freddie." A minute later while he was in the bathroom, he yelled, "I think he packed up and left! I can't find him!"

I laughed all over again.

"Don't you laugh, young lady!" he admonished. "This is serious! 'cause if I can't find Freddie, I can't pee!"

I laughed harder.

"Okay," he began, "when I come back, you stay over there on your side of the bed, and I'll stay on my side because Freddie and I need a break."

I tried not to giggle, but I snorted instead.

When he came back from the bathroom, I got up to go. It hurt to pee a little, and I was extremely sore. I noticed I was bleeding again, and I washed myself up and put on some baby-doll pajamas and a sanitary napkin. He took one look at me and groaned. "Do you have to put on those pajamas? Don't you have a pair of coveralls or something?"

I turned my head to the side and looked at him inquisitively.

He pointed down and said, "I gotta keep Freddie from rising up again. We need the rest!"

I laughed so hard I passed gas. I felt my face turn red that I had passed gas in front of him. I always figured that my husband would be the first one to slip. He laughed and grabbed me, and then I laughed and cut another one.

"Oh, Sweet Thing, you're making Freddie rise up again. You're going to hurt me. Uh-oh, uh -oh." Then he looked down and hollered, "Stay under cover, Boy! Run for our lives!"

I was rolled up in a ball laughing so hard; and every time I laughed, I cut one. I tried to stop; and Harold said something funny, and I laughed and cut another one. This went on and on until my gut hurt so bad from laughing, I had to convince him to stop. "Stop it, Harold. Please! I can't laugh anymore! My stomach hurts! Please!" I begged.

He stopped for a few minutes, and then he cracked out something else funny, and I laughed again. We finally fell asleep in each other's arms.

Promptly at 6:00 a.m., the alarm woke us up. We both jumped out of bed naked as jaybirds and grinned at one another. Harold took a quick shower and dressed for work. I said a little shamefully, "I wanted to fix you some breakfast, but we never made it to the grocery store."

Harold laughed and looked down at his pants and said, "You hear that, Freddie? I do not want to see or hear from you until we get some groceries in the house!" he admonished his pants and we both burst out laughing.

"We have a coffee pot," I told him, "but no coffee."

"How about I take you to get a few things before work?" he asked.

"Okay."

I noticed I was extremely sore when I moved around. Harold noticed I had bruises all over my legs, hips, back, and arms. He slipped his pants down, and he had the same bruises.

He raised his red head from looking at his bruised legs and looked down at me and exclaimed, "Okay, that's it! You can't have me on the floor! Not one more time! Do you hear me, Young Lady?" We busted out laughing again. Years later, I came to appreciate all the laughing we did back then.

"I'll tell you what," Harold said. "When I get home, I'll behave myself, and you behave yourself this evening, and we'll make it to the grocery store."

A little more seriously he asked, "Do you want me to go get you something for breakfast before I go to work?"

"No. Just bring me something for lunch."

"Okay, Sweet Thing. See you at noon." I heard him jump down the stairs and start up his Chevrolet and peeled out of the yard.

A few minutes later Leona, our landlady, knocked on the door. I wrapped a robe around myself and went to the door. "Harold is on the phone," she said politely. "He wants to ask you something."

I stepped gingerly down the stairs with her and picked up the phone from the counter. "Yes?" I asked a little nervously.

"Hi, I got this idea. See what you think? I was going to leave my car with Mildred, and she can come by and take you grocery shopping. We're behind schedule at work, and I'm going to have to work a little late."

"I guess so, but I wanted to go with you," I said hopefully. I could almost hear him grin on the line.

"I'm sorry, Sweet Thing. She'll be there in a little while. By the way, Mildred will have to bring her twins and be back before the other kids get home from school."

"Okay. I'll try and hurry."

"Bye, Sweet Thing."

"Bye, Honey. See you tonight."

I thanked Leona, and she said, "Anytime you need anything, Donna, just let me know. I can take you to the store or whatever else you need. Maybe we could go shopping sometime?"

"Sure, I'd like that." I walked toward the door to get ready when Mildred came over. "See you later and thanks again," I said over my shoulder.

"No. Thank you, dear."

I turned and looked at her inquisitively.

"For moving upstairs." Then she smiled sweetly.

After I got back upstairs to our apartment, I opened the blinds (I love a lot of light in the house—it must have had something to do with that wall again), straightened up the kitchen and bedroom, jumped in the shower, and got dressed to go shopping. It was July 17, and it was warm that day. We had married on July 12, 1957. *Wow!* I thought, *I've been married for five days!*

I was still a little sore, and I hoped that no one noticed I walked funny while I was shopping with Mildred.

A few minutes later, I heard Mildred climbing the stairs with her twin boys. I opened the door and said, "You could have blown the horn, and I would have come down."

"Oh, no," she said. "I wanted to see your new place."

She looked around at our little apartment and said, "It's nice! A lot better than what Leroy and I started off with. We had to live with his mom and dad a while and then with my mommy and poppie for a little while."

"Really?" I asked.

I enjoyed talking with Mildred. She was very down-to-earth and very fun loving, like Harold. She had beautiful red wavy hair and soft brown eyes. She stood maybe an inch or so taller than five feet and didn't weigh more than 105 pounds soaking wet. She had freckles all over her face and body, just like Harold and his mother. "Yeah, I like this place." She nodded. "You and Harold are very lucky."

She glanced over at the kitchen counter and said, "I see you have our coffee pot. We bought you the best one. Oh, I see you put Mommy's quilt on the bed. You know, she made that a long time ago for Harold when he first decided he was going to get married. She put it in his hope chest in hopes that someday he would bring home a bride. She was delighted when he told her he was getting married but a little apprehensive because you are so young."

Mildred could talk, let me tell you. Once she got started, it was hard to get her to stop.

She eyed me a little and nodded, "But," she continued, "I can see you know your way around. Mommy need not worry. You seem like a very capable person to me."

That made me feel good. I smiled at her.

"So, do you want to make a grocery list, or what?" she asked.

I shrugged my shoulders, "Okay, I guess so. But I don't know what Harold likes."

"Who cares!" she said and laughed. "Just get what you like."

I must have looked aghast; I said, "I couldn't do that! I want to please him as well as myself."

She laughed, "'Well, here's the money for groceries he gave me." And she handed me five twenties.

"I won't need that much, will I?" I asked.

"Well, let's go see," Mildred said as she opened the door and let her boys down the stairs, holding each one of their little hands.

After we were in the car, Mildred continued, "Harold called me this morning and said, 'Hey, sis, what're you doing today? I said, 'Nothing in particular. Why?' He asked me, 'If I bring the car over, will you go and pick up Donna and take her to the grocery store?' I said, "Sure, but I'll have to bring Mickey and Andy along.'" She glanced over at me. "Harold said you wouldn't mind."

"No, I don't mind. I love kids."

She turned back to the road and said, "I asked him how it was going, and he told me what a wonderful person you are and how God had truly blessed him. He said that you're not only beautiful, but that you were loving and caring, and not only that but also a wonderful housekeeper. He also told me that you've been through a lot, but he said that he was going to make sure that you will never have to worry again."

It was nice to hear how much your new husband cared about you and how good he talked about you to someone else. I smiled brightly, very content with life just then.

"He told me he was going to get a phone for your apartment," Mildred said. "I told him that since he already had a phone at Mommy and Poppie's that all he had to do was have it transferred to the apartment. But he said he couldn't take away Mommy and Poppie's phone. I told him to call the phone company and have a phone put in your new address and combine the bill, and he could pay them both each month on one bill."

I realized then just how smart Mildred was.

We drove quietly for a few minutes, and then she turned to me and said, "You know, Donna, when you get a little older and get your license, I'll help teach you how to drive. Do you want to learn?"

"Yeah. Wow!" I exclaimed. "I would love that!"

"Okay, it's a date then," she grinned. "We won't tell Harold, and you can surprise him."

As we walked down the grocery store aisles, I put milk, eggs, bacon, sausage, bread, bologna, cheese, mustard, and mayonnaise in the cart. I stopped and thought for a minute. I only had breakfast on my mind because I hadn't eaten yet.

"Don't forget about the coffee," Mildred reminded me. "Harold likes eight o'clock coffee. Oh, he puts sugar in his coffee, so you'll need that too."

"Oh, yeah. Thanks, Mildred." I put those items in my buggy.

"What are you going to fix for supper?" she asked.

I nodded and put potatoes, pork chops, chicken, beans, cake mixes and icing, and a roast in the cart.

"You know how to cook a roast?" she asked.

"You bet! I watched my mom enough. She's the best cook in the world!" I said proudly.

I bought tea bags to make iced tea. Next, I bought washing powders, bleach, and clothes softener in my buggy. I got some face soap, dish soap, shampoo and cream rinse, and some cleaning supplies. When we got to the checkout counter and the girl rang it all up, the bill came to $79.40.

"Oh, you're good," Mildred commented dryly.

I turned and looked at her. "Why do you say that?" I asked as I handed the cashier four twenties.

"'Cause whatever the groceries come to you, keep it a secret unless they ask. That way you always have spending money for birthdays or whatever. Or if you hit hard times, you can surprise him with it."

Boy, I thought, *this gal is smart.*

As we made our way through the parking lot to Harold's car, she asked innocently, "I noticed you're walking a little funny, Donna.

73

Is something wrong?" She smiled and continued, "Too much of Freddie last night?"

I stopped dead in my tracks, and I felt my entire face and body turn red all over.

She laughed.

"How did you know what he calls it?" I asked astonished.

She laughed again. "That's an old family nickname someone gave it a long time ago, and it's been handed down for generations." She shrugged her freckled shoulders. "I don't know how it got started, but the story has been passed down throughout the family ever since."

She helped me put the groceries in the car, and I asked her, "How did you know I was sore?"

She grinned. "I don't have six kids for nuthin'!"

"I thought it was five?" I asked.

She pointed to her abdomen and said proudly, "One in my belly. I'm four months pregnant."

I was astonished. "You've got to be kidding? You're so slim!"

"Yeah. I don't usually start showing till I'm in about my seventh month. And then I blow up overnight like a blimp." Then she puffed her cheeks out to look fat.

I giggled.

As we got in the car to go back to the apartment, she said, "Your soreness will go away in a few days. If you have any Epsom salt, take a bath and just sit in the water for a while for the next few days. By that time, you'll stop spotting, and the tissues will heal, and it won't hurt any more when ole Freddie comes a calling." We both giggled.

She was a lot like Harold. I loved her silliness and humor.

"My husband is a preacher," she told me.

"Oh yeah?"

"Yeah," she said. "He's the pastor at the First Baptist Church. Do you go to church, Donna?"

"I did back home. I'd like for Harold and I to attend a church down here."

"What denomination are you?"

"Baptist," I said proudly.

A few minutes later, we were back at the apartment, and she helped me carry all the groceries upstairs. "Okay," she said, "if you need anything, here's my number. Just call me." She handed me a note with her phone number on it. "Harold said he's going to get a phone in for you. I'll call the phone company when I get home."

"Okay," I replied. "Thanks, Mildred." I really like her.

"Any time, dear." She hugged me and said, "I'm very proud to call you my sister-in-law." Then she left to go home and take care of her family and call the phone company for us.

I got busy putting everything away before Harold got home. Mildred had placed a box of Epsom salt in my cart when I wasn't looking, thank God. After I straightened up, I took Mildred's advice and poured some Epsom salt into a tub of hot water with some bubble bath I had brought from home. I slipped into the hot tub and leaned my head against the rim. The hot soapy water, along with the Epsom salt, felt wonderful on my soar body.

I had turned on the radio before I slipped into the tub, and I lay there listening to the music and thinking about my life with Mom and Dad and then my new life with my new husband. Married. I still couldn't believe that I was Mrs. Clouse—Mrs. Donna Clouse. *Gee*, I thought, *that makes me sound old*. And I giggled.

I noticed it was starting to get late and Harold would be home soon. I climbed out of the tub and got dressed to start supper. Even though we had a small fan in the window, it wasn't enough to cool the apartment. It was still too hot to cook, so I made us some sandwiches and coleslaw. I lay down on the bed to get rested up before Harold came home. I must have been more tired than I thought because I feel into a deep sleep.

Harold came home sometime while I was sleeping, and I woke up the sound of the shower running. When I first woke up, I had forgotten where I was, and when I finally came to my senses, I smiled and lay back down. *This is so nice*, I thought. We had our own little apartment, a great car, and all that we needed to set up a household. God had blessed us, and we were grateful. I thought about the wonderful husband I had and how loving and kind his family was. I already felt like I belonged. They had been so good to us and had accepted me as part of their family and as Harold's wife—even though he was eight years older than me. I thanked God that afternoon for all He had done for me and for giving me Harold.

I was lying on my stomach across the bed when Harold got out of the shower and came up behind me. He smelled wonderful—clean and fresh. I loved the smell of him. I rolled over and gazed at him. He had a towel wrapped around his midsection.

"Did you get to the grocery store today?" Harold asked.

"Yeah," I replied sleepily.

"Did Mildred treat you well?"

"Oh, yes! I really like her! She's a lot like you."

Harold chuckled and sat down on the bed. "I know. When we were kids, people thought we were twins. She's actually one year older than me."

"Really?"

"She's always been my favorite sister and always will be."

I raised a dark eyebrow inquisitively.

"Now, don't get me wrong!" he said defensively. "I love my other sisters too! It's just that we can tell each other everything, and we don't have to worry about it getting around to the whole Clouse clan."

I smiled. I had never had a sister like that, but I was glad that he did.

Then he asked me a little too innocently, "Are you sore, Honey?"

I turned my eyes away from him a little embarrassed and answered honestly, "Yeah, a little, but I took an Epsom-salt bath and soaked for a while."

"How did you know to do that?"

"Mildred noticed I was walking a little funny," I confided.

Harold laughed.

"You know what she said?" I asked him. I felt my face turn red.

"What?"

"I almost fainted. It embarrassed me so much!" And I rolled my eyes

"Too much Freddie?" he finished for me.

"Yeah!" and I slapped his arm in mock anger.

He laughed and said, "Well, you won't have to worry about him for a few days, anyway."

"Why?"

He grabbed his towel and whipped it off and poor Freddie was bandaged! "Oh my Gosh! What did you do?" I hollered.

He laughed harder and said, "He got his neck wrung last night!"

Then we both burst out laughing. It felt good to laugh so much.

"I got to thinkin' while I was in the shower. I decided to wrap it up to surprise you," he told me.

I shook my head and said, "You're nuts! You know that?"

"Yeah, ain't it great?" And he smiled that huge dimply smile that I loved so much.

"Let me see if I can get it off for you or you'll hurt yourself," I said and started picking at the tape.

"Damn!" he hollered when the tape pulled the sensitive skin.

"Sorry," I murmured.

"Damn!"

"Sorry," as I continued to pick away at the stubborn tape.

"Damn, Honey!" he hollered. "That hurts!"

I stood up with my hands on my hips and glared at him completely exasperated. "I can't get this stuff off. Go sit in a hot tub and see if it will dissolve any."

"You think that will work?" he asked me with one raised eyebrow.

"Well, if it doesn't," and I tried to say this with a straight face, "we'll have to amputate, and you can grow another one."

He rolled his hazel eyes and groaned, "Funny. Ha ha ha. Very funny."

I giggled and said, "You really have to think before you pull one of your practical jokes."

He shrugged his shoulders. "Guess so." Then he reached for my hand and asked, "Will you stay in the bathroom with me and talk to me?"

"What are you? A two-year-old?"

"Don't get smart," he growled and pretended to slap my behind as he followed me into the bathroom.

"Okay. But don't do that again!" I admonished him.

"I can promise you that!"

It took about an hour, but the hot water finally loosened the tape, and he was able to peel the rest of the tape off.

"I can't wait to tell Mildred about this one!" I teased.

"You better not!" he warned and we both laughed.

After he was dressed, we sat down at the kitchen table and ate our sandwiches and slaw. "What do you say we go to the movies tonight?" he asked.

"I'd rather just stay here and enjoy our apartment together," I told him honestly.

"Sounds good to me," he replied.

We finished our dinner and settled in like an old married couple in front of the TV. A few minutes later, Harold said, "You know, Honey, I've never let my car get as dirty as it is now. We have to take time and wash my other baby, you know?"

"Oh, so my competition is your car, huh?"

"Yep."

Then he smiled that heart-melting smile of his, and I drowned in the love and affection that radiated from the man that was my husband. I would have done almost anything for him. "Okay," I finally replied. "How about tomorrow evening when you come home? Do you want to do it as soon as you get home, or do you want to wait until the sun goes down some?"

He shrugged, "I guess as soon as I get home."

"Okay. I'll have everything ready, so we can start on it."

The next evening, I was downstairs waiting with a bucket, the water hose, soap, and towels as soon as he pulled in. He was grinning from ear to ear, and he hugged me and kissed me before we went to work on my rival. When we finally got done cleaning her up, she really did look pretty. Harold whistled and exclaimed, "Wow! Now that's sharp!"

It pleased me that he was happy. I felt like I had accomplished something for him, and I made a solemn vow to myself to always try and please him.

When we got to the top of the stairs, he grabbed me around the waist and lifted me up and said, "You know, I forgot to carry you over the threshold."

I gazed up at him and whispered, "I guess you did."

"Oh, and one other thing," he began.

I cocked my head to one side. "Oh?"

"Yeah, don't ever climb the stairs in front of me with those shorts on again unless you want ole one eye to stand to attention."

"Oh, Harold!" and I slapped at him. "You're bad. But I love you anyway."

"Thank God," he whispered and leaned down and kissed me tenderly.

We showered together, and I fixed some dinner, and then we lay down on the bed to watch his favorite Westerns on TV. Harold was your typical shoot 'em up bang, bang cowboy. It was nice to just stay home and enjoy each other's company. It just felt right.

"Harold?" I asked.

"Yeah?"

"I'd like to start going to church again."

"Okay. Where did you want to go?"

"I noticed there's a Grace Baptist Church not too far from here. Can we go there and at least try it."

"Okay. I think that's the one Peevine and Lil go to."

I smiled. Harold was so easygoing and easy to talk to. I loved him so much already.

The following Sunday morning, we were up early, and Peevine and Lil came by and picked us up, and we all went to church together. I really enjoyed the service, and the people were so wonderful and friendly, and everyone welcomed us to their church. But when Harold's mother found out, she got a little upset. She scolded him, "You should come back to our church, son."

"Mommy," Harold said, "Donna was raised in a Baptist Church, and what's the difference as long as they teach the truth about God?"

"Okay," she replied, "but I do not approve." And she shook her head.

"Why?"

"Because they believe that you can't lose your salvation and we believe that you can."

"Well, I don't believe Donna and I are going to be that big of sinners. Besides, Donna gave her life to God when she was nine years old, and I gave my life to God when I was a little boy. And that's what counts!"

Mrs. Clouse could tell he was getting upset about it, so she dropped it.

I loved him more for taking up for me on my choice of denomination. Harold was my best friend, husband, father, big brother, and uncle all rolled into one. I loved him so much. I had never known anyone like him nor anyone since.

Chapter 5

We were settling into married life very well. Harold's family invited us to their homes for dinner all the time. Sometimes we accepted, and sometimes we just wanted to stay home and enjoy each other's company. Weather permitting, we usually spent Saturday washing and polishing the car. We went to the drive-in movies two or three times a week.

One evening, Peevine called and told Harold that his wife, Lil, was having a birthday and wanted us to come over and celebrate. On Saturday evening, we got all dressed up and went out to dinner and a club to dance. Because I was underage, Harold ordered me sodas, and he had a beer or two. Harold and I danced—and boy could he dance! It was all I could do to keep up with him. When the band played a slow dance, he wrapped me in his embrace and sang softly in my ear. I melted in his arms. I noticed that the other people had stopped dancing and watched us. As soon as the dance was over, they applauded every time.

Harold and I were very competitive with each other—always trying to outdo the other—whether it was on the dance floor or in bed making love. We both tried very hard to make the other one cry uncle, and we loved it.

Sometimes on the weekends, we went over to Uncle Eugene's and Aunt Edna's to play ball with the kids. Ronnie told Harold once, "You know, you married the girl I wanted. But as long as you're good to her, I'll let it go." Then he looked at me with such longing that it embarrassed me.

Always one to encourage someone else, Harold patted him on the back and said, "You'll find another."

"Not like her," Ronnie muttered.

Harold's brother Clifford told him once, "Well, if she can cook as good as she looks, I'm going to kill you and take her away."

Harold gut punched him, and they wrestled around for a few minutes on the ground to everyone's amusement.

On most Sundays after church, the Clouse family would get together (usually at Uncle Eugene's house because they had the biggest house and yard) and have a big lunch and play games like volleyball, softball, football, or horseshoes. I liked to take charge of every situation (and still do). I was ordering everyone around while we were playing. Once, Clifford, Harold, Paul, and Eddie picked me up and put me in the basketball hoop. I was screaming at Harold, "Harold! Get me out of here!"

He cocked his head and glared playfully at me and asked, "You promise to keep your mouth shut and just play the game?"

I was furious but helpless to do anything about it. "Okay," I muttered.

"Alright. Now remember, you promised. Okay?"

"*I said okay!*"

"If you don't keep your promise, we're going to throw you in the creek," he warned me as he reached up to help me out of the hoop.

As soon as he had me out of my embarrassing predicament, I stomped off in a huff to help the other ladies with the food. I needed time to cool off. I had a temper (still do).

We always stayed late because we thoroughly enjoyed getting together with his family. They were so much fun to be around. Everyone was good-natured and loving—always caring for one another. I really miss the Clouse family, even to this day.

One night when we left, it was about ten o'clock, and Harold had to go to work the next day. As usual, he took the long way home with the top down. We had to drive under a tunnel that had a waterfall that flowed from the mountain onto the road. When we got to the waterfall, Harold pretended that the car died and stopped right under the waterfall.

"Harold!" I cried. "You're going to ruin the car!"

He shrugged. "Can't," he replied with his arm around the back of the seat. "It's leather."

"Get us out of here!" I whined. "We're getting all wet!"

"Kiss me, then."

"Okay." I knew it was useless to argue with him, and I gave him a quick peck.

"No. I mean *really* kiss me," and his eyes sparkled in the moonlight.

I sighed and leaned over to him and gave him a nice, hot, tongue-wrapping kiss as the water pounded on both of us. He started up the car and pulled away from the waterfall, and we busted out laughing because we were soaking wet.

"What's the landlady going to say when she sees us coming home looking like a couple of drowned rats!" I asked.

Harold shrugged. "She's probably in bed by now anyway."

"Why did you do that?" I asked.

"'Cause I love it when you get mad and then laugh." And he grinned at me. Then a little more seriously, he continued, "Donna, Honey, my Sweet Thing, you've had enough pain and tears and hard times in your life, and I want to give you all the laughter I can for the rest of your life."

"You mean our life," I corrected and snuggled up to him.

When we got home, all the lights were out downstairs. We tried to be quiet while we dried down the car and put the top up. We crept quietly up the back stairs and took our showers. Harold took his first. When I got finished, I had a robe on and my hair wrapped up in a towel; Harold was watching the news. I lay down beside him on the bed.

Harold looked over at me and asked, "How can you come out of the shower wearing a robe and your hair wrapped up and still look so beautiful?"

"Oh." I slapped his arm. "You know that's not true."

"Yes, it is, Honey. Honest," he said truthfully.

"They say love is blind, you know," I retorted as I shook my long black tresses out.

"Uh-oh, here comes Freddie!" he cried. "He's peeking his one eye at you!"

I cocked my head to one side and smiled dangerously, "Really? Well, Fuzzy Wuzzy is all ready for him."

"Fuzzy Wuzzy?" he asked. "That's her name?"

"Yeah. I figured you can name yours, so I can name mine," I replied cockily.

Harold chuckled, "Wait until I tell the family!"

"Don't you dare, Harold!" I threatened.

"Well, let me see." And he acted like he was contemplating the consequences. Then he started singing using the melody of *Frankie and Johnny*, "Freddie and Fuzzy were lovers. And oh boy could they love!"

I grabbed a pillow and hit him upside the head with it, and we both cracked up laughing. Next thing I knew, he grabbed the other pillow, and we were in the middle of a heated pillow fight.

August 1957 was such a hot month. The little fan we had in the kitchen window just wasn't enough to keep the apartment cool. One afternoon, Harold brought home this massive refrigerator motor with long metal blades attached to it.

"Harold!" I exclaimed. "What're you doing with that thing? It will get my floors all dirty."

"Honey, we're roasting in this apartment," he answered while he set the monstrosity on the living room floor.

I eyed him with arms crossed hoping that the "fan" wasn't going to ruin my clean floors.

"I found it behind the plant. It's one of those commercial refrigerator motors," he said proudly. Harold was a machinist by trade and knew what he was talking about.

I couldn't help but say sarcastically, "It looks like one that goes on a commercial plane."

"Oh, Honey, I'll build a box with a screen over it tomorrow. Meanwhile we'll stay cool tonight," he said, still trying to convince me.

"Yeah, if we don't fly away," I retorted.

I was turning into a pretty good cook, and I fixed us a great dinner. I was proud of everything except my biscuits. They smelled and tasted good, but they just didn't rise very much. Harold picked up the biscuit and took a bite and said, "Well, they make one hell of a cracker, you might have just invented something new here." We both laughed.

Sweat poured down our bodies by the time we finished eating. Harold saw how hot and miserable I was and said, "Let's clean up the dishes and go for a cool ride out in the country."

We went for a ride and came home a little while later and started watching TV. A few minutes later, Harold got up and sauntered over to the fan and said, "Let's crank this baby up." When he plugged the fan in, it made a loud whooshing sound, and the air shot straight up to the ceiling.

"Hmm…let me see." He looked around and spotted our little tin trash can by the bed. He unplugged the fan and picked it up and set the motor down in the trash can. He stepped back, looking proudly at his work. "There," and nodded, "that should work." Then he plugged the fan back in and watched the air blow right on the bed. My hair was blowing around my face like we were in the car with the top down.

He climbed back into bed and said, "Come here, Sweet Thing." And he wrapped his arms around me, and we fell into a deep sleep. The air felt so good blowing on us.

Sometime during the night, we suddenly woke up to a loud crash and then a bang, bang, bang. I started to jump out of bed to turn the light on, but Harold grabbed me and said worriedly, "Don't get out of bed, Honey. You might step right into it."

I felt the blood drain my face as I realized the danger we were in. "Can you reach the curtains on your side and pull them back a little. Maybe the street light will shine in here, and we can figure out where that thing is before it chops our legs off?"

I stood on the nightstand and reached for the curtains while Harold held on to me. I gasped when I saw where the fan was. If Harold had not stopped me, I would have stepped right into the middle of it and been hacked to death. He jumped out of bed, turned the light on and unplugged the fan.

Suddenly the landlady was knocking at the door. We looked at each other, and Harold groaned, "Oh, boy." He slipped on his pants and opened the door.

"Is everything okay up here?" she asked.

"Yeah, Donna plugged in this stupid fan to try to get cool, and it made a lot of noise, but I'll get it fixed," he assured her.

"Okay," she replied, "as long as you two are okay."

I hit him with the pillow as soon as she left.

"Aw, Honey. That's all I could think of to say at the time." And then he started tickling me, and we wrestled around for a few minutes until I cried uncle.

The next day, he went to the lumber yard and bought some wood and built a nice frame for it. Even though it was noisy, it kept us cool for a long time. After a while, we got used to the noise, and the landlady assured Harold that she couldn't hear it downstairs.

Mom and Dad called a few times to check to see how things were going. I told them that I was very happy, and that Harold was a wonderful husband. I told them not to worry about me, that I was doing fine. Mom told me that if I needed anything that they were there for me.

We had been married for about five weeks, and I had not had a period since the week before we got married. I did not say anything to Harold yet because I wanted to wait a little while. Then I noticed that my breasts were getting tender around the nipples, but I still didn't think too much of it because Harold loved my breasts.

A few days later, I called Mildred and told her my symptoms.

"Sounds like you have a little one on the way," she said.

"Really?"

"Yes, why don't you wait another few weeks and then go see Dr. Welch. He has delivered all my children. He's gentle and very experienced."

A few weeks later, I started getting morning sickness. I put some crackers on the nightstand and ate one or two before I got out of bed every morning. Harold watched me curiously one morning but didn't say anything. I took his hand and said nervously, "I'm pretty sure I'm pregnant."

"Are you sure?"

"Well, Mildred gave me a book to read, and I have all the symptoms," I confided, holding my stomach and feeling a little nauseous.

Harold grinned and jumped out of bed. "Hot dog!" he exclaimed, "I'm going to be a daddy!" His smile brightened up the room. It made me feel better just seeing how happy he was. His excitement was contagious, and I couldn't help but smile back at him.

He plopped down on the bed and took my hand, "Okay, we'll hold off telling anybody until we go to the doctor and find out for sure."

"Okay."

"And I'll tell Mildred not to say anything yet." Then he jumped back up and jogged over to the phone. "Better yet, I'll call her now."

We made an appointment with Dr. Welch, and Harold went with me. I was so nervous that when the nurse called for "Mrs. Clouse," I didn't realize she was asking for me. Harold nudged me, and I called as though I was still in school, "Here!" As soon as I realized my mistake, I felt my face flush, and Harold snickered.

"The doctor will see you now," the nurse said, and then she looked at Harold and said, "Mr. Clouse, please stay in the waiting room."

Harold grinned. "Sure."

I glanced over my shoulder at him as she led me into the little examining room. There was a small examining table in the middle of the room with steel stirrups. I wasn't sure if I was going to saddle up and ride the table into the sunset or what. The nurse interrupted my musings when she said, "Take your clothes off from the waist down, Dear, and put this on." She handed me a paper shirt. "Oh, on second thought, Mrs. Clouse, please go ahead and strip all the way. The doctor will want to check your breasts too."

Why? I thought. *They're still there.*

In a few minutes, there was a light tap on the door and a short heavyset balding man walked in, looking over the forms I had filled out earlier. As he flipped through the papers, I noticed he had short stubby fingers, and I wondered how in the world he could perform surgery with such short fingers. When he glanced up at me over the top of his black rimmed glasses, I noticed that his eyes were a beautiful sky blue and very kind. "When was your last menstrual day, Mrs. Clouse? Do you remember?" He asked.

I squirmed a little and said, "Yes, it was July 1 through the 4th. Just about a week before I got married."

"Okay, let's examine you, shall we?" Then he pushed a button on his intercom, and his nurse walked in a minute later.

"Lie back, Mrs. Clouse," she instructed me, "and put your feet in the stirrups."

I did as I was instructed.

"Now, scoot down a little."

I scooted a little.

"A little farther…a little more…"

As I scooted farther down, my face began to burn in embarrassment. After they had me situated like they wanted, I felt as though I was exposed to the entire world. I turned my head away and tried to look at the wall. And then a horrible thought came to me. "Please, dear Lord," I silently prayed. "Please don't let me cut one right about now."

The doctor slipped on a pair of latex gloves and put his hands on my knees and started pushing them apart. "You must open your legs as much as possible, Mrs. Clouse. I need to see your opening."

I groaned inwardly, but I did as he instructed and began to cry. I was scared and humiliated all rolled into one. The nurse held my hand reassuringly, which made me feel better. "It's okay, Honey," she crooned. "No one likes this procedure."

"Don't worry, Mrs. Clouse," Dr. Welch said. "I will not hurt you. Just breathe normally."

When he was finally finished with his examination of the lower part of me, he took his gloves off and threw them in the trash, washed his hands and put on another pair. Then he came up beside me, pulled the paper shirt to the side exposing my breasts and stomach. He pressed down on my stomach and around my breasts and asked me if it was sensitive, and I nodded. Then he pressed down on my lower abdomen and said, "Oh, yes. You can sit up now, Mrs. Clouse."

The nurse helped me sit up.

"You can get dressed," he told me, "but I want you to give the nurse a urine sample before you leave. You can step into the bathroom over there. There are cups available for you in there and then give it to the nurse. When you are finished, you may go back out to the waiting room and sit with your husband." He glanced at me over the rim of his glasses and asked, "He is here with you, right?"

"Yes,"

"Splendid!" He smiled.

When I finished providing the urine sample (which is no easy trick for a woman!), I went back out to the waiting room with Harold. The blood had drained from his poor face, and he was fidgeting around. He picked up a magazine and then set it back down. His right leg was jumping all over the place. He held my hand and then let it go and squirmed around in his seat. He tried to smile at me but it came out as a grimace. He was not helping my nervousness one bit.

About twenty minutes later, the nurse called Mr. and Mrs. Clouse and escorted us into the doctor's office. Dr. Welch shook hands with Harold and introduced himself. Then we all sat down, and Dr. Welch said, "Well, I have some good news for you Mr. and Mrs. Clouse," and he paused for special affect I'm sure. Harold and I were holding our breaths. "You are pregnant. About six weeks from what I can tell."

I thought Harold would have whopped for joy, but he just sat there. I glanced over at him and he was smiling, but I couldn't tell if he was happy or not, and that made me nervous not knowing what he was thinking.

"I'd say we're looking at April 8 or 9 for the birth," the doctor continued and then looking at Harold he said, "Your wife is very young. Her body will be doing a lot of changes and growing in the next seven and a half months that she would have had several more years, but now she has to change in a shorter time."

Then at me the doctor continued, "Before the baby is born, you are going to feel tired, and that's normal. But stay as active as you can because that produces a healthy baby. I want you to go for walks every day, even it's for a short walk. Do it. It will make for an easier delivery."

I nodded and said, "Okay."

Harold shook the doctor's hand again and thanked him. At the front desk, we paid the co-pay and walked out the office door. As soon as we left the office, Harold pulled me around the side of building and grabbed me, hugging and kissing me. I noticed that there were huge tears rolling down his cheeks. I hadn't realized I was holding my breath, and I exhaled in relief. I reached up and touched his face tenderly. I truly loved this man with all my being.

"Oh, Honey!" he exclaimed. "Honey, Honey, Honey!" And he whirled me around the sidewalk in his arms. A few people grinned at us, and a few thought we were insane, but we ignored them.

"We're going to be a mom and a dad!" He looked down at me with love shining in his eyes; I almost melted right there on the sidewalk.

As we made our way to the car, he said, "This is great! Isn't this great?"

He didn't give me a chance to answer. "God's been so good to us. So very good!"

He helped me in the car and continued, "Now I'll have you and a great baby of ours!" I don't think his feet touched the ground as he raced in front of the car to the driver's seat. "We'll have to drop by Mildred's and tell her first." His poor hands were trembling on the steering wheel.

After we told Mildred, she just smiled knowingly and said, "I knew she was. She just has that glow about her." Then she winked at me.

"We can't stay long, sis. We have to get these prescriptions he wants Donna to take filled. Plus, he wants her to take these vitamins he gave us."

Next thing I knew, he was rushing me back out to the car. As soon as we pulled out of the drive at Mildred's he said, "Hey! Let's go tell Mommy and Poppie!"

"Can't we just call them?" I asked. I was tired and wanted to go home and absorb in private that I was going to have a baby.

He shook his head, "No, we better tell them in person."

As soon as we pulled up into their yard, the front door burst open and his mother ran toward us with her arms stretched wide. She was hollering, "Oh, son! Oh, Donna! Oh, Son!"

I was barely out of the car when she grabbed me and buried me in her bosom jumping up and down and kissing my face. I could hardly breathe. Next thing I knew, she had Harold and me both in her embrace. "Congratulations!" she was hollering. "I'm so proud of you!"

Poppie bounced out the screen door with a wide grin on his face. "We knew you could do it, Son!"

Harold grinned at his dad.

"You all come on in and have some dinner with us," Mommy said. "We have to call the rest of the family!"

I rolled my eyes. Harold had a *big* family. This could take the rest of the day. I resigned myself to it and smiled. I knew eventually Harold and I could be alone to revel in the wonderful news.

As she walked us toward the house, she asked, "What do you want, Donna, Harold?" She glanced from one to the other waiting for our answers.

Harold said, "We don't care. Whatever God chooses for us is fine with us."

"Well, us to," she replied. "But you know the heat is on for you to give us a boy sometime because there hasn't been a boy born that will continue the Clouse name."

I looked up at her inquisitively as we went inside.

"All my other sons had girls. Only Ed gave us a boy, and all the girls had lots of boys, but they will carry the names of their fathers." She pushed her glasses back up on her face and looked at Harold and said, "So, the ball is in your court."

Harold leaned back on the sofa and crossed his feet in front of him all cocky-like and replied, "Well," he drawled, "I'll do my best. In fact, I have already done my best. Now it's up to Donna to deliver." He grinned down at me.

I looked at everyone in the room and replied, "I know I will do my best to have a healthy baby. But I read somewhere that a woman does not determine the sex of the baby. The *man* does." I made sure and emphasized the man part. "So, that puts the ball back in your court, Honey." And I smiled sweetly at him. Everyone laughed.

Mommy said, "I know one thing. If it looks anything like its mommy, it's going to be the prettiest thing in the family, boy or girl."

I smiled at the compliment.

"Hey," she continued as a thought struck her, "maybe we'll get lucky and have twins!"

I shook my head, "Please don't say that, Mommy. Our apartment is too small."

After dinner and calling all the family, we went home and took a shower together. Harold kissed my belly, my hips, my heart. "You have made me so happy," he murmured. "So very, very happy."

"We did this together, Harold," I reminded him.

"I know. It's just you are so very special, and I love you so much."

I stroked his hair and said, "I feel the same for you too, you know?"

"I know." Then a worried expression crossed his face, and he asked, "Are you sure you're okay?"

"Yes, I feel fine," I assured him. "I wouldn't even know I was pregnant except for my breasts are very sore, and the doctor said that would go away in my third or fourth month."

As we got out of the shower and dried off, I glanced around the apartment and asked, "Where in the world are we going to put the baby bed and all the things that a baby needs?"

Harold shrugged and said, "I don't know, Sweet Thing, but we'll figure it out. We might have to start looking for another place. I don't want you climbing these stairs after you get bigger and further along."

I didn't like the picture that created in my head. I was always so slim and trim.

"We should probably start looking for an unfurnished place, it's cheaper," he said. "Besides, we've got plenty of time. When the paper comes in, you start looking through it and circle some places that you think sound good, and we'll call them when I get home."

"But what are we going to do about furniture, Honey?"

"I don't know, but God will provide." That was one of the things that I loved about Harold—he was so positive no matter what the situation.

"That's true," I agreed.

If it were possible, my pregnancy made us even closer than before. We didn't make love as much because we were afraid of hurting the baby. The prenatal book the doctor gave us said we could have intercourse up until seven months of pregnancy but not after that. Harold was happy just holding me in his arms. At night, he laid his head on my belly and talked to our baby and often sang to him or her. I loved his voice.

In fact, he paid so much attention to my belly that I began to feel neglected, and I wasn't even showing yet! One evening he had his lips up close to my belly button and he said, "Hello! Are you in there! Hello!"

Then he put his eye up to my belly button and exclaimed, "I can't see you!"

I reached down and tugged on his red hair and said, "Hey, I'm here too, you know!"

"I know, Honey! But I'm just so excited about our little one! I just can't wait! It's like Christmas in August!"

I rolled my eyes and stuck my tongue out at him. He laughed and kept talking to my belly button.

Every morning, I got up and packed Harold's lunch because he wasn't coming home as much as he used to. I missed him, but work was getting busier, and the overtime helped a lot; plus, he received another raise. To help with the loneliness, I took my walks every day, often going by Mildred's house after I had cleaned up the apartment and did any laundry.

Mildred was a great person to be around, but her house was always a mess. The kids ran around with no diapers on half the time. Flies buzzing all around all over the place. I'm such a neat freak that it drove me crazy. Sometimes she asked me to watch the kids for her while she ran a quick errand. While she was gone, I cleaned her house for her and did a little decorating such as move a plant here and put a picture there. She always loved everything I did and was delighted with the cleaning.

The first time I cleaned house for her, she exclaimed, "How did you do this so fast?"

"I don't know," I shrugged my shoulders. "I guess I just have a knack for it."

"I know one thing. My brother is very lucky, or should I say blessed to have you."

I smiled at her, drinking up the compliment.

"I'll bet the two of you will have a bunch of kids, and your house will be spotless as well as the kids!"

The family nicknamed me "Mrs. Clean." I didn't mind; I liked it.

September came around, and it was getting closer and closer to my birthday—my sweet sixteenth birthday. I didn't say anything to Harold, but I knew that I was going to throw a fit if he forgot.

I noticed that Harold was on the phone a lot in the evenings, but I didn't think too much about it because he had a large family and lots of friends. As it got closer to my birthday, I noticed that whenever we visited Mildred, she and Harold were in a corner whispering. Whenever I approached them to see what they were talking about, they stopped talking. And whenever we were with Peevine and Lil, the three of them huddled together whispering. It was really starting to get on my nerves.

One afternoon I asked him, "What is all this whispering about? It's driving me nuts!" I was really getting exasperated.

"Oh, Mommy and Poppie are celebrating their 50th wedding anniversary," he replied coyly.

I placed my hands on my hips and snorted, "Well, you don't have to keep that a secret from me!"

"You're right, Honey. I'm sorry," and he dropped it.

On September 15th (just three days from my birthday), when Harold came home from work, he announced, "Mommy and Poppie's fiftieth wedding anniversary falls on September 18th, so we got a huge party lined up for them."

I felt my gut twist. He had forgotten my birthday, but I hid my disappointment.

He grinned at me and continued, "We're having it at the ice cream factory. My boss said we could use the factory for their wedding anniversary. Wasn't that nice of him?" He seemed so excited about the anniversary party, but he had forgotten *my* birthday!

"Yeah, great," I muttered absently, too absorbed in my own disappointment. I hoped that perhaps—just maybe—he still had plans for us the next day.

"We'll all get dressed up, and I've ordered the band that the company always uses for the Christmas parties. Edna, Mildred, and Nancy are going to decorate and do the cooking." He glanced down at me and said, almost like an afterthought, "You can help too if you feel like it. You know how much they love your cakes and pies and potato salad."

I nodded absently, "Yeah, I can do that."

The next day, when I got to Mildred's for my morning walk, she said, "I have to get paper plates and cups for Mommy and Poppie's party. You want to go with me?"

"No." I was feeling forgotten. "I'll stay here and watch the boys for you."

"Okay. But don't worry about the house. It will still be here when we are long gone."

After she left, I couldn't stand the mess, and I straightened up her house. I loved taking care of her sweet little boys. They were so cute with their big brown eyes and blonde curly, wavy hair. I had just sat down when she got back from the store. She took one look around and said, "What did I tell you?"

"If you need any help with the party on Saturday, just let me know," I told her.

"I might ask you to watch the boys Saturday morning while Nancy and I decorate."

"Okay. Are you dressing up for it?"

"Yeah, we thought we'd give them a big surprise and put on our Sunday best!" She smiled and clamped her hands together and exclaimed, "We've got a band coming, and there'll be plenty of food! It's going to be so much fun!"

I was really starting to feel let down. I tried not to let it upset me, but I just couldn't help it.

"Oh, don't tell any of the grandkids because they will tell Mommy and Poppie about it. They can't keep a secret," she concluded, shaking her head.

Harold had his dark blue suit dry-cleaned, and when he brought it home from the cleaners, he asked me "What're you going to wear, Honey?"

I thought about it for a minute and then asked, "Do you think I can still wear that pretty white dress I got married in?"

"I don't know. Let's try it," he said.

I had started to gain a little bit, and I was disappointed when I couldn't zip my dress up. I couldn't help myself, but between Harold forgetting my birthday and the dress not fitting, I cried. "Don't worry about it," he reassured me. "I'll give you some money, and you can go shopping with Mildred tomorrow and pick out something you like."

He thought I was crying about the dress!

The next morning, after Harold left for work, I called Lil, Peevine's wife, and asked her if she wanted to go shopping. I walked over to their apartment after I had straightened up, and we caught the downtown bus. We tried several dress shops, but I couldn't find anything I liked. Finally, I spotted a dress in the window of a shop across the street, and they had a sign that read *big sale*. We crossed the street and went in and asked the salesgirl if they had the dress in the window my size.

The dress was white and showed off my dark skin and black hair. The neckline was a little low but respectful. It had a full skirt and tight bodice, and Lil said I looked smashing in it. My white pumps go perfect with it.

Lil found a pretty two-piece maternity outfit for herself because she was six months pregnant by then. She looked great in it. I couldn't wait until I had to buy maternity clothes. I wasn't happy about going from a size 8 to a 10, but I knew I'd be able to lose it after the baby was born.

"What do you want, Donna?" Lil asked me while we were standing in line at the check-out counter.

"It doesn't matter, as long as it's healthy," I replied honestly. "His family is hoping for a boy to carry on the Clouse name."

"Yeah, we don't really care either. It's nice to have a boy first so he can take care of the next one if it's a girl. But whatever the Lord blesses us with is fine."

While we waited outside for the bus, I asked her, "Is Peevine as happy and anxious as my Harold is about the baby?"

"I honestly don't know," she answered. Her eyebrows knitted together while she thought about it. "He never says too much about it."

"Really?" I was surprised.

"Yeah, I guess men are all different in some ways."

The bus pulled up to the curb, and we headed back to their apartment. I called Harold as soon as we got back to see if he could pick me up there after work because it was getting late in the afternoon and very hot.

Lil had a sudden idea and asked, "How about if we fix dinner here, and you and Harold eat with us? Peevine gets home about the same time Harold does."

I loved the idea. "Sounds like a plan to me!"

I wasn't looking forward to going home to that hot apartment. Lil and Peevine's place was cooler than ours because it was on the first floor and had lots of windows for a cross draft to blow through. The boys showed up, and Harold was delighted that we were eating with them. We had a nice evening with two very close friends.

Saturday morning came, and Harold said, "I'm going to be really busy today, setting everything up for the party tonight for Mommy and Poppie. Mildred is going to pick you up around 6:00 p.m. and bring you over. I'm taking a change of clothes with me, and I'll clean up and get dressed down there. Okay?"

"Yeah, okay," I tried to keep the disappointment out of my voice. "I'll be ready."

I was drying off the lunch plates when he gave me a quick peck on the cheek and left around noon. As soon as the door shut behind him, I threw the dish towel I had in my hand at the door. "Oh!" Then instead of picking up the towel, I walked over to it and kicked it. It was my birthday, and he hadn't even mentioned it! A tear slowly made its way down my cheek, and I plopped down on the floor feeling sorry for myself.

At 6:00 p.m. on the dot, I heard a horn blow. I looked out the living room window, and Lil and Peevine were sitting outside waiting on me. "I thought Mildred was going to pick me up." I called down to them.

"Harold called and told us to pick you up!" Lil called back.

Hmm…that's strange, I thought. "Okay, I'll be right down!" I ran around the apartment and made sure everything was turned off, grabbed up the pies and potato salad I had made, and locked the door.

When we pulled into the parking lot in front of the factory, there were cars everywhere! I could hear people laughing and talking through the open windows, and then I heard some shhhh shhhh, and everything suddenly got very quiet. Peevine parked the car and then said, "Here, let me take those pies for you." And Lil reached for the potato salad and opened the door for me.

The lights were out inside, and as soon as Peevine opened the door and we walked in, the lights flipped on, and a banner dropped from the ceiling that read, "Happy Birthday, My Sweet, Sweet Thing!" Harold was standing by the band, and they started to play "Sweet Sixteen" by Billy Idol and Harold began singing it to me. Suddenly, everyone jumped up from their hiding places and started applauding and wishing me a happy birthday. I started to cry. Harold sauntered over to me, and I looked up at him through the tears and sniffled, "I thought you had forgotten."

"I know," and he smiled down at me.

When the band finished "Sweet Sixteen," they began to play "Oh Donna." Harold grabbed me around the waist and spun me out to the middle of the room. He held me close and squeezed and asked, "I'm not hurting you, am I?"

I shook my dark head, ashamed for feeling so sorry for myself and thinking that he had forgotten my birthday. I really had a wonderful husband. Then everyone joined in the dancing.

"I thought it was your Mommy and Poppie's anniversary," I reminded him.

"It is. They're on their way. They'll be here around 7:30, but I wanted to celebrate your birthday first."

"Oh, Harold!" I chided him. "You're so crazy!"

"It was Mildred's idea."

I didn't matter whose idea it was. It was my first surprise party, and I couldn't have been happier. Harold had made a large ice-cream cake for my birthday and another one for his parents' anniversary. Everyone celebrated both occasions at once. It was a lot of fun. Most of my presents were for the baby I was expecting, and that was fine with me. It was almost like a birthday party, anniversary party, and baby shower all rolled into one.

Harold and I danced that night to a lot of our favorite music. I was completely surprised, pleased, and happy all at once. I thought about how wonderful his family was. They were a close family, which I needed in my life. I felt wanted, needed, respected, and loved. It was a wonderful time in my life, and I thanked God over and over for blessing me with such a husband and family.

The next few months went by very quickly, and I started to grow out of my jeans, shorts, and dresses. Harold took me shopping for maternity clothes. It was getting close to Christmastime, and we went shopping for our first Christmas tree. Harold loved the holidays. He was like a big kid during those times. I guess it was because he was so family oriented.

We had also been watching the paper for an unfurnished downstairs apartment to rent. One afternoon, Lil told us that her mother was getting married again and moving in with her fiancé. Her mother lived in a nice apartment that she had to move out of at the end of the month. We asked if we could see it, and her mother said that she should be glad to show it to us. It was perfect! It was an old brick house with a large porch, two bedrooms, living room, kitchen and a fenced-in backyard. Across the road was a Catholic church that had been converted to housing for nuns; plus, it was on a quiet street.

We loved it. It had a large kitchen and lots of windows for a good breeze. After the baby got older, he or she could play in a nice big backyard. The rent was seventy-five dollars a month. I didn't like the color of the walls, but I knew we could paint it. There was an upstairs apartment where a mom and dad and their little nine-year-old girl lived. As a bonus, the woman was an RN. That would be convenient if we had any trouble with the baby.

Lil's mother called the landlord to tell him she found someone to take the apartment when she left. She gave us his number, and Harold couldn't wait to get home and call him. The landlord spoke with a broken accent, and Harold had a hard time understanding him. Harold was finally able to talk him into renting the apartment to us with no deposit and no first and last month's rent. We were truly blessed.

We hated leaving our little place because the landlady had been so sweet and nice to us. We gave her plenty of notice. She was crushed, but she said she understood because the apartment was too small for a baby and all. "But wherever you go," she said, "you have to come by and see me and let us come by and see you."

"Most definitely," I assured her. "Maybe we can pay you to babysit for us once in a while."

Her faced lit up the room, "Oh! I can't wait! Thank you so much!"

There was only one problem left—we still needed furniture. We spent a few sleepless nights discussing how to come up with a solution, and we had a month to do it in.

Lying in bed one night, I said to Harold, "Let's just concentrate on getting a bed for now, and the rest later. We can get it piece by piece if we need to. We have all our pots and pans, a coffeepot, mixer, dishes, toaster, and our towels and linens. We'll need a shower curtain because it belongs the landlady."

I was getting so excited talking to Harold about the new place. I just had to keep talking about it. "We will need a lawn mower too because now we have to start doing the yard. Oh, Honey, I just love it! And we have all those large windows for a nice breeze and lots of light during the day. And I just love that marble fireplace. I can make that place into a showplace. I just know it! And that large kitchen, I just love it!"

The closer it got to the end of the month, the more excited we became. While we're at Mommy and Poppie's for Sunday dinner with the rest of the family, we mentioned we had found a real nice unfurnished first-floor apartment.

Eugene said, "We have some stuff in the attic. You're welcome to it."

"What's up there?" Harold asked.

"Well, there's a double bed and mattress, some chairs, and things."

"Okay. I'll come by sometime this week," Harold assured him. Harold glanced over at me and winked.

After we got home that evening, we laughed about how everything just seemed to be falling into place for us. "Okay, we got one bed. We can go ahead and move in after the painting is done. We can paint it in one day with the both of us working on it," I told Harold.

"Not you," Harold said. "I don't want you smelling any paint in your condition. I'm not going to move in until three days after we have it painted, and I'll raise all the windows and let it air out. We have a nice couple upstairs to keep an eye on it for us while we let it air out."

"Oh, Harold!" I said with exasperation. "You're so cautious."

"It pays to be that way, Honey. You and that little one are my whole life, and I'm not going to take any chances with our future."

One evening we were over at Peevine's, and he said, "Hey! I have a great idea. Let's have a painting party. You furnish the beer, and I'll furnish the grill and hot dogs and hamburgers. I have enough paint rollers and brushes, and the girls can make some baked beans and potato salad. I'll invite my pals from work and you invite your friends and we will have it done on Sunday afternoon!"

I clapped my hands together and exclaimed, "Oh! That's a great idea!"

On Sunday afternoon, everyone showed up, and they started painting. They had two coolers of beer and plenty of food. Lil and I went shopping for her baby because it was due in three months. While we're out shopping, I bought a quart of yellow paint. Lil asked me, "Why are you getting that?"

I just smiled and looked at it knowingly and replied, "You'll see."

When Lil and I got home, they had just started on the kitchen. When Harold wasn't looking, I opened the yellow paint and poured it into the pan of white paint. Harold came by and said, "You and Lil get out of here. I don't want you to smell the paint."

"Okay. I'm going!" And I smiled sweetly.

We walked back out into the yard where the guys were cooking hamburgers and hotdogs.

"Hey!" exclaimed Don. "Who made the potato salad and deviled eggs?"

"My wife," Harold boasted.

"This is the best potato salad I've ever had. And the baked beans are great!"

Harold said, "Lil made those." And he smiled at both of us.

A few minutes later, Harold went into kitchen to get something. When he came back out, he asked, "Honey, what did you do?"

"What do you mean?" I asked innocently.

"The paint has yellow in it."

"It's okay," I assured him. "The landlord said as long as it's white"—I shrugged my shoulders—"and it has white in it."

Harold gave me that look. "Don't worry," I told him. "I'll call him and talk him into it, okay?"

"Okay."

The kitchen turned out a beautiful pale yellow—even Harold loved it. The landlord stopped by the next day and asked, "Why didn't you paint it all white?"

"Because I wanted the kitchen to be a little different," I told him.

"It's nice," he said. "I like it. You did such a good job painting. I tell you what, I'll give you one month free rent. You go ahead and move in and there will be a lawn mower under the porch. If you can get it up and running, you can have it."

The problem of needing a lawn mower was solved. I couldn't help but smile smugly at Harold.

Lil's mother called me and said that she had a lot of things up in the attic and storage, and that Harold and I could have anything I wanted. I called Lil and told her about it, and she came over the next morning. She had left all kinds of pretty plants, drapes, throw rugs, some little tables, lamps, a couple of chairs, some dishes, pans, and some old clothes. I was delighted, but I gave Lil first choice—after all it was because of her mother that we found this great place. Lil took what she wanted. I prayed the whole time that she left the rugs and potting plants or the lamps and tables. She took all the pots and pans and dishes but left all the things I wanted including some knickknacks.

We let the apartment air out for two days before we moved in (Harold was overcautious about my smelling the paint). Our first night in the apartment, Harold measured where to put the baby things. "Where are we going to put the baby things?"

"We don't have a baby yet," I reminded him.

"No," I could tell he was getting a little aggravated with me, "but he or she is coming, and we want them where we can see them no matter where we are in the house." He was such a worrywart. I just rolled my eyes.

All of Harold's friends and Peevine's friends helped us move in and gave us a house warming party, which we didn't know anything about. Everyone just started coming over with food, sodas, and beer for the guys, of course, and we had a cookout in the backyard. Lil helped me put the dishes and canned goods away in the cabinets and put the groceries in the refrigerator. Everyone surprised us by buying a bunch of groceries to fill up our pantry and refrigerator.

Peevine said, "We were going to give you gifts, but we thought that since we come over here a lot that food would be best." Then he grinned.

"We know you have special taste, Donna, so we decided to let you pick out your own style for the house," Lil interjected and laughed.

My new kitchen had a large stove, sink, and refrigerator. The appliances in the little apartment we just moved out were all gas. Our new apartment was all electric, and I felt much better about that. Yes, we loved our new apartment.

We were too far away from Mildred for me to walk to her house every day now. There was a little used-furniture store up the street that I started walking to every day. I had my eye on an old-fashioned washing machine he had. The owner of the furniture store had a price of fifteen dollars on it. He was a small Asian man who tried to act tough, but deep down he was really very sweet. His name was Mr. Lee. I told him I that I wanted it for seven dollars. He said no. He also had a sofa and chair for twenty-five dollars. I told him I wanted it for twelve dollars, and he said no. I went back every day for at least a month.

One time when I came in, I asked him, "Does the washer work?"

"No."

"Then why are you asking fifteen dollars for it?"

He rolled his eyes and shrugged, "I don't know, lady. It seemed like a good price to me."

"Then why don't you fix it?" I asked him.

"I don't have time," he said and looked back down at the receipts he was adding up.

"Well, you know, my husband can fix anything."

"Is that right?" I could tell he was getting annoyed with me and just wanted to shut me up. "I tell you what, lady. I have a lawn mower out back. If he can fix it, I'll give you the washer free."

I smiled ever so sweetly and turned around to leave. "My husband will be here Saturday morning."

That evening I made Harold a very nice dinner. After dinner, I told him about my visit with Mr. Lee that day.

He said, "You did what?"

"Harold, we have no way to do our laundry except to go to the laundromat every time. At the other apartment, the landlady let me use her washer in the basement."

"Okay," Harold said, "let's just say I fall for your little scheme. What if I can't fix it?"

"You can," I assured him.

Fifteen minutes after we arrived at Mr. Lee's on Saturday morning, Harold fired the lawn mower up, and it worked like a champ. Mr. Lee offered Harold a part-time job working on Saturday, but he shook his head and turned Mr. Lee down nicely. Because the washer machine had rollers on it, we rolled it down the street to our apartment. We made such a good deal on the washing machine, I went back every day.

I noticed he had a dresser and chest out back. It was in bad shape and had an odor. I casually sauntered back in and asked Mr. Lee as I motioned to the back of the building, "Hey, what're you going to do with that junk back there?"

"Well, I don't know. What you think?"

"I tell you what"—I was so sure of myself—"you give me seven dollars, and I'll haul it away for you."

"It's a deal!"

When I got home, I called Harold at work and told them to bring home a dolly. After work, Harold and I walked down to the furniture store together with the dolly. "I'm here to get the junk outside," Harold told Mr. Lee who opened his cash register and handed me seven dollars. Harold's jaw dropped open, and he looked at me quizzically, but he didn't say anything. I smiled sweetly and took the money from Mr. Lee.

When we got outside, Harold took one look at the chest of drawers and dresser and said, "Honey, you can't do anything with this stuff!"

"Yes, I can. Just put one piece at a time on the dolly and take it home and put it on the porch, and I'll work on it as I get time."

When Mr. Lee noticed that we were going to walk the furniture home on the dolly, he asked Harold, "Do you want to use my truck?"

"Sure," Harold replied.

"Here's two dollars for gas." Then Mr. Lee nodded over at me and said, "That's some woman you go there."

Harold just smiled that big smile of his and said, "Yeah, don't I know it."

The next day while Harold was at work, I took all the hardware off and washed the dresser and chest of drawers inside and out with disinfectant. I bought paint and stain stripper and asked Harold if he could put on the stripper, and then we waited a few days to take it off. When we took the stripper off, the wood underneath the ugly paint was so beautiful. Harold was amazed. We sanded down the rough spots, and Harold fixed the drawers, and they slid in and out easily. He refused to let me varnish or scrape the paint. He worked on our little project each evening after he got home from work.

When we had it all done, we went to the hardware store and picked out some knobs and handles. After Harold put them on, he stepped back and exclaimed in amazement, "It's beautiful! Not only did you get it for free, but he paid you to carry it off." He shook his head. "You are something!"

Every day I kept taking my little walk down to Mr. Lee's. After a while, he started calling me Mrs. Clouse. "So, what you want for free today, Mrs. Clouse?"

I had my eye on a living-room suit he had. "I tell you what, Mr. Lee. For that one living-room suit and that rocker, I'll come up here every Saturday for the next few weeks, and my husband and I will get this place cleaned up for you, and you might sell something. What do you say?"

"Deal!"

Harold wasn't very happy with the deal I had made, but after a couple of Saturdays, we had everything looking good, cleaned, and put up neatly. Now when people came into the store, they could see what Mr. Lee had. After we got the living room set home and cleaned up, it looked nice in our apartment. Harold was proud of me.

As time went on, my baby kept getting bigger and bigger. One morning, Harold dropped me off at Mildred's. I was sitting in her rocking chair holding her little baby boy when suddenly I felt something punch me from inside. I jumped out of the chair and screamed. Mildred ran into the room and looked at me funny. I looked up at her and exclaimed, "I felt something punch me from inside!"

Mildred relaxed and smiled and said, "That's your baby, Sweetie. He or she is waking up."

I just looked at her in bewilderment.

"As your baby continues to grow," she continued, "you will feel that more and more."

I didn't say anything to Harold that night. As usual, after I got out of the shower, Harold got out the measuring tape to measure my belly. At the exact time he got the tape around my middle, my baby drew up into a big ball. It scared him so bad, he jumped back and banged his head on the wall. "What was that!?"

"The baby is starting to move inside of me," I said.

"Doesn't that hurt?"

"No, not really," I shrugged my shoulders. "It's a little bothersome sometimes. But it doesn't really hurt."

He made me stand still for thirty minutes while he watched my tummy, waiting for the baby to move again. When the baby finally moved, he dropped down to his knees and wrapped his arms around me and said, "Hello, Little One, this is your daddy. I'm waiting impatiently for you."

Then he lightly taped my stomach and crooned, "Hello? Hello?"

Then he started singing softly, "Hush little baby, don't you cry…," and he looked up at me with those beautiful hazel eyes. "Aren't you going to sing to our baby?"

I shook my head, "No. I'm not that crazy."

He grinned at me and said, "Aw, Honey, I'm just singing to our baby."

He put his eye up against my navel like he often did, and the baby kicked. He jerked his head back and asked in amazement, "Doesn't that hurt?"

"No," I assured him and ran my fingers through his curly red hair.

When we went to bed at night, Harold would turn his back to me, and I would snuggle up as close to him as I could with my arm around him and my stomach pressed up against his back. We would sleep that way; and every time the baby kicked, Harold could feel it. He just loved that. If the baby didn't move in five or ten minutes, Harold would whisper, "Okay, Little One, let me know you're okay." Sometimes the baby would move in response.

When the baby still didn't move, Harold would ask, "Honey, it's been fifteen minutes. Do you think the baby is okay?"

"Harold! The baby sleeps too, you know!"

"Okay."

While we waited for the baby to come, we continued to work on the apartment. We polished the wood floors and they turned out beautifully. Harold got the washing machine working like a new one, and I got better and better at cooking. I started making homemade pizza, and Harold loved it. He wanted it all the time. I got tired of flipping the dough around for thirty minutes to make it stretch. One day I cut my time in half by using French bread instead of pizza dough. Harold loved it. "Honey, you have to let Betty Crocker or somebody know about this French bread pizza idea you came up with!"

"Oh, Harold, it's just something I came up with to save me some time."

Harold kept saying. "I'm telling you, Honey, this could make us a fortune!"

"Oh, Honey, shut up and leave me alone about this and just enjoy it," I told him. (Guess what? You can buy French-bread pizza now. I should have listened to Harold.)

The baby continued to grow, and I took my daily walks. Occasionally, there were days when I felt a lot of pressure, but I didn't let Harold know because he worried unnecessarily. On the days when I felt bad, I stayed home and walked around the apartment. On real nice days, I washed down the porch and sat in one of the folding chairs we had out back. Shirley from the apartment upstairs sometimes came downstairs and visited with me. As the baby grew, Shirley checked on me more often. If she didn't see me outside or hear me in the apartment, she knocked on the door to make sure I was all right.

We had a huge bay window in the living room that went all the way across the wall. I loved it. Lil's mother had left the drapes up, and we didn't have to buy any new ones for it. I gave Mommy (Harold's mother) the size of the kitchen window and the material I wanted the curtains made from and drew her a diagram of how I wanted them to look, and she made them for me. They were perfect. The curtains brightened up the whole kitchen and matched the pale yellow on the walls.

We still didn't have a kitchen table, and I hadn't found anything I liked at Mr. Lee's. One afternoon, Uncle Eugene called and said that Aunt Edna had bought a new kitchen table, and if we wanted their old one. I said yes, of course. Harold brought it home, and it was cracked a bit, and some spokes were missing out of the back of some of the chairs. He put it on the back porch and worked on it every evening after work. Harold had all the spokes fixed and patched the cracks in the table, and we sanded it down with steel wool, and he varnished it. I had enough material left over from the curtains that I took it to Mommy Clouse along with some foam, and she made me the cutest pillow seats for the chairs.

The kitchen looked great. We had plenty of counter space for all our electric appliances. We loved our apartment. Harold couldn't wait to get home each day from work to see what I had done that day.

I was feeling pretty good one day, and I decided to take a walk down to Mr. Lee's to see what was new in his shop. As soon as I walked in the store, he looked up and his eyes got big. He exclaimed, "Hey! Mrs. Clouse! Your baby growing big! Yes?"

I smiled and nodded.

"I have something special I put back just for you." He took me over to the counter and pulled out from beneath it the prettiest canister set. It was yellow with different kinds of fruit on it. I loved it, and I knew they matched my kitchen perfectly.

"How much?" I inquired.

"For you, Mrs. Clouse, nothing. You show me the American way. Since you and Mr. Clouse clean up my place, I sell lot more things! My business pick up good." He bowed slightly and continued, "I am in your debt. Thank you."

"Thank you, Mr. Lee." I felt slightly humbled and happy that we had helped him.

"If I get some things for the baby, I put to the side for you."

I was delighted. "Oh, thank you!"

I couldn't wait to get home and clean up my new canister set and display them on the kitchen counter. I was starting to hurt a little around my hip area. When Harold came home that evening, I was standing by the stove cooking supper. He came up behind me and put his arms around me and kissed my neck. He loved to surprise me that way. "Hi, Honey. So what have you been up to today?" he asked.

I laughed and kept on stirring the potatoes. He was starting to know me pretty well, and he began looking around. When he finally noticed the canister set, he asked, "Where did you get those?"

"Mr. Lee. He gave them to me for nothing."

Harold raised his eyebrows.

"He said they were free because we had done such a good job cleaning up and organizing his place that his business picked up. He thanked us and said he was in our debt." I smiled at him sweetly.

"Well," he drawled, "I'll say one thing, Mrs. Clouse. You sure do work miracles."

I just laughed.

As the baby got bigger and bigger, we stayed home more because it was getting more difficult for me to get around. Shirley, the nurse from upstairs, was always checking on me. Sometimes after church, if I was feeling up to it, we would drive out to his parents' for dinner. After dinner, Harold would go fishing for a while. I wouldn't mind because I knew he needed to relax. He had been so worried about me. Hunting season had started, and I knew he wanted to go so bad, but he was afraid to leave me alone for very long.

The closer it got to my due date, Harold called me from work two or three times a day; and if he wasn't calling me, he was calling one of his family members to check on me. It never failed that whenever I would lay down to rest, the phone would ring. Finally, I rearranged the furniture, and the phone was next to the bed or the sofa, and I could answer it without getting up.

Late one morning, Mildred called me and asked, "Hey, Donna, how about I come over and pick you up and we go bug Harold at the plant?"

I wasn't feeling well that day. "No. I'm not feeling that good today."

"Oh, come on! Let's surprise him! He's always bragging on you at work. Let them see you! I'll help you get ready. We won't stay long. I promise."

Mildred was just one of those people you couldn't say no to. "Okay. I probably should get out of the house." I showered and dressed and fixed my hair. I wanted to look as presentable as I could. Mildred showed up with her little ones, and we drove to the factory to "see Harold."

As soon as we walked in, I saw big sign strung across the ceiling that read, "Welcome, Little Clouse!" Harold had pulled off a baby shower for me! I was so surprised that tears sprang into my eyes. All I could manage to exclaim was, "Oh my goodness!"

All the Clouses were there as well. We got a basinet, a stroller, a baby toilet seat, a complete baby set from Sears: six pairs of little shoes, bottles, nipples, and a bottle sterilizer. We got everything—receiving blankets, baby gowns, T-shirts, belly bands, baby clothes—everything we needed for the next couple of years. We wouldn't have to buy a thing, except for maybe a few dozen more diapers.

I was overwhelmed by his family and friends. Nobody had a lot of money, but they looked out for each other. I have learned over the years that a loving, caring family is what counts in life—nothing else, except God, of course.

We got so many things that we had to borrow Mr. Lee's truck to get it all home. After we got all the gifts back to our apartment, we picked out what we were going to use right away and put the rest in the closet for later.

As March rolled in, it became more difficult for me to bend over, and I could no longer tie my shoes. Whenever we went anywhere Harold had to tie my shoes for me. One day he said, "Well, I guess you'll have to stay home during the day while I'm at work. You can't tie your own shoes anymore." He laughed at me.

I winked at him and replied, "I'll think of something." That wiped the smirk off his face.

The weather the beginning of March was beautiful, but it went out with cold and snow. April 1, 1958 came, and spring finally arrived. The trees in the background began to bloom, and the honeysuckle smelled so nice while I was hanging the laundry out on the line.

On a Tuesday, April 8th, around one o'clock while I was hanging laundry out, I suddenly felt tremendous pressure and a cramping-like pain. I was afraid to call Harold because he had told me not to do anymore laundry when he wasn't home. I had felt great that day, and I went ahead and started the laundry. It didn't seem like a bad idea at the time.

I called out, and Shirley heard me upstairs and ran down the stairs to me. She tried to usher me inside, but I wouldn't go until the laundry was all hung up. She gave up and finished hanging up the laundry and then helped me inside. I called Harold and told him he had better come home. He got so excited he rushed home.

The pains were fifteen minutes apart, and Shirley suggested that we go on to the hospital. She offered to call Dr. Welch for us to let him know that we were on our way to the hospital. When we got to the hospital, they put me in a wheelchair and gave Harold a stack of papers to fill out. Suddenly, my water broke, and the nurse jumped up and started wheeling me down the hall. I was so embarrassed by the stream of water that followed me down the hall that I kept my eyes averted to keep from looking at anyone. When I looked up at Harold, his face was red. I wasn't sure if it was from embarrassment or worrying about me and the baby.

When we got to the labor room, Harold followed me inside. The nurse put her hand on his chest to stop him and said, "You can't come in here. We have to get her undressed and prepared for the baby's birth."

"I can't leave my wife!" Harold protested.

"Mr. Clouse, you will have to."

She must have recognized the concern on his face because she said softly, "Don't worry. We'll keep you informed of her progress as she comes along."

Harold glanced down at me and leaned down to kiss me. "Everything will be okay, Honey. I won't leave. I'll be right here waiting on you." And he kissed my hand.

I tenderly squeezed his hand with one hand and touched him softly on the cheek with the other hand and said, "I know, Sweetheart."

Then she ushered him out of the room and down the hall to the father's waiting room. I hated that he couldn't be with me, and he hated it even more. She wheeled me into the labor room, and there was another lady also in labor who was probably twice my age. As the nurse helped me out of the wheelchair, I asked, "Can I go to the bathroom and get cleaned up?"

"Okay, but make it snappy." She handed me a hospital gown and said, "Take everything off and put this on."

When I got into the bathroom, I noticed that there was a shower. I took off my clothes and got into the shower and proceeded to clean myself up. The nurse opened the bathroom door and said, "Mrs. Clouse, I did not say take a shower."

"I know, but I felt very unclean with all that stuff running down between my legs."

"Please, Honey. If you get dizzy or weak, just push this button." And she indicated a red button beside the commode.

I took a shower as quickly as I could, even though it was very difficult for me to bend over. I felt a lot better, but I realized I hadn't felt the baby move. The nurse helped me into the bed, and I was extremely worried because it had been a while since I felt the baby move. I sat up in bed, and I asked the nurse, "I'm a little worried. The baby hasn't moved. In fact, it's been a couple of days since he or she has moved much."

The nurse smiled and answered, "That's common. Just before birth, Mother Nature puts them into a deep sleep." I relaxed a little.

She wheeled over a monitor and said, "We're going to hook you up, so we can monitor you and your baby's heart rhythms."

While the first nurse was hooking me up, another nurse came in and said, "Mrs. Clouse, I am Patsy, and I'm going to shave you and get you ready for the baby's birth."

I touched my face and exclaimed "Shave me? Are you crazy?"

She smiled sweetly and said, "No, Dear. Down here." And she pointed at my groin area.

"My private area?" I asked.

"Yes, the doctor has to be able to see the birth canal clearly while he is helping you give birth to your baby."

When Patsy finished, the first nurse came in and said, "Dr. Welch is out of town, and Dr. Jamison will be in a few minutes."

About a minute later, a tall man wearing a white coat came into the room. My stomach knotted because he resembled the man who tried to rape me as a child. He frowned and introduced himself. He was very gruff and not friendly at all. He was very rough as he pushed down hard on my stomach. He was hurting me, but I was afraid to say anything. He suddenly jerked the sheet down and demanded, "Open your legs and bend your knees."

He began to examine me further. He shouted at me, "Why are you so stiff? Relax! How the hell do you think you got this way anyway?"

I felt my heart pounding in my chest, and sweat broke out on my forehead. He made me feel like I was being violated and not examined; and when he hurt me again, I slammed my legs down on the bed and screamed, "Get out! I don't want you for my doctor!"

He stood there dumbfounded. I looked over at the nurse, "Get my husband!"

"Mrs. Clouse, please. You have to understand—"

"Go get my husband, or I am going to start screaming as loud as I can!" I threatened. I guess all those years of being treated badly as a child reared its ugly head. I wasn't about to stand for it now.

"Okay, Mrs. Clouse, okay. I'll get him." She ran out of the room, and I could hear her white nursing shoes beating a path down the hall.

Within thirty seconds, I heard another pair of heavier shoes running down the hall, and I knew it was Harold. I started to feel better already. Harold burst into the room and ran to my side where I was sobbing uncontrollably. I grabbed him and held on to him as tight as I possibly could. He stroked my hair and kissed the top of my head and asked softly, "What's wrong, Honey?"

"D…D…Dr. Wel…Welch is out…out…of…t…t…t…town!" I managed to spurt out.

Harold looked at me with this bewildered expression on his face. I felt better just having Harold with me. I whispered to him, "The other doctor was rough with me and he hurt me."

I shook my head and pleaded with him, "I don't want him, Harold. I don't want him to deliver our baby!"

"Okay, Honey. Calm down. I'll see to it." He stood up and walked the nurse over to the counter and said, "I don't care what you or the hospital thinks. If my wife said he hurt her, he hurt her! We refuse to let him deliver our baby. You get somebody else here, now!"

The nurse hurried out of the room, and they let Harold stay with me to help get me calmed down. In a few minutes, another nurse came into the room and gave me a shot to relax me, and Harold had to leave again.

About an hour or so later, another doctor came in who was older and kinder. He had a nice voice. "Good afternoon, Mrs. Clouse. I'm Dr. Janis, and I am going to examine you now and see how you're doing." He smiled warmly, and I nodded.

When he finished examining me, he said, "You are only four centimeters, so it will be a little while. You're doing just fine, Mrs. Clouse." And he left the room.

Eighteen hours later, the morning of April 9, 1958, I was at ten centimeters, and the nurse rolled me down the hall to the delivery room. As we passed the father's waiting room, the nurse told Harold that he could come with us as far as the delivery-room door. Right before they wheeled me in, Harold kissed me and said. "I'll be waiting for you right here, Honey."

I smiled weakly at him. As soon as they wheeled me through the door, Dr. Welch was standing there in an operating gown and putting on his mask. I was so relieved he was there. He smiled and said, "Show time, Mrs. Clouse. How do you feel?"

"A little weak."

"Well, I'm here now and it will soon be over," he reassured me.

As he snapped on his gloves, he said, "Because you are so young, we are going to put you to sleep. When you wake up, you will have a beautiful baby!"

I was lifted on to the operating table, and a man behind my head put a gas mask on me and said count from one hundred backward. I could feel someone putting my legs in stirrups or something and telling me to scoot down a little more. I started counting one hundred, ninety-nine, ninety-eight, ninety-seven, ninety-six, and then blackout.

A few hours later, I woke up in my room, and all the Clouses were standing around my bed. Those that could find chairs were sitting down. Because of Harold's insurance coverage, he managed to get a private room for me. Everyone was congratulating me and

Harold; and at first, I was little bewildered. Then I remembered and immediately reached down to feel my stomach, and it was almost as flat as it once was!

Harold came up to the bed and hugged me and exclaimed, "Great job, Honey! And Dr. Welch made it just in time and delivered her!"

"Her?" I asked.

"Yeah! She's beautiful, Honey! Just perfect! She weighs eight pounds, nine ounces and measures fifteen inches long! Oh, and she has the cutest little feet and hands! Just like yours!"

"Did we get a redhead?"

"No."

"My color?"

"No."

"What then?"

"Well, what little there is, it looks sort of blonde from what I can tell." He patted me on the arm. "I only got to see her for a few minutes before they took her down to the nursery. I couldn't even hold her." He just kept on babbling.

"She's beautiful and healthy. Oh, and she had all toes and fingers. I checked." He announced proudly. I rolled my eyes. "When you're ready, Honey, we'll walk down to the nursery together and see her."

I heard Mommy Clouse in the background saying, "She's perfect, Donna. Just perfect!"

"The rest of the family is down the hall, gaping at her down at the nursery," Harold said.

"The whole family is here?" I groaned.

"Of course. This is a big deal. Everyone wanted to be here."

If it were possible, he was grinning from ear to ear.

In a little while, the nurse came in and told everyone they had to leave except for the father. When everyone had left the room, the nurse brought the baby in for me to see. She was wrapped up in a pink blanket with a tiny pink hat on her head. She grunted and growled, trying to stretch her arms and legs. The nurse placed her in my arms and stepped back. Then she made Harold put on a hospital gown and mask.

The baby started squirming in my arms, grunting and rooting at my left breast. She sounded like a little baby pig. "What's she doing?" I asked the nurse.

"She smells the milk in your breast and she's trying to get at it," the nurse said.

"Oh, no! We're going to bottle-feed." I told her.

The nurse looked over at Harold, and he nodded. "She's right." I could tell he was smiling behind the mask because his eyes were twinkling, and I knew he was about to say something to embarrass me.

She shook her head and said, "Dr. Welch is not going to like that. He wants all of his new mothers to breastfeed."

Harold said, "Look nurse, if she breastfeeds me and the baby, we're going to bumping heads all night."

She must have been used to father's like Harold because she replied, "You'd better not tell Dr. Welch that, my boy!" Then she turned around in a huff and marched out of the room.

As soon as she left, we opened the blanket and checked her all over. She was perfect. Harold said, "Do you remember that list of names we had picked out?"

"Yes, I know them by heart."

"Which ones did you narrow it down to?" he asked.

"I've got it down to several. Theresa, Debbie, Vickie, or Cheryl. Which one do you like?" I asked.

"I don't know. Hey, let's let her decide." he said.

I rolled my eyes. "Now how are we going to do that?"

"Watch this." Harold put his head down next to the baby and said very softly, "Hey, little girl. Remember me? I've been talking to you for months now. We're getting ready to pick a name for you. So you let us know which one you like by your response to them, okay?"

I just shook my head. I couldn't believe what I was hearing.

Very softly he said, "Theresa Gail?" She scrunched up, and a little frown puckered her forehead. We laughed at the sight.

"I guess that's a no. How about Vickie Kay?" She squirmed and frowned again.

117

"I guess that's out. Okay, I get the point. How about Cheryl Ann?" She scrunched up even more and cut gas and frowned. We both cracked up.

"Okay," Harold said, "I want you to know, Daddy's Little Girl, that we're running out of names. Okay now. How about Debbie Lynn?" She grunted and opened her eyes real big and smiled the biggest smile I had ever seen.

Harold smiled too and said, "There you go, Honey. Debra Lynn it is!" She smiled again when he said her name and we both laughed. We named all our children that way.

Just as the nurse walked in, Harold bent down to pick her up out of my arms. The nurse said, "No, Mr. Clouse. The fathers aren't allowed to hold them until it's time to go home."

Harold stood up with his hands on his hips, and I could tell he was fuming behind the mask because she stopped him from picking her up. "Okay!" he exclaimed, "pack us up! We're going home!"

"Back off, Mr. Clouse. I haven't had to call security on a father yet, and I don't want the first to be you."

Harold wanted to hold her, but we had to stay three days. I was very sore because the doctor had to give me so many stitches. The doctor explained that I ripped as the baby's head was coming through. He said that the baby was very large for my first baby, plus the fact that I was so small down there, he had to cut me. He said I had to keep the stitches dry, and he gave me instructions on how to care for them over the next few weeks. He also said that the stitches will start to come loose and fall out on their own. As he was writing up my care on the chart he said, "You must clean your breast and nipple every time before and after nursing the baby." He kept on writing.

"Uh...uh...uh...," Harold began, "we're not going to nurse."

Dr. Welch glanced up from the chart and said, "Yes, the nurse told me, but with breasts like your wife's, who do you think you are to withhold that from your baby?"

Harold stiffened, "I'm sorry doctor, but that's how we feel."

"Hmm. Well, I don't like it, but the closest thing to breast milk is Enfamil. It's a little expensive, but it's better for your baby. At least for the first five months." He continued scribbling on the chart for a few more minutes and then said to me, "I'll see you in a couple of days to release you."

The nurses brought Debbie in to see me in the mornings, at lunch time, and at dinner for her feedings. Between those times, they fed her in the nursery every three hours. I watched the clock on the table beside me just waiting for those times. The plant wasn't far from the hospital, and Harold took off from work and ran over to the hospital and was there for every one of her feeding times. The nurse told me that they hadn't seen a father like him in a long time. The nurse also told me that after they made him leave at night, he hung around the nursery window watching Debbie until the nurses closed the curtain at 10:00 p.m. He was so anxious to get us home.

Finally, the big day came. Harold was at the hospital at 6:00 a.m. to take us home. When he walked into the room, the nurse told him, "It's going to be a while."

Harold sat down in the chair and said, "That's okay. Just give me the baby, and I'll sit here and wait." And he smiled that charming, dimply smile of his.

She shook her head, and his smile faded. "We can't do that, Mr. Clouse. We have rules."

"Well," he said as he smiled again. (I gulped, not sure what was about to come out his mouth.) "You know, I had a part in her birth too. She wouldn't be here if it wasn't for the part I played in it all."

The nurse smiled sweetly and said, "Yes, Mr. Clouse, we are all aware of the part you played in the act." Then she cocked her head to the side. "By the way, how bad did it hurt?"

Harold snorted. "Okay. I'll wait patiently," and he looked over at me and grinned. That was one of the things I loved about Harold; he knew when he had been beaten.

In a little while, the nurse rolled a wheelchair into the room, and Harold helped me into it. Then he wheeled me down the hall to the nursery. They had her right up front where we could see her. The sign on her clear plastic baby bed read, "Baby Girl Clouse—8lb, 9oz. 15" long." We stared at her in total awe for a few minutes.

I couldn't get Harold away from the nursery. "Humph!" I growled. I wheeled myself back down the hall to my room. I was a little jealous of my little baby girl.

Finally, Dr. Welch came in and signed off on the paperwork, so we could go home. He leaned down and whispered to me, "Good luck with Mr. Clouse. We haven't seen a father like him around here in a very, very long time."

I nodded. "So I heard."

"Good luck to you and your family," he said to Harold, and then he turned to me and said, "I'll see you and the baby in six weeks for you and your baby's checkups."

"Okay."

We were so excited when the nurse brought Debbie in. Harold laid out the blanket and gown set I had picked out to take our baby home in. I chose a pale yellow because at the time I packed it, we didn't know if it was going to be a girl or a boy. Harold got everything ready and laid it out on the bed. He hoped he could dress her. Harold turned to take the baby from the nurse.

"Oh no, Mr. Clouse. I have to dress her."

Poor Harold. His face literally fell, and his shoulders slumped in defeat.

"You just sit down over there in that chair and put your mask on."

"You know," Harold said quietly, "we are getting really close to coming to blows, you and me."

She smiled pleasantly and said, "And you will lose."

Harold and the nurse glared at each other for a few minutes, and suddenly Debbie cut a big one, and they burst out laughing. Harold laughed and said, "That's right, Baby Girl, you tell her, 'Leave my daddy alone!'"

At last, Debbie was dressed, and we were ready to leave. Harold said, "Let me push the wheelchair."

"No," the nurse replied, "we have rules."

"Yeah," Harold said. "Too many stupid ones too."

Then he asked, "How about I carry the baby?"

"No. You carry the flower and the bags."

"Okay, okay."

When the doors of the elevator slid open, the nurse said to Harold, "Go get your car and bring it around to the front of the hospital, Mr. Clouse."

"Okay!" Harold bolted and ran down the hall. I shook my head. For a minute I thought I saw wings sprout out at his ankles.

The nurse, Debbie, and I waited on Harold out front of the hospital. He wheeled the car around and parked and jumped out and ran up to the nurse who was still holding our baby.

"Now?" he asked. He was really getting impatient.

"No. You help your wife get into the car."

"Okay." He opened the passenger door and helped me into the front seat. "Now?"

"No. Get in your car, Mr. Clouse."

He ran back around the front of the car and slid into the driver's seat, and the nurse handed me the baby and said, "Good luck with those two, Mrs. Clouse." And she closed my door.

Harold put his seat back and reached over and took Debbie from my arms. He lay her carefully on his lap and started checking her all over. He couldn't seem to get enough of her. "Can we just go home now? You can hold her all you want and check her all night if you want to once we get home."

Fifteen minutes later, there was a line of cars behind us with horns blowing and hands waving. Finally, Harold wrapped her back up and handed Debbie back to me. There were tears in his eyes, "Oh, Honey, she's really ours. Yours and mine. Ours. Wow, wow, wow!"

When we pulled up in front of our apartment, the front steps were bombarded with Clouses everywhere. They had been waiting for us, and they couldn't wait to hold our little Debbie. She was passed around like a football. Harold kept saying, "Okay, it's my turn. Okay, it's my turn." And everyone kept telling him to go away, that he would have her for the rest of his life, but they could only see her on Sundays.

All I wanted to do was to get out of the car and go inside. Everyone seemed to have forgotten about me. Finally, Uncle Eugene noticed that everyone was so wrapped up in the baby that I had been forgotten. Uncle Eugene rushed up to the car and helped me out and up to the front door. Harold finally realized he had forgotten about me, and he was sorry. But I was proud that he felt that way about our precious child.

When I got into the apartment, I went straight to the bathroom and freshened up and slipped into some decent pajamas and lay down on the bed. I was exhausted, and the last few days were catching up to me. Before I knew it, everyone poured into the apartment raving about Debbie and taking pictures as they continued passing her around.

The hospital had only given me enough milk bottles for one day, and we had to make up some bottles of milk for Debbie. Mildred went into the kitchen and filled the bottle sterilizer with water and some empty bottles and boiled the water for ten minutes to sterilize the bottles. She made up another bunch of bottles to last about twenty-four hours.

Several hours later, everyone began to leave, and it was so nice being with just my husband and our little girl. Poor Debbie was exhausted because she couldn't sleep from being held by so many different people! She was turned every which way except upside down and shaken by her heels. Bless her heart.

After everyone left, I said, "I want to give her a bath."

Harold's eyes lit up, and he fixed the little baby tub with luke-warm water. I laughed when he dipped his elbow in the water to check the temperature. He ignored me and took Debbie from my arms and gently placed her into the water and supported her with one hand while washing her with the other. I told Harold "Don't get her navel wet. The doctor said it had to stay dry."

He was very careful. She loved it. She giggled and cooed the whole time. He shampooed her little head and rinsed it. He washed her all over and patted her dry and rubbed baby oil on her. When he was finished oiling her, she looked like a greased ham. I shook my head and took another cloth and wiped some of the excess off. He struggled with her diaper, and I helped him fasten the pins. "You are doing a great job, Honey," I complimented him. He just beamed. "I am so proud of you."

Harold took a shower, and we ate and settled down to watch a little TV. Suddenly, the doorbell rang. "Who in the world could that be?" I asked. Harold shrugged his shoulders and got up to open the door.

It was Mom and Dad! They had driven all the way from Ohio to see the baby!

Dad said, "We have something for you." He went out to the trunk of the car and came back inside with a new white baby bed and mattress set.

"Oh, Dad!" I was overwhelmed. "It's beautiful!"

Harold was speechless. He simply nodded and shook Dad's hand.

At the baby shower, Aunt Edna gave us a basinet, but we knew Debbie wouldn't be able to use that for very long. They stayed for a few hours and poor Debbie was passed around again. About ten o'clock, Dad announced that they were going over to Uncle Eugene and Aunt Edna's, and they could come back tomorrow. They just loved our little apartment and our new little girl.

I was the happiest woman in the world—if you consider a wife and mother at sixteen a woman. I had a great husband, a beautiful baby girl, and a nice home. Our apartment was more like a home than an apartment. Our upstairs neighbors were always delighted to watch Debbie for me if I needed to run down to the store for something. We really enjoyed taking Debbie with us whenever we could. She was such a good baby. She only cried when she was hungry or needed changing.

From the time Debbie was first born until she was about nine months old, whenever Debbie was sleeping peacefully, Harold always tiptoed over to her crib to make sure she was still breathing. I think he hoped to wake her up, so he could play with her.

Dr. Welch was very pleased with her progress. When she was four months old, the doctor took her off Enfamil because he said she didn't need that rich of a diet anymore. He started her on Carnation and told me to keep an eye on her because sometimes a diet change will cause a baby to get diarrhea or constipation and sometimes spit up, and that I should call him. But none of those things happened. She took to the change in diet very well.

Harold loved to feed her. As soon as Debbie finished her milk, Harold lifted her up over his face, and she burped and spit a little milk on his face. Harold laughed and said, "Um, Um, good!" Debbie laughed and giggled, very pleased with herself.

It seemed every time she laughed, she got the hiccups. And the more we laughed, the more she laughed and hiccupped.

Harold had more fun with his baby girl than anyone can imagine. Debbie was my little girl when we were home during the day while Harold was working, but the minute he came home she disowned me and was Daddy's girl. My little girl had all the love and affection that I never had when I was very young. We made sure of that.

When Debbie was three months old, our first anniversary was coming up. Harold loved to throw big parties—like my 16th birthday and our baby shower. I expected him to have a big shindig cooked up for our very first anniversary or maybe a night out and dinner with just the two of us. I had exercised and watched my weight and was back down to 112 pounds. I was pleased with myself and thought Harold wanted to show me off.

The afternoon of our first anniversary, I showered and fixed my hair. I picked out a nice outfit that I knew Harold liked, and I bathed Debbie and dressed her in one of her nicest outfits. As soon as he pulled up outside, with Debbie in my arms we stood by the front door waiting on him. He bounced through the front door with flowers in one hand and a rocking horse in the other.

My jaw hit my chest and my eyes started to burn as I fought back the tears. I felt a wave of disappointment flood through me. I couldn't help but spit out, "She can't ride that!"

Harold stepped back for a moment and replied, "Sure she can." "How?"

He shrugged his broad shoulders and beamed, "I'll hold her!" Debbie reached her little chubby arms out to Harold. He set the rocking horse down and took her into his arms. He bent down and helped her place her chubby legs on either side of the plastic saddle and helped her rock back and forth.

Debbie laughed and cooed. It was easy to see that she loved it. My disappointment subsided as I watched the pure joy my husband and little girl were having with that little rocking horse. That first night, Harold couldn't get her off it. Every time he tried to take her off, she cried. He looked up at me for help, but I just smiled and said, "Oh, no. You brought it home, you deal with it." Eventually, she fell asleep on her little horse that night, and we put her to bed.

One night we had trouble getting Debbie to go to sleep. It was getting late and Harold had to go to work the next day. We tried everything—a warm bath, rocking back and forth, singing softly—nothing worked. Finally, Harold got a bright idea, and he bundled up to take her outside. Panic struck me, "Harold! Where are you going with Debbie?"

"It's okay," he reassured me. "I'm going to take her for a lap around the block and see if that works. She usually always falls asleep when we go somewhere."

He was back in ten minutes with our sleeping baby girl in his arms. Harold grinned and placed her gently in her crib. From then on, whenever Debbie was fussy and couldn't go to sleep, Harold would bundle her up and take her for a short ride. It worked every time.

When Debbie was five months old, my seventeenth birthday was just around the corner, and I noticed that my breasts were getting tender. At first, I didn't think too much of it because I knew that it was getting time for my period.

On my seventeenth birthday, I was sitting in the living room feeding Debbie when Harold strolled in with a baby walker. I looked up and exclaimed as sarcastically as I could, "Oh, yeah! A baby walker! Oh, Harold! You shouldn't have!"

He grinned that dimply heart-wrenching grin of his and whipped out from behind his back a bouquet of flowers. My heart melted, and I laughed at him. He was so pleased with himself.

A week later, Harold strolled into the kitchen while I was washing baby bottles and wrapped his arms around my waist and kissed my neck. "I love you," he whispered against my neck.

I figured now was as good a time as any to tell him what I suspected. "Honey, I think I'm pregnant again."

He stepped back from me and exclaimed, "No way!"

I turned around and nodded. "I think so."

With a funny little smirk on his face and a twinkle in his eyes, he asked as innocently as he could, "How'd that happen?"

I splashed soapy water on him from the sink and groaned, "Oh!"

He laughed and wiped his face off with a dish towel. Then more seriously, he asked, "Really, Honey? Have you missed a period?"

"Not yet." I shook my head. "But I don't think I'm going to get it."

"When's it due?"

"Three days." I was one of those women who were always regular. I turned back around the sink of bottles and said, "Let's get through the holidays, and then I'll go see Dr. Welch."

"We can't wait that long, Honey. If you are pregnant, you need to start taking your prenatal vitamins. I want us to have a healthy baby like Debbie." He was always so caring about his family.

"Okay. If I miss my period this month and next month, then I'll make an appointment."

Harold agreed, and we settled down into our usual routine.

I made the appointment with Dr. Welch when I was a week late in October. I knew the drill. He examined me, and then I gave the nurse a urine specimen, and I waited in the waiting room with Harold for the results. In about twenty minutes, the nurse called us into Dr. Welch's office, and Dr. Welch confirmed our suspicions.

"Maybe we'll get a boy this time!" Harold was excited.

I rolled my eyes. I had just got my figure back and was looking and feeling good again. "Oh, Harold!"

Dr. Welch cleared his throat and said, "As far as I can determine, you're looking at around June 7th for this one. Take your vitamins, and we'll probably have another healthy birth, okay?"

Then he looked at Harold and continued, "And, Mr. Clouse, take it easy. She's not a free ride, you know?"

Harold smiled broadly and replied, "It's not me, Doc. She's all over me!"

I slapped his arm.

After we were outside, I accused him, "You're going to have our doctor thinking we're sex maniacs!"

"Now, Honey," he pleaded defensively, "you have to admit, we do enjoy each other."

I felt my face redden, and he laughed.

"God has truly blessed us, and He is going to give us a beautiful healthy son this time. You wait and see!"

When we told his parents about the baby, his mother confided, "I had a dream you had a son, and he had dark hair and dark eyes and looked like a little Indian."

Harold turned to me and exclaimed, "That means this one's going to look like you, Honey!"

"Debbie has my nose and body build and my small hands and feet," I replied. "Her eyes are the same shape as mine, but they have her grandmother's pretty blue." I smiled tenderly at him and continued, "I hope this next one is as good a baby as Debbie," and hugged our little girl to my chest and kissed the top of her blonde head.

As the holidays approached, the baby inside of me continued to grow. This time, I didn't get morning sickness like I did with Debbie. That was a blessing. We didn't have to look through all the baby names because we knew if it was a boy, we would name him Harold, Jr. If we had another girl, we still had three other girl names to go through.

We started getting Debbie used to the idea that she had a little brother or sister coming. Harold patted my stomach and said to her, "Baby's coming."

Debbie grabbed his hand and pushed them off my tummy and cried, "My da da!" She refused to allow any of her cousins to sit on her daddy's lap. She tried to pull them off as best she could and shrieked, "My da da!" But it was okay if I held them. If her da da wasn't around, and I tried to pick up one of Mildred's little ones, then she would have a fit and screeched, "No! No! My mommy!" She was jealous if we gave anyone the slightest attention but her.

Whenever Harold talked to my stomach and said, "Hey, little guy, this is your papa. I love you, and I'm waiting for you. We'll go fishing and hunting and play ball—"

Debbie crawled over and pulled his hands away and said, "No baby! Me baby!" and pointed to herself.

As time went on and my stomach continued to grow, Debbie got used to the idea of a new baby since she saw how much her daddy loved it already. She crawled over and patted my stomach and said to my belly, "Me baby too." Then she laid her head on my stomach like she saw her daddy do and talk softly to it. It was mostly gibber, and we weren't sure what she was saying, but it was so cute.

When Debbie was old enough, we put her in the baby walker, and she took to it instantly. She realized immediately that if she moved her chubby little legs that she could venture out into places she had never been before. And the faster she moved her little legs, the faster she flew through the house. She could practically fly on those hardwood floors. We heard her laughing above the squeaking of the wheels as she flew from room to room.

After a while, she knew what time Daddy came home, and she rolled over to the bay window and stand on tiptoes to peek out and wait for him. As soon as Harold pulled up outside, Debbie clapped her hands and stomped her little feet and hollered, "My da da! My da da!" Then she'd make a beeline for the front door, screeching the whole time because she couldn't wait for him to come in the front door. Harold had to carefully edge his way in because he didn't want to knock her down or bang her poor little toes against the door.

Every time I went to the doctor for my checkup, Dr. Welch said, "I think we have a seven-pound boy here." Harold's face beamed.

The Clouse family was counting on a little boy to carry on the Clouse name. Harold's oldest brother, Ed, had a son who drowned that summer when he was nineteen. So now the Clouse family was really counting on Harold and me to have a son. Every present that we received was either blue or had something to do with being a boy.

One afternoon as Harold was talking to his son, I reminded him, "You know, Honey, it could be another girl."

Harold looked up at me and smiled. "No, it's a boy, and he's going to look just like you. You'll see."

I started wondering what the family would do if it was a boy. They threw such a shindig when Debbie was born, I couldn't think of any bigger party they could have.

As I grew, I noticed that I was carrying this one a little differently. My hips started to spread, and my breasts were enormous! Harold didn't mind. I carried Debbie all in front, but this one I carried a little lower, and it kicked all the time. I was very uncomfortable all the time with this one. Sometimes I thought there was a soccer match going on inside of me. The baby kicked on one side of my stomach and then rolled over to the other side and kicked that side.

One morning I was holding Debbie, and the baby kicked so hard, she bent down in my arms and pointed at my stomach and said, "Be nice, Baby!" I couldn't help but laugh. She was repeating what Harold and I always told her. Debbie learned to talk very fast. I think it was because we started talking to her from the time she was in my womb. She was very smart and very opinionated. She had no hesitation about telling you what she liked or didn't like. (Hmm, I wonder where she got that from?) Debbie was a true blessing to us and was very special.

Whatever Daddy did, Debbie did. She talked to my stomach as much as Harold did. Some of it was gibberish, but some of it I could make out. And she always kissed my belly when she was finished talking to the baby and patted my stomach—just like her daddy.

One evening when Harold came home from work, he wasn't his usual self. I could tell immediately something was bothering him as soon as he walked in the door. "What's wrong?" I asked.

Harold plopped down on the sofa beside and picked up Debbie and held her tight. She squirmed and smiled and patted his scruffy cheek. "Mr. Ball sold the company to Borden Company." He rubbed his eyes and kissed the top of Debbie's blonde head. "I started working there after school and on the weekends when I was sixteen years old."

I didn't say anything. I rubbed his arm and listened. He took a deep breath and continued. "After I graduated, I went to work for him full-time. After I was drafted, Mr. Ball told me not to worry, and that as soon as my term was over, I could go back to work for him full-time. When I came back, he put me right back to work and kept my seniority just like I never left, plus he gave me a raise."

Harold shook his head. "I just can't believe it. Mr. Ball has always been so good to his employees." He looked over at me and said, "He treats us like we're family," then he shrugged. "I know he's getting old but..."

Harold was really upset that Mr. Ball had sold out, but he also understood that he had to look after his health. He found out the next day that Mr. Ball agreed to stay on as acting president for the first two years because he wanted the changeover to the new ownership to go smoother for his employees.

We began trying to wean Debbie off the bottle to baby food because we didn't want two children on the bottle at the same time. I started mashing up her food and feeding her at the table with us. She learned to use a sippy cup, and she liked that. It made her feel like a big girl.

One evening for dinner, I had fixed baked chicken, mashed potatoes, green beans, and biscuits. Harold set Debbie in her high chair and shoved her up to the table without putting the leaf of the high chair on. We dug into our dinner, and she sat quietly for a few minutes watching both of us with her big blue eyes. Suddenly she reached over with her chubby little hands and grabbed a biscuit and a bunch of mashed potatoes and crammed it all into her mouth.

Harold burst out laughing, "Well, I guess we can stop buying baby food for a while."

One morning in church, as the offering plate was being passed up and down the aisles, Harold tossed our envelope into the plate. Debbie reached in the plate and pulled it back out. We had a difficult time trying to convince her that it needed to go back into the plate. My face turned red as I heard people laughing. It was funny. Thinking back on it now, I should have laughed with them.

Harold reached over and took an empty envelope out of the back of the pew in front of us and handed it to her, hoping that she would relinquish her hold on the other one. She was determined to keep them both. Then he reached in the plate and took out a quarter and said to her, "Change," and handed her the quarter. She dropped the offering and took the quarter. Harold then reached in his pocket and put another quarter in the plate and quickly passed it to the next person while Debbie was engrossed in her wealth. Everyone laughed and applauded. We watched her until she grew tired of it to make sure she didn't put it in her mouth.

On the way out, she reached over and handed to the pastor and said, "Thanks." From then on whenever the offering plate was making its rounds, one of us kept her occupied with something else until we had a chance to put in our offering and pass it on.

Debbie's first birthday was coming up, and that was all Harold could talk about. I was sure it was going to be big. We went all out for her and a gigantic cookout for her at his parent's house. Every Clouse that was ever born that was still living made it to her first birthday party. She got all kinds of toys to play with and learning toys; but of all the toys she got, she loved the little baby doll her Aunt Mildred gave her most of all. It was the kind that a little girl could button up and zip, and it had Velcro on the shoes.

Debbie loved to undo all the clothes and shoes and take it off and then put it all on again. She just laughed and played with her little dolly. A look of concentration creased her brow as she tried to button the dress back on it. As soon as she had it all dressed again, she'd look up and laugh and clap her hands. She loved it so much, I couldn't pry it out her hands with a crowbar. She took it everywhere with her.

One day, she sat it on her potty chair and pointed her finger at it and said, "You can do it." When she started walking and accidentally messed up a throw rug, she straightened it back up again and said, "There now," and continued on her way, dragging her dolly behind her. The only time I could wash it was after she fell asleep at night.

Mom and Dad had been trying to talk us into letting them take Debbie home to Columbus when the baby was born to give me time to recuperate. We knew I wouldn't be able to lift her like I was after the baby came. We didn't like the idea of not seeing her for a couple of weeks, but they finally convinced us. They threw the guilt factor in there. You know the one where "his family gets to see her all the time, but we only get to see her every few weekends?" We decided when I went into labor that Harold would call them, and that should give them plenty of time to drive down from Columbus to Lexington.

Around 6:00 p.m. Sunday evening on June 7th, I started having some cramping. It didn't feel like labor pain, just some cramping in my lower back. Harold went ahead and called my mom and dad, and they started down. While we were waiting to see if the pains got any worse, Harold got this bright idea. "Hey, Sweet Thing?"

"Uh huh?" I asked absently. I figured he was just going to pop off something smart like he tended to do.

"How about we shave you? That way, the hospital won't have to!" He was excited about playing nurse.

"You're crazy, Harold!"

"Oh, come on! It'll be fun!"

Just to shut him up, I agreed. My cramping got worse around 8:00 p.m., and we went to the hospital. After the admission nurse had me situated in my room, the CNA came in to shave me. Before I could say anything, she whipped the sheet off and took one look at my private and asked, "Okay, who beat me to the punch?"

My face turned crimson, and I laughed, "My husband."

She nodded and said, "He did a pretty good job. Unfortunately, I have to do it again."

I looked at her quizzically.

"Hospital policy."

I rolled my eyes and snorted, "Great."

Harold waited in the "big boy's room," as he like to call it, worried to death about me, the baby, and Debbie. The nurse kept coming in every few minutes to check me, and finally around 10:00 p.m., the nurse called Dr. Welch. I kept telling her, "I'm not in any pain. It just feels like cramping. That's all."

She looked at me and said, "You are ready, Mrs. Clouse. You are eight centimeters. And besides that, the head is peeking out, and its hair is black."

Junior was born as we went through the delivery room doors. Dr. Welch cried, "Now that's what I call a close call!" He weighed seven pounds two ounces. He was the most beautiful baby I had ever seen. The doctor showed him to me right away before they put me under to extract the afterbirth.

When I woke up in my room, I could hear all this commotion outside in the hall. Harold bent down and kissed me on top of the head and whispered, "Hi, Sweet Thing, we have a son. He's beautiful." Harold had tears in his eyes, "He looks just like you, Baby."

"What's all that noise," I asked.

"It's my family waiting to see you."

"All of them?"

He nodded. "All of them. They are ecstatic about us having the first boy Clouse in over nineteen years!" he proclaimed proudly.

"Yeah, you certainly worked hard on this one, didn't you, Dear," I said a little sarcastically.

Harold laughed.

The nurse started letting the Clouses come in a few dozen at a time. Just kidding; it was probably five or six at a time—it just seemed like a dozen. All any of them could talk about was the first baby Clouse boy in years. Mom and Dad came a little later with Debbie. After a few minutes, Mom bent down and asked, "Are they always this loud, dear?"

I nodded. "Yes, Mom. Always."

"Boy, did they go this nuts over Debbie when she was born?"

"Yes, Mom. This is normal for them."

When it was time for everyone to leave, Mrs. Clouse refused to leave the hospital and Mr. Clouse never went anywhere without her. They sat out by the nursery and made sure that no one made off with little Harold Jr.

When the doctor asked me about circumcising the baby, I said, "Of course." Harold just looked down at me, but he didn't say anything. The first time the family was in the room after his circumcision, they threw a Pentecostal fit on me. But I stood my ground and explained to them that it was healthier and cleaner for the baby, and it caused them a lot less trouble when they grew up.

Harold's mother looked at Harold and said, "Italians, Greeks, and Jews do that to their babies because it gives the boys more pleasure when they start...you know!"

Harold snorted and replied, "If that's true, then I think I'll have the doctor do me!"

After a while, they forgave me when they realized it was better and more sanitary.

About twenty-four hours after giving birth to Junior, I started having labor pain symptoms. I couldn't believe it! The nurse told me that I had such an easy birth, and the bones were starting to go back together. The afterbirth pains were worse than the labor pains I ever had with Debbie. I had to stay in the hospital an extra day with the baby.

On the third day of my hospital stay, Mom and Dad came by, and they had all of Debbie's things all packed up and were ready to take her back to Columbus for two weeks. Everything was fine until Mom tried to take Debbie out of her daddy's arms. She threw a fit. We listened to her scream all the way down the hall. I started to call them back, but I knew I needed the time to heal.

Junior turned out not to be the little sleeper Debbie was as a newborn. He had his days and nights mixed up. He slept all day, and then around 7:00 p.m. he was wide awake and wanted constant attention. After about three days of staying up all night, I decided that it had to stop. It was nice he slept during the day because I could get my house work done, but at night I couldn't get any rest for having to look after his needs.

I usually gave my babies a bath twice a day, one in the morning and one right after dinner. This time, I decided to turn Junior back around to the correct time of day. I didn't give him a bath to keep him from getting sleepy. Every time he drifted off to sleep, I tickled him or picked him up or talked to him. The nurse upstairs helped me keep him awake that day while I got a few things done.

By the time Harold came home, Junior was one cranky baby. I told Harold what I was doing, and he joined in on the fun. At 10:00 p.m. we gave Junior a long warm bath and played with him and rubbed him down with baby lotion and baby powder. When I fixed his 11:00 p.m. bottle, I filled it with a few extra ounces, and Junior drank it all. He gave us a big burp or two, smacked his lips, filled his pants (I changed him), and off to la-la land he went. End of problem.

We got worried when he didn't wake up for his 6:00 a.m. feeding after missing all his nightly feedings as well. Harold placed his hand on the baby's belly and shook him. He woke up and looked up at us with those huge dark eyes and smiled. I fed him while Harold got ready and left for work. I changed the baby, and he drifted back to sleep.

When I went into the bathroom, I noticed that I was bleeding very heavily, and that I was passing large blood clots. I called the upstairs nurse, and she came down and said, "We have to get you back to the hospital, Donna. You're hemorrhaging." She called Harold at work, and he called Mildred to stay with Junior. By the time the ambulance came to rush me to the hospital, Uncle Eugene showed up with Mommy and Poppie Clouse who volunteered to stay with the baby.

I had lost a lot of blood and was in the hospital for three days. I was anemic, and they gave me blood and iron shots to build my blood levels back up again. The doctor told Harold I had to have plenty of rest and not to lift anything over three pounds for a few weeks. I couldn't rest because I was so worried about the children and our little apartment.

When we walked into the apartment, Junior was happy, but the house looked like a cyclone went through it. There were diapers hanging on the lamp shades and on the arms of the chairs and sofa. Mommy Clouse shrugged and said, "His pee doesn't smell so I hung them up to dry and use them again to save on laundry."

Harold felt me tremble beside him. He knew it wasn't from fatigue but pure, unadulterated anger. I was furious to say the least. He rushed me out the living room and straight to the bedroom to avoid another feud like we had at the hospital about Junior's circumcision.

"Harold!" I whispered angrily. "This house is a mess!"

"Shhhh…I know, I know. Just calm down, and I'll get them to leave, so I can straighten it up for you." He helped me undress and put me to bed.

I heard him in the other room make excuses to his parents, and then he called Eugene, and Eugene came right over and took them home. After they left, I heard Harold stacking dishes in the sink and the water turn on. Exhaustion finally got the best of me, and I fell asleep. When I woke up, the house was straightened up as best he could, and Junior had his bath, and Harold was rocking him asleep with a bottle. He smiled tenderly at me. I couldn't help but smile back. He was such a good dad and husband. God had blessed me beyond my wildest dreams.

Mom and Dad kept Debbie another two weeks, and I thought Harold got impatient wanting to see his little girl. He wanted his family together. I missed her too, but I knew if she came home too early, I would try to pick her up and maybe start hemorrhaging again. During the day, the nurse upstairs stayed with me and handed Junior to me after I sat down because I couldn't lift him. On days when she had to work, her mother came over. After a few weeks, I finally had our cute apartment back in shape with the help of Harold and the nurse upstairs.

At last, my parents were bringing Debbie home the following weekend. Harold and I were so excited to finally be able to get our family together. As soon as Dad carried her in the room, she saw Harold and laughed and ran straight to him, but she ignored me. She loved to see her daddy and rocking horse, totally ignoring me. I was crushed. Tears sprang into my eyes and threatened to spill over onto my cheeks. She had changed so much in the last few weeks, and I just couldn't get over it. My baby girl left and came home a little girl—it was frightening.

I had Junior in my arms, and we showed him to her and said, "Baby brother."

She looked over at us and said, "Okay." Then she wobbled over to me on the sofa and raised up my shirt to look at my belly. A puzzled expression crossed her features, and she looked over at Junior again. Then she patted my stomach and said, "Baby?" and pointed to Junior. She shook her head and cried, "No! No! No! I baby! I baby!"

Harold and I looked at each other; we knew we had a job on our hands.

The next day when Mom and Dad came by to say goodbye and drive back home, Debbie dropped her toy and wobbled over to them. She wanted to leave with them. Dad had taught her to say grandpa and grandma. Debbie grabbed his finger to go with him. She was crazy about Dad. I glanced over at Harold, and I could tell he was a little jealous.

We didn't want Debbie to get jealous of her little brother, so I let her help me bathe Junior and feed him and change his diaper. One time while she was helping me change his diaper, she pointed at his penis and asked, "What's that?"

I said as calmly as I could, "That's his pee pee."

She shook her blonde curls and demanded, "No it's not. Take it off!"

After a while, Debbie learned to love her little baby brother; just don't mess with her daddy or horsey—as long as you stayed away from those two things, you're fine.

I was sixteen and had two kids now. I wanted children, just not that close together. Mildred talked me into getting a diaphragm for contraceptive. Dr. Welch advised me that I was too small, and that it could cause me discomfort during sex. Well, I had to have one. After all, my sister-in-law had one, and she should know. Besides, she had seven kids (hello, stupid).

When my baby boy was three months old, I was turning seventeen. Harold came home that day with a twin stroller. After that I could take both children at the same time when I went on my daily excursions. I used to leave Junior with the upstairs neighbor while I took Debbie to the market and shopping. Sometimes I went out just to get out of the house.

I was overwhelmed with a new stroller for my seventeenth birthday—not! "Oh, Honey!" I exclaimed sarcastically. "Now I *know* you love me!" Then I put my hands on my hips and grumbled. "You know you're going to pay for this."

He smiled and said, "I know."

"By the way, where are my flowers?"

"Flowers?" The smile was suddenly wiped off his face. I couldn't help but laugh.

Chapter 6

Harold's job was getting stressful. The new owners were weeding out all the employees that had been with the company a long time and made pretty good money. Harold had worked with the company ten years and was making pretty good money back then. As people began quitting, the new owners hired new people, starting them at the bottom. Then they stopped paying for employee insurance. Mr. Ball had always paid the employees' medical insurance, but the new company refused to. That became a real problem for us, and it was getting harder to make ends meet. Harold started working part-time for Mr. Lee to help cover our bills and take care of any extras we needed.

In August 1959, Poppie Clouse got sick, and Harold's brother Robert and his wife came down from New Jersey with their three kids. They had a daughter, fourteen, and two boys, eight and twelve. They were great kids. Harold talked to Robert about the owners of the factory and the changes they were making and getting rid of people. I think he tried to hide a lot of things from me because he didn't want me to worry. Robert convinced Harold to move to New Jersey, and he helped Harold get a job in the Government sector. There wasn't much industry in Lexington at that time and most people who lived in Lexington went to Ohio to work. Harold told Robert that he would think about it, and the following week Poppie got better, and Robert and Janet went back home to New Jersey.

Harold worked as hard as he could at the factory and for Mr. Lee, but we continued to struggle financially because of the medical insurance we had to pay and the doctor's bills, food, etc. One evening in January 1960, after dinner, Harold admitted, "Honey, we can't make it here anymore."

I was crushed. I loved our little apartment, and I had fixed it up so pretty. But I didn't want my husband to keep struggling and worrying about his family. "Okay, Harold. Whatever you think is best."

He kissed me on the forehead and said, "I'll call Robert."

Everything happened so fast after that. Harold worked a two-week notice, and during that time we began packing up our clothes, the babies' clothes and things, house wares, linens, etc. We talked to the landlord about leaving our furniture until we found a place and Harold continued to pay the rent until we could afford to come back and get our things. Junior was just seven months old, so he was too young to understand what was going on, but Debbie was a real trooper. She handled it better than I did. She was always a pioneer and loved to go on to new and adventurous places. I had been moved around so much as a child, and I had a home at last; it was harder for me to leave, but we had our children to think about.

On the day we got ready to leave, Harold loaded the car down with as much of our things as we could carry. Then he made a bed in the back seat for the babies. Debbie stomped her little foot and refused to leave without her horsey. Harold tried to convince her that her horsey could come on the next trip, but she cried so hard it broke his heart. Harold gave in and told her that he had to take it apart because it wouldn't fit in the car. She cried and cried as he broke it down into pieces and put it in a box. The whole time Harold was taking it apart, she kept saying, "You broke it! You broke it!"

"No, I didn't, Honey. We'll put it back together when we get to Aunt Janet's, okay?"

Because she kept on crying, and he couldn't seem to convince her that he could put it back together at Janet's, he reassembled it in the living room. "See? Daddy can fix it once we get to Aunt Janet's."

Debbie began to understand then, and she nodded and wiped the tears from her face and patted him on the shoulder. "Okay." Her daddy was a genius.

When Harold knew that Debbie understood, he took the rocking horse apart again and put all pieces in a box.

"Okay, Honey. Daddy and you will put it back together, and it will be as good as new."

Harold carried the box of "horsey" parts out to the car and strapped it on top and helped Debbie in the back seat. Then he held Junior while I got in and handed the sleeping baby to me, and he slid into the driver's seat and asked me, "Ready?"

I nodded and turned to look at our apartment. I couldn't help myself. I burst out crying. I loved our place. I was so happy there. Poor Harold had to deal with three babies that day. I felt bad later, and I kept apologizing to him. He held my hand and smiled that dimply smile of his and sang "Oh! Susanna." "Oh, Susanna. Oh, don't you cry for me. 'Cause I'm going to Louisiana with a banjo on my knee!" Debbie joined in the fun, and I couldn't help but sing too. Harold had a way of bringing out the best in any situation.

Kentucky is such a beautiful state. I think mostly it didn't have large factories to darken the skies with pollution. Robert, the most successful of the Clouse family, lived in Dayton, Ohio. He and his wife worked in the same factory together. Janet worked the day shift, and Robert worked the night shift. They had two little girls, and one of them is always home with them.

Robert managed to get Harold a job working in the same factory he did on the same shift. That worked out well for all of us. Harold had a lot in common with his brother, and they got along great. Janet was a sweet person, and she loved our babies because she couldn't have any more children. She worked in the insurance department at the factory. Harold and Robert slept during the day, and Janet worked. I did the housework, cooking, laundry, and looking after the little ones. They had a huge three-story house. Janet was a bit of a clutter hound whereas I liked things neat and put in their proper places (still do).

While Janet was at work and the husbands were sleeping, I cleaned and organized every room. I worked on one room at a time, and when I was satisfied with the results, I moved on to the next room. It took me a while, but I finally had the place spotless and well organized. Robert and Janet's kids helped watch my little ones during the day, which gave me more time on the house.

One day, I finally made it to their beautiful dining room. You couldn't see the furniture because of all the "stuff" cluttered everywhere on the table and chairs. There was stuff all over the server and china cabinet. I cleaned the table off and found the most beautiful oak dining table I had ever seen. I polished it up, and it shined beautifully. Next, I took all the china and wine goblets out of the cabinet and washed them and placed them all back in the cabinet nice and neat. I cleaned off the server and polished it inside and out.

As soon as Robert and Harold walked in the door, he noticed the dining room. His eyes grew big as saucers and a huge grin crossed his face. "Donna!" he exclaimed. "You're amazing! I haven't seen that table in years!" He walked into the dining room and saw the clean cabinet and all the clean china and glassware and whistled appreciatively. "I appreciate what you did, but you didn't have to do all that."

"I didn't mind. It keeps me busy."

Harold walked up and placed his arm around my shoulder said proudly, "Yep, she's somethin', all right."

Robert and Janet wanted to pay me, but we refused to take their money because we were living with them for free at the time. We enjoyed living with Robert and Janet. The children were happy because they got a lot of attention. We lived with them for three months, and Harold had managed to save up some money for a down payment on a house. A house came up for sale about six houses down the street from Robert's. One evening at dinner, Robert said to Harold, "Let's take a look."

Harold shook his head and snorted, "I don't have enough money yet to buy a house!"

Robert wasn't one to take no for an answer, and he pressed, "It can't hurt to talk to them. If you can get the house, then we'll be close together."

It seemed every time we went to look at a place to rent, Robert always came up with excuses for us not to get it. The house was too small, too big, bad neighborhood, no yard, small yard, no garage—it was always something. I think it was because Robert wanted his little brother to live close by.

Robert called the number on the sign and made an appointment for us to go down and see it. We went down and looked at it. It was red brick and needed some repair, but I knew it had great possibilities. It had four bedrooms and a bath upstairs, and downstairs there was a living room, kitchen and dining room with a large basement. It only had one bathroom, but Harold figured in time we could install another one downstairs. There was a beautiful fireplace between the living room and dining room. The windows were huge in the front and let in a lot of light. All the rooms in the house were large—plenty of room for our family. The carpeting was dirty and smelled, but I knew we could tear it out. We were still paying rent on our apartment in Lexington where we were storing all our furniture. After looking around, Harold shook his head and said, "I don't know, Robert. I don't think we can afford it."

After checking into it further, we found out that the owner, Mr. Smith, had some medical problems and was six months behind on his payments. He was having a hard time selling the house because it needed some repair. In the end, we got the house at a great deal, and the payment was only eighty-five dollars a month, which was ten dollars a month higher than our rent for the apartment in Lexington. Harold put five hundred dollars down, and we took over Mr. Smith's payments. We lived with Robert and Janet another month while we worked on the house.

One afternoon while Harold, Robert, and Janet were at work, I took all the kids and walked down to the house to look it over. I noticed in the basement that the Smith's had left some tools. I asked little Jan to watch the kids for me the rest of the day. I helped her get the children all back up to Robert's, and I fixed everyone lunch.

After I settled Debbie and Junior down for their afternoon nap, I asked Janet's boys to help me down the street, and we all walked back down to the house. We started pulling up all that nasty carpet, and there was the most beautiful hardwood floor underneath. I couldn't believe it! I had hit the jackpot! They needed sanding, but I knew Harold and I could do that, and then we could varnish them. I didn't say anything to Harold about it because I wanted to surprise him.

The boys and I went back down the next day, and we started tearing down a wall by the entry way. The wall was about six feet wide and eight feet high. The boys and I took a sledge hammer and knocked it down. I used Robert's tools and wheelbarrow and hauled the garbage over to the neighbor's house. I had paid their boys to help me, and I used their garbage cans. It took several days to get the deed accomplished, and I kept stalling Harold from going down in the evening to look at the house until I could finish my handiwork.

Robert kept asking Harold to walk down to our house, but I kept stalling him. Robert got so insistent that I took him to the side and told him I had a surprise for Harold, but I needed a few more days. Robert agreed and helped me stall Harold a little more. Harold and Robert had planned on going back that weekend to Kentucky to rent a truck and bring our furniture back. They left on Friday evening after work, and I knew then that I had enough time to finish cleaning up the mess before Harold and Robert got back.

I told the boys not to tell anyone, and I paid them for their help. We all worked like troopers the rest of the week and the weekend and got everything swept and cleaned up and disposed of. I talked Janet into calling one of her friends that had a truck to haul away all the carpet and mess from the torn-down wall. Her friends lived in the country and needed the carpet and stuff to fill in some holes on his farm. He refused to take any money and said, "I do you a favor, and you do me a favor. That's as it should be."

Janet came down and couldn't believe what we had accomplished. As soon as she walked in, her eyes lit up and she exclaimed, "You did all this by yourself?"

"No. Your boys helped me," I chuckled.

She walked around and shook her head. "I'll say one thing. You are one hell of an interior decorator. It looks much better without that wall, and the floors look great!"

I beamed at the compliment.

"How did you know what was under the carpet?"

I shrugged my shoulder and smiled. "I just pulled up on one corner. And the more I pulled, the prettier the floor got underneath."

"I love it!" Janet exclaimed. She bent down and ran her hand over the hardwood surface. "I know Robert and Harold are going to love this."

"Don't tell them!" I admonished. "I want to surprise Harold."

All the rooms in the house were different colors and dull and cracking in various places. I bought a bucket of semigloss white paint and convinced Janet and her boys to help me paint. It took us all weekend, but we finally finished it up.

We began to worry about Harold and Robert because they had been gone for several days, and we hadn't heard from them. We didn't know it at the time, but Harold and Robert had called work and took an extra five days off due to bad weather and driving conditions. What do you know? They took a wrong turn and ended up in a hunting and fishing camp. Hmm…I wonder how that happened? Since they were there, they might as well do a little hunting and fishing.

When they did finally pull up in the driveway, Janet and I ran outside to meet them. I had Debbie by the hand and Junior in my arms. Robert jumped out of the driver's side and Harold popped out of the passenger side. They hugged and kissed us. Harold's stubbly beard rubbed my face raw, and he smelled. "Ew! Harold! What's that stink?" And I pushed on his chest.

He smiled and sauntered to the back of the truck. There on the rear bumper were tied two big bucks they had shot. When he opened the back door, there was a cooler filled with fish and ice.

I looked at him quizzically and asked, "Where'd those come from?"

"What, these?" he asked pointing at the deer and the fish.

I nodded.

"Oh, the deer just jumped right out in front of us, and we couldn't just leave them lying there. And the fish were hitchhiking, so we just had to stop and give them a ride."

I had to laugh. He grinned and picked up Debbie, and she timidly felt his whiskers. Then she wrapped her little arms around his neck and hugged him.

"We'll unload the truck tomorrow. Robert and I have to get the deer dressed and clean the fish and put it all in his freezer in the basement."

Robert called his friend Lucas, and he came over with some of his buddies and a case of beer. They picked up Harold and Robert along with the deer and fish, and off they went to Lucas' farm to "dress the deer and clean the fish."

I didn't mind because I still had some trim work left to do. Janet picked up some hot dogs, hamburgers, buns, ribs, and some steaks, and she and the kids went over to the farm to start a cookout. An hour or so later, I called the Lucas farm and told Janet that I was ready. She came by and picked me up.

When we got there, the guys were finishing up the deer. They decided to just throw the fish on the fire. They were delicious. I had never had campfire fish before, and they tasted delectable.

As we were munching on our fish, Harold said, "Just think, Honey. One more night, and we'll be moving into our very own house."

I nodded and smiled sweetly.

"Did you go down there while I was gone?" he asked.

"Yeah, I scrubbed the bathroom and floors and windows and cleaned out the fireplace and tried to sweep out the basement, and I washed down the stairs," I replied innocently.

"I'm going to try and get you a new washer and dryer just as soon as I can," he promised.

I didn't tell him then, but the Smith's had left their washer and dryer in the basement and worked fine.

Finally, around 10:00 p.m., Janet and I decided to take the kids home. We helped Mrs. Lucas clean up, then we proceeded to load up the kids. Debbie didn't want to leave her daddy, but the mosquitoes were eating her alive. She had bites all over her poor little arms and legs. She missed her daddy, and she wanted his undivided attention. Janet and I finally managed to get her in the car, and she cried all the way home for her daddy. "Da, Da, Da!" she cried. "Mommy! Da, Da, Da!" After about five minutes from the house, she fell asleep. Janet carried Debbie in, and I carried Junior. I didn't fool with their baths that night because I was so exhausted.

Robert and Harold made it in around midnight and stuffed enough deer meat in the freezer to last a year—maybe two. Harold came in the bedroom I was in and fell across the bed. I growled, "Oh no, Big Guy. You get in the shower or out of my bed and on the couch tonight!"

"Oh, Honey," he groaned. He rolled over and peeked at me with one eye.

"Yeah, I know how tired you are. So am I," I reminded him. "But I don't want to smell that dead animal on you all night." I pinched my nose and pretended to wave off an extremely offensive odor.

"All right, all right." Then an idea occurred to him. "Will you undress me?" he asked as innocently as he possibly could.

"Okay."

"Will you run my shower for me?" He figured he might as well get as much as he could out of me.

"Okay, but I'm not going to shower you or shave you!" I let him know that real fast.

"Do I have to shave tonight?"

"No, but don't expect any kisses from me till you do!" I huffed.

"But it's been five days!" he whined.

"No crap, Dick Tracy!" I got a kick out of giving him a hard time. I loved that man. I think he enjoyed aggravating me as well. He groaned and moaned for a while, but he finally got his shower and shave.

The next morning, our bedroom door burst open, and Debbie ran up to the bed and jumped into the middle of it screaming, "Da Da! Da Da! Home!" He covered his head up with the pillow and rolled over groaning, "Not yet. Maybe by nightfall."

I patted his behind and got dressed and made a large breakfast for everyone because we needed a lot of energy to unload the truck. Janet was still in bed, and I let her sleep for a while. Mr. Lucas and his wife came over to help.

Harold drove the truck down the street while the rest of us walked down. Little Jan watched the children while we unloaded the truck. Robert walked up the front porch with the key to unlock the door. I asked him to wait and let Harold do it.

After Harold had the truck backed in the driveway and walked up to the door, we were all standing around, "Honey," I said, "you open the door."

"Why?"

I stomped my foot. "Just do it!" I exclaimed.

He shrugged and took the key from Robert and unlocked the door. As soon as he swung open the door, he saw all the hard work we had put in to it. "Honey!" he exclaimed, "did you do all of this yourself?"

"With Robert's boys and the boys next door."

"I love it! It really opens up the whole house!" The wires were hanging down from the ceiling from the outlets that weren't there anymore. He smiled that big dimply grin of his and asked, "What were you planning on doing with these?"

"I figured you'd know what to do with them," I shrugged. "I knew you'd probably Harold Rig them."

Robert laughed, "She has your number, Harold!"

Harold scooped me up into his arms and carried me to the back porch and back in again and kissed me passionately and said, "I love you, my sweet, sweet wife, and I admire you greatly."

"Aw, cut out the mushy stuff," Robert growled, "or I'll have to go see Janet."

We both laughed, and then we all began to unload the truck. The boys helped by carrying in the small stuff and the things that went into the basement

When we finished unloading, Harold asked Mr. Lucas, "What do I owe you?"

"Aw, you don't pay friends. You do things for friends just because they're friends."

Harold shook his hand and said gratefully, "Thank you."

Mr. Lucas replied, "I'm sure if I needed any help, you wouldn't hesitate to lend me a hand."

Harold nodded and said, "Anytime. Just let me know."

They became good friends. Harold always helped Mr. Lucas keep his car and truck and farm equipment tuned up. Mr. Lucas bought the parts, and Harold did the work. We were always going out to their farm, and Debbie and Junior loved to go out there. They even started calling them Uncle and Aunt.

Our house turned out lovely. Harold sanded the floors, and he and Robert varnished them. They turned out beautifully. We had enough furniture for three rooms—living room, bedroom, kitchen, and two baby beds. We loved our new house. It was so spacious. The steps leading up to the second floor were hardwood, and Debbie was scratching up her little legs as she climbed up and down them. We were afraid that one of the kids might fall and tumble down them. We decided to carpet just the stairs, and we placed a plush rug at the bottom of them just in case.

After a while, the neighbor wives began coming over and asking for my help to rearrange their furniture or make a room bigger. I think it was because Janet was always bragging about my talent for decorating.

Robert and Janet had a lot of friends, and their friends liked us, and we liked them. We fit right in. We weren't real crazy about New Jersey, but we loved our home, and Harold enjoyed his job. We had good insurance, and Harold had a wonderful retirement plan. We figured on staying in New Jersey until Harold's retirement.

One afternoon while the four of us and our children were having a picnic, I casually asked Janet, "Where's the nearest used-furniture store?"

Harold jumped up and yelled, "Don't tell her! Don't tell her!"

Janet and Robert busted out laughing, and Janet asked, "Why not?"

Then Harold proceeded to tell them the story with Mr. Lee. They loved that one. Janet piped up, "You should be proud, not complaining."

Harold shook his head and admitted, "I'm not complaining. She saved us a fortune."

Janet shrugged and said, "Then what's the problem?"

"She's embarrassing sometimes with all her wheeling and dealing. That's all." Then he plopped back down beside me.

"Nothing wrong with that," Robert said. "I wish Janet had a little of that in her. I'd be a whole lot richer if she did." Janet poked him in the arm, and we all laughed.

Janet turned to me and asked, "Would you consider cleaning our house once a week for us. You could do it any day you want. If Jan's not in school, she can watch the kids for you. When she is in school, you could do it on the weekend. Maybe Saturdays, if you want to. We can leave for a while, and you would have the house all to yourself and work undisturbed."

It appeared she had been thinking about this a lot. "I would love to!" I told her. "If it's all right with Harold?" And I turned and gave him the most imploring look I could.

He laid back on the blanket we were all sitting on, placed his arms behind his head, and said, "Sure, Honey, if you don't think it's too much for you."

I leaned down to kiss him, and he grabbed me and pulled me on top of him. Robert and Janet groaned, "Here we go again."

Harold chuckled and released me.

My part-time job worked out wonderfully. Robert and Janet paid me thirty-five dollars a week to clean their house. Jan watched the children during the summer and during school; Harold watched them on Saturdays for me. Occasionally, Robert and Janet went somewhere and took our children with them. Now I had some spending money, and I didn't have to keep asking Harold for money all the time.

A few weeks later, the factory decided that everyone had to work rotating shifts. Harold and Robert had to work two weeks on night shift, two weeks on day shift, and two weeks on third shift. They decided to carpool with two other men because they had to drive from Lambertville to Trenton, which was about twenty-five miles each way. It became more difficult for me to get to the store because either Harold was working or sleeping, depending on which shift he was on.

One evening while the guys were working, I mentioned to Janet that I needed to go to the store. She piped up, "Hey, why don't I teach you how to drive?"

"Yeah, that's a great idea!"

In the afternoons when Harold was riding with the other husbands to work, the car sat in the driveway. I took the kids up the street to Janet's and fixed everyone dinner. Then little Jan babysat the children while she took me out to a parking lot to teach me how to start, stop, turn around—all the basic rules. We didn't mention to the children what we were doing because we didn't want them to tell their fathers. It took Janet about two weeks to teach me how to drive, and now I had a way to go when Harold wasn't home but his car was. I took the car for a spin just to enhance my driving abilities.

Janet showed me where the used-furniture stores were located that were not within walking distance. Just across the bridge on the other side of town was Pennsylvania, and there were a lot of secondhand stores there. I was looking for bedroom suits. We had four bedrooms, but only one bedroom suit and two baby beds. We also needed a dining room set.

I started cleaning an older couple's house that lived next door to Janet because they were too old to keep it up anymore. While I was cleaning their house one day, I mentioned to them that I was looking for some used furniture. The older gentlemen said, "I have an old dining room suit downstairs. You're welcome to it."

I went downstairs and looked at it. It was dark mahogany wood with a few cracks and scratches, but I knew Harold could fix that. I noticed an old bedroom suit that looked like it came from Abraham Lincoln's days. It was also dark wood, but I thought that I could change that if I wanted to. "How much do you want for that?" I asked.

He snorted, "You can have too if you want it."

When I finished cleaning their house, they were delighted with my services and tried to pay me. I shook my head and said, "No, you don't have to pay me because you gave me so much."

They made me take the money and asked me to clean for them once a month.

Robert was amazed at how clean I kept our house, the old couple's house, cooked all our meals, and worked on the furniture that the couple had given me. I also wallpapered the kitchen, bathroom, and the upstairs. Harold loved it, as well as Janet and Robert. They loved it so much that they decided to wallpaper their living room and dining room. Harold and I helped them, but Janet pooped out, so the three of us finished it. They were so good to us and the kids.

One afternoon while Harold as at work I called little Jan and asked her to babysit for me, but she wasn't available. I walked out on the porch and the neighbor's, Gus and Mary, were swinging on their porch swing. They must have heard me on the phone because she hollered over to me, "Donna! We'll watch the kids for you for a while."

"You will?"

"Sure, where're you going?"

I walked over to where they were sitting, so we could hear each other better. "I'm looking for some bedroom furniture. All we have is our bedroom suit and the two baby beds for the kids. Oh, and we also need a dining room suit."

"Just bring 'em over, Honey. I have all day! Besides, I'd love to look after your two beautiful children anytime—just to be able to love on them for a while."

I took the car and drove around to some of the used-furniture stores. I found a nice bedroom suit that included the dresser, chest, two nightstands and a headboard but no mattress. He wanted thirty-five dollars for the entire set, and I gave him a twenty-dollar deposit to hold it for me until Saturday when Harold could pick it up for me.

I drove down to the next store, but I didn't see anything I liked. I knew I needed to get home and start dinner, so I decided it was enough for one day and headed home. When I got home, I parked the car in its usual place, picked up the kids from the neighbor, and started supper.

Before I had a chance to tell him that Janet and I found a bedroom suit and put a deposit on it, he looked up from his plate of food and said casually, "Lucas's wife told him she saw you driving today, and you were doing a real good job."

I choked on my plate of food.

He laughed and said, "Honey, I don't mind you driving, but you have to get your driver's license because if something should happen to the car while you're driving it, our insurance company isn't going to pay for any damages."

"Okay," was all I could squeak out, and I nervously shoved another forkful of food in my mouth.

The following Saturday, Harold and I went to the driver's license bureau to get my license. I passed the written test and was given a permission slip to drive with a licensed driver. They told me I had to come back in a month to take the driving test and get my official driving license.

While we're gone, Janet and Robert had a new bedroom suit delivered for Jan's room. We stopped by to see it, and Janet said, "She's outgrown her old bedroom suite, so we want you to have it."

We were delighted! It was white provincial with a canopied twin bed with a matching chest and dresser. It had the cutest little glass top dressing table with a mirror to match and two nightstands with two trim-laced lamps. Debbie loved it.

We folded her baby bed up and put it in the spare bedroom to get it out of the way. I didn't say anything to Harold at the time, but I noticed my breasts were getting sore again, and I had missed October's period. A few days had gone by, and we were upstairs placing the bedroom furniture in one of the bedrooms after we had stained it, and Harold said, "Honey, I think I'll take Debbie's baby bed to the basement to get it out of the way."

I turned and looked at him a little sadly and said, "Never mind. We'll be using it again pretty soon, and I don't want that basement smell to get all over it."

He stopped midway through pushing the dresser in place. "What? Please tell me you're joking!" he begged.

I shook my head. "Afraid not."

"But...but...but...," he stammered.

"You know we didn't like that diaphragm," I reminded him. "And we used that cream, which didn't work either."

At the ripe old age of eighteen, I had another one on the way. I had just gotten my weight back down and looking good again, and here we go again. We were very happy with our little boy and girl, but I guess God had other plans for us. We searched around for a good obstetrician and found Dr. Johnson in Trenton. I had a hard time with my third pregnancy. Dr. Johnson said it was because I was having my babies too close together, and my body didn't have enough time to bounce back.

I told Harold not to ever touch me again, but I got over it. I didn't gain as much weight with this one, and I was tired all the time. I spotted the whole time, and I began having edema, and the doctor wanted me to stay off my feet as much as possible. We hired the neighbor's mother, Betty, to live with us during this pregnancy. We gave her the spare bedroom, and she was a big help lifting and chasing after the other two.

Harold built Debbie and Junior a sandbox at the corner of the yard and a water slide. I missed going to the beach. We used to take Robert's station wagon and all his family, and our family went to the beach on the weekends when the weather was nice. Debbie loved the beach almost as much as her horsey. We got her a tricycle, and she flew down the street to Uncle Robert and Aunt Janet's every chance she got. We had to watch her constantly. Debbie and Junior got along reasonably—at least as well as siblings do. She eventually got over her jealousy. They were smart kids and easy to raise and take care of.

I went into labor on July 28, 1960, and she was born seventeen hours later. She weighed six pounds two ounces and was seventeen inches long with golden red hair all around the back of her head. Her eyes were the prettiest blue, like Debbie's. She was a dry birth, and her little arms, legs, face, and body were chapped and dry. I had to pour baby oil on her every day and let it soak into her skin. The hospital kept her in an incubator for the first two days until she started breathing better. Harold went to the nursery every day and talked to her. After she got out of the incubator, the hospital let Harold hold her.

When it came time to name her, we did the same thing we did with Debbie. We gave her the other three names, Theresa Gail, Vickie Kay, and Cheryl Ann. Every time we said Cheryl Ann, a big toothless grin crossed her face, and she laughed. Harold laughed and said, "Okay, Honey. That's it, Cheryl Ann."

After we got her home, Janet spoiled her to death. She and Robert came down the street to pick her up and kept her the whole weekend. Cheryl had a hard time with her baby formula. No matter what we put her on, it did not agree with her, and she spit it up or had diarrhea or constipation. The doctor eventually put her on a formula for sensitive stomachs, and she slowly came out of it by the time she was four months old. When she was first born, Harold was afraid to hold her because she was so tiny. I put her on a pillow, and he held her that way. Our insurance paid for all the hospital and doctor bills, except for $75.

We went back to church and rededicated our lives and were baptized again at the Grace Baptist Church in town. I was glad to get back to church. We had been so busy working and raising our family and fixing up the house. Harold and Robert went hunting and fishing whenever they could. They were constantly helping each other either on the houses or keeping the cars running.

We were doing pretty good and paid cash for just about everything we needed, except for the car and house, of course. Back then, if you didn't have the money, you didn't buy it—period. We bought a 1958 green and white four-door Chevrolet Belaire. It was two years old, but we loved it. We had to park it on the street, which was a main road for trucks going in and out of Trenton. The speed limit was thirty-five miles per hour, but they flew up and down the street.

In January 1962 we had a new president and a new baby on the way. I gave birth to our fourth child on January 8, 1962. Cheryl Ann was eighteen months old. We had a different doctor this time, and Theresa Gail was born in Doyle Town, Pennsylvania. She was a dead ringer for Junior. She looked just like him and me. She had big dark eyes and black hair with beautiful long eyelashes. I knew for sure that this one was our last. She was such a good baby. She never cried unless she was hungry or wet. She played for hours in her baby bed, looking up and talking to something. Harold whispered to me one day while we were watching her, "She's talking to angels. She sees angels."

I poked him in the ribs and snorted, "Yeah, you get me knocked up again, and you're gonna see stars too!"

He laughed. "Well, Honey, you have to learn to leave Freddie alone!"

"Humph! I'm buying bunk beds, and you can take the top bunk," I chortled.

One Sunday morning while we were getting ready for church, Cheryl was just starting to walk. Harold had put some things in the car for the kids and left the door partially open. I was trying to dress all the kids and myself, but when it came time to dress Cheryl, I couldn't find her. It was extremely warm that day, and we couldn't find her anywhere.

Finally, Harold went out to the car and looked in the back seat, and she was either passed out or cried herself to sleep. She must have pushed the lock button, and the door and couldn't get out. Harold started screaming, "Get me the keys! Get me the keys!"

I grabbed the keys off the dresser and ran outside with them. Harold's hands were shaking as he frantically unlocked the door and jerked it open. He grabbed her, and she was soaking wet with sweat. Harold ran back into the house and up the stairs to the shower and got in holding her. Then he turned the water on cool and let it run over them. She woke up crying, and we knew then that she was all right. We didn't go to church that day. Instead, we took her to the hospital to make sure she wasn't hurt. We were scared to death. When we got back home from the hospital, we gave all three of them a lecture about getting in the car alone. No one tried that again.

Cheryl adjusted to her older sister and brother, but I think they had a hard time adjusting to her. She was quite a character. She bit them when she didn't get her own way, which was usually all the time. She fought constantly with her older brother. Debbie avoided her like the plague.

Chapter 7

We really loved our house, and Harold enjoyed his job, but we missed the Clouse Family and the beauty of Kentucky farms. The air in Kentucky was so pure and fresh compared to the smog in New Jersey.

Harold's factory went on strike for two weeks, and we took the kids to Kentucky to visit with his parents and the rest of the family. Robert and Janet loaded up their car and kids as well, and we all traveled back home together. His parents had aged a lot in the few years we were gone. We also stopped by to see Peevine and Lil. It was so nice to be back. I think we missed it more than we thought. Peevine was working for Borden's driving a delivery truck between all the stores. He was making good money and enjoyed the job.

When we visited Uncle Eugene and Aunt Edna, they talked us into moving back home. It really didn't take much convincing. Deep down we both wanted to come back. Robert and Janet were devastated. We hated to hurt them, but we had to do what was best for us. I stayed at Uncle Eugene and Aunt Edna's with the children and Harold went back and put the house up for sale and worked a notice at his job.

He sold the house almost instantly and got back all the money we spent on the renovations and made a profit. This time, we sold the furniture with the house, and then he came back to Kentucky and looked for work. Since he had several years working in industrial, he got a job working as a machinist at Parker Seal Company making small parts for Boeing, GE, Westinghouse, and Frigidaire. He was making pretty good money.

He called our old landlord to see if he had any houses available. He had a little house in Winchester, Kentucky. The house was in an old neighborhood and needed a lot of work, but we were confident that we could make it look nice. It had its own driveway, and Harold liked that. It only had three bedrooms, but the rooms were large.

We looked through the house, and I imagined all things we could do to make the house look nice. As we walked out to the back porch, we noticed that it was rotting away, but the yard was huge and fenced in. We knew that would be excellent for the children. Harold rubbed his chin and said to the landlord, "We'll paint and fix it up, if you'll buy the materials."

The landlord's face lit up, and he said, "I'd be glad to do that, and I'll also give you six month's free rent for the work."

They shook hands, and we had a place to live, and Harold went to work. Harold tore down the back porch and steps and built a brand-new one. There was a door that led under the house, and it had a type of well that never got filled in. Harold put a padlock on the door, so the kids couldn't get under there and get hurt. The landlord bought the paint, and Harold scraped all the old paint off the outside of the house, and then he had to sand it all down. He spent most of his days off working on the house. Peevine, Rodney and his wife, and Harold's brothers Eugene and Ronnie came over one weekend and helped Harold get the entire outside painted white. We trimmed around the windows and doors in black. It looked like a different house when we finished.

While Harold was at work, I started on the kitchen wood that went all the way around the kitchen halfway up the wall. I painted it a nice warm brown, and then I wallpapered it with a pretty kitchen print. It turned out beautifully.

The entire family was delighted to have us back. Mom and Dad were happy that we had moved closer also. Harold was happy with his job and was being trained for tool and die. He had to go to school at the plant in the evenings, but we knew that it meant more money for us when he finished.

Once again, we had to start from scratch. Since we got most of our furniture before for almost nothing, we knew God would bless us again. Our first battle was to get a lawn mower. We had a large front and backyard to mow plus the side was long. Harold rummaged around underneath the house to see what was all under there, and he found an old lawn mower. He tore it down, replaced a lot of the parts, and it worked like a new one. I admired how he could fix almost anything and make it run like new.

The children loved the house. They had plenty of room to run and play—they liked that, and so did Harold. He ran and played with them like a kid himself. Sometimes I thought I had five children as I watched them play from the kitchen window as I was cooking or washing dishes. He loved to tease them.

One afternoon after cutting the grass, he was sitting on the back steps talking to Debbie. She had a fascination for birds, and Harold told her that if she was quiet and sneaked up behind a bird after it landed and shake some salt on its tail, then it couldn't fly away. She ran into the kitchen and grabbed the saltshaker off the table. "Debbie what are you doing?" I asked.

"I'm gonna catch a bird!" And out the door and down the porch steps she flew! She waited endlessly on the side of the house for a bird to land. A while later, a little mockingbird landed in the yard under some bushes. She glanced over at her daddy nervously, and he motioned for her to sneak up behind it. As stealthily as she could, she snuck up behind the bird, but before she could get more than six or seven feet from it, the bird flew away. She tried several times, and Harold just kept laughing watching her. Finally, she stomped her little foot and placed her hands on her hips and said, "You can't catch a bird that way, Daddy!"

"Yes, you can. You just have to be fast."

She tried a little while more, then she got tired and came over and sat down next to him.

"I'll tell you what," he said, "I'll make you a bird trap."

She looked up with those big blues eyes and asked innocently, "What's that?"

"You get a box and stick and tie a string to the stick. When the bird lands under the box you pull the string, and the box drops on top of the bird!"

Debbie wanted her daddy to fix it then and there. She hid behind the house again and waited forever for a bird to land under her box. Huh! Image that! No bird landed under her box. She got bored with it after a while and wandered off to play games with her siblings.

Sometime later, Mr. Clouse got sick and was in the hospital and had to stay the night, and Mrs. Clouse spent the night with us. The next morning, Debbie was out in the yard picking wild daisies in her night gown and had gotten dew all over the bottom of her hem. Grandma looked outside and saw her and shouted, "Hey! Debbie. Debbie dew drop! Whatcha doing?" She looked up from her flowers and grinned. And that name stuck. I still call her that every now and then.

Grandma started calling Junior "Peter Gun" from the time he was three years old. I asked, "Why do you call him that?"

"Because there's a detective show I like to watch, and the detective is real good looking and pretty like Junior is going to be, and the detective's name is Peter Gun." That name stuck too. She called him that until the day she died.

Terry loved to play in the dirt and get under the car with her daddy and ask questions, "What's that, Daddy? What're you doin' that for?" She got almost as greasy and dirty as he did. Harold nicknamed her Dirty Gertie. That name stuck for years. Cheryl was always fighting with her sisters or brother, and she loved to scream at the top of her lungs if something didn't go her way, and Harold named her Tiger Lil. She's now a grandma herself and she still has a temper.

Because we didn't have to pay rent for the first six months while we fixed up the house, we were able to buy a new living room suit and bedroom suits for the kids and our bedroom. Harold also bought us a new washing machine. I was thrilled. I still had to hang our clothes outside on the clothesline, but I had been doing that since I was a little girl. I didn't mind. Sometimes in the winter, after Harold came home from work and I had the kids bedded down for the night, I took the clothes to the laundry mat and dried them.

We bought our first twenty-four-inch color TV set in 1963. We really couldn't afford it, but we didn't go to the movies as much as we used to. When we did go to the drive-in, we always took our own popcorn and soft drinks. Sometimes I cooked wieners and put them in a thermos bottle and bring along some buns. Harold walked up to the concession stand and told them he needed mustard and ketchup for his hot dogs and they always gave it to him.

One summer night it rained all night. When we woke up the next morning, our entire backyard was flooded. My biggest child, Harold, got the big idea of telling the kids we had a swimming pool, and they all went swimming. He had them all out there teaching them how to swim. I groaned because I knew all their underwear was ruined. I finally gave up and just joined in, and we were all kids for a short time. Looking back on it now, I'm sure our neighbors thought we were a strange bunch.

Our children were our life. We lived for them. We loved playing and entertaining them. Hearing the laughter of a child is like listening to beautiful music. Everyone should take the time to listen to a child laugh. It's the most beautiful sound in the world.

Harold loved to take us all to the Frostie Root Beer stand where he proposed to me. Kids' root beer was free as long as the adults bought one. We always got curb service, and the carhop brought me and Harold the big mugs, and the kids got the little ones probably about the size of a shot glass. Harold told the kids not to drink it all. And when we ordered again, she would see that they were still sipping on their first one and left the new ones. After doing that several times, she got confused as to how many mugs we had, and Harold stuffed a few under the seat to take home. Those little mugs were our most treasured items in the house. The kids refused to drink their milk or anything unless it was in one of those mugs.

I wanted to get my tubes tied because our last two children were birth-control babies. The doctor refused to tie my tubes because back then you could not reverse it, and he said that I was just too young. By then, I was the ripe old age of twenty. After a lot of pleading and begging and finally refusing to let Harold touch me again, he agreed to get a vasectomy. We went to see Dr. Avery there in Winchester, who was a reputable physician, and he agreed that we should do something because the children were coming pretty fast. It was also hard on my health and our finances.

After Harold's surgery, he was in a lot of pain and had some major swelling. The doctor told him not to do any lifting over twenty pounds for the next six weeks, and no sex until the doctor saw him again for a checkup.

About a month after the surgery, Harold came home from work and one side of his testicles were red and swollen. I asked him, "Did you do any lifting?"

He eased himself down on the bed and moaned, "Honey, I have to lift every day. What am I going to say? I can't lift today?" He shook his head. "I can't do that. Besides, I don't want everyone to know what I've done. It's embarrassing."

I begged him to go to the doctor, but he refused.

After about eight weeks we figured we were safe, and sex was even better for me because I didn't have to worry about getting pregnant. Two weeks later, after enjoying each other and relaxing even more than ever before, my breasts began to get sore, and then I missed a period.

"No way! Honey, it has to be something else!" Harold groaned. All I could do was cry.

We made an appointment with Dr. Avery. I knew the drill, and so did Harold. I cried when the doctor told us. Poor Harold, he sat there dumbfounded. The doctor checked Harold's sperm count, and he was showing ten thousand sperm. The doctor said that an average woman couldn't get pregnant with that few cells. Lucky us, huh?

I never told Harold, but I just did not want any more children. When the doctor confirmed my fifth pregnancy, he gave us a whole new layette and didn't charge us for the delivery, nor did we have to pay for the hospital bill. I think the doctor was afraid that we would sue him.

I blamed Harold for not going to the doctor earlier when he had that swelling. I was furious with him, and I didn't let him touch me. I was so upset that I wouldn't even sit across the table from him. I know now that I shouldn't have acted that way, and I regretted it for years. I had just gotten myself slim again, and I know that I was being very selfish, only thinking of myself and not his feelings. I've wished a hundred times over I could have done that differently.

Harold bought the kids a swing set, and he had a friend come over and help him put it together. After a case or two of beer, it turned out okay. The kids played on it all the time.

We bought our second car it was a black and red Oldsmobile. Harold usually drove the Oldsmobile to work and left me the Chevy. I was scared to drive the Oldsmobile because it was like driving a tank, and I could handle the Chevy better. It was nice to be able to go places during the day with the kids if I needed to go to the store or something.

August 26, 1964, I gave birth to my fifth child. She weighed eight pounds ten ounces. I had run out of girls' names that I liked. Harold had begged me when Terry was born to name her Donna when she was born because she looked so much like me, but I refused. She was just too pretty to be named Donna. I didn't name this one until the day we were leaving the hospital. The nurse told me, "You have to name this child before you are released from the hospital!" I named her Donna after myself and Kay for Mildred because that was her middle name.

Donna Kay looked a lot like Harold. When I first woke up after giving birth, I hadn't seen her yet and Harold was beside my bed shaking his head. When I looked at him, he buried his face in his hands, and he moaned, "I've ruined this one!"

"What do you mean?" I was beginning to get worried.

"Every time you got pregnant, I have prayed to God while you were carrying our baby that it would look like you and your family, and not like me or my family."

I touched his shoulder gently and said, "Harold, that's silly. We have beautiful children."

"Oh, Honey!" he cried. "She looks just like me! The poor little thing."

"We had another girl?"

He nodded.

"Is she healthy?"

"Yes."

When I finally did get to see her, her poor little head was lumpy with knots all over it. The doctor had to take her with forceps. The doctor told us that while we were watching TV and just sitting around to put on a soft white glove and rub her head in a circular motion and showed us how to do it. She also inherited the Clouse thick neck. Harold and Mildred were the only ones in the Clouse family that didn't have the thick neck.

I didn't take her out very much the first four to six months of her life until her little head started straightening out. There was nothing we could do about the thick neck since that was hereditary, but when she was six months old, she was as cute as a button. She had my brown eyes and dark lashes, but she had the Clouse reddish blonde hair and still does.

Harold made the tool and die department at work and everything was going along well for us. Harold took little Junior hunting and fishing with him as much as he could.

Harold and Peevine saw a speedboat for sale one afternoon, and they pooled their money together and bought it. It needed some work, so they both worked on it for about a month refinishing it and putting on a new windshield and rebuilding the engine. The boat seats six, so we took turns riding in it.

Peevine and Lil and their two kids went with us and our five kids to the river on the weekends and we'd make a picnic out of it. Lil and I made potato salad and baked beans. There was a grill at the boat dock, and we brought along wieners and hamburgers and grilled out. We brought along a couple of playpens for the little ones and kept eyes on the older ones. We usually stayed all day and sometimes rented a cabin, and all of us stayed the night in one cabin. That was tight, but we still had fun.

Harold let Peevine drive the boat while he water-skied. Sometimes he skied with just his feet. I couldn't believe that anyone could ski without skis, but he did it. After Harold made a few rounds, he drove the boat and Peevine and Lil skied. I never skied because I couldn't swim. I never did learn how.

One afternoon, a large wooden crate was delivered. Curiously, I looked at this shipping label and it said the crate was from Germany.

When Harold came home and saw the crate sitting on the front porch, he hollered, "Woo-hoo! It's here!"

The kids heard their father and all those who could ran out to the front porch jumping up and down with him.

"What is it, Daddy!" Debbie asked.

I stood at the screen door and watched all the commotion for a few minutes, then I asked, "Yeah, Daddy, what is it?"

Harold looked up at me grinning and said, "It's that new Volkswagen car from Germany."

I couldn't believe my ears. "There's a car in that box?"

"In pieces," he nodded as he began to use a crow bar and open the crate. "This is just part of it. More pieces will be coming as we pay for them."

"You're going to put that car together one piece at a time?"

"Yeah. Peevine and me."

I shook my head and went back into the house to finish dinner.

Every few weeks, a new piece would come in; and with each new piece, Harold and Peevine slowly built a Volkswagen in the backyard. He loved to tinker on things. Harold was not the kind of person to just sit around and do nothing. He was always coming up with big ideas. After it was built, they got bored with it and sold it a few months later.

About a month after they sold the Volkswagen, I glanced out the living room window when I heard him come home from work, and he was pulling a 1927 Packard Roadster with a rumble seat behind the Oldsmobile.

"Harold!" I hollered. "Now what are you doing?"

He grinned at me as he jumped out of the Olds and unhitched the Packard. "Ain't she a beauty?"

"You're kidding, right?"

"Aw, Honey. How can you not think this isn't the most beautiful car in the world? She's a classic!" And he patted the pile of rust on the fender.

It looked like junk to me. The body was rusty, and the interior was torn up and faded. Obviously, it didn't run.

"You're not leaving the pile of junk in the front yard!" I scolded.

"Why not?"

"Please take it to the backyard," I begged.

He shrugged, hitched the junk back up and dragged it around to the backyard.

The kids loved to "help" their daddy build the "new" car. They couldn't wait to ride in the rumble seat. Harold worked on the car every afternoon after work. When we could afford it, Harold bought used parts from the junkyard and rebuilt the engine. In a few weeks, he had that pile of junk running. Next, he bought some good used tires from the junkyard. When he started on the interior, I helped him reupholster it and put new carpeting in it. Harold patched the rust holes, and we sanded it down and got it ready to be painted. We couldn't afford a fancy paint job, so one of Harold's buddies who worked at a body shop cut him a deal, and they sprayed it black.

That old Packard turned out to be one of our favorite cars. The older kids took turns riding in the rumble seat. They thought their dad was a genius. I must admit, I did too. I don't think there was anything Harold couldn't do once he set his mind to do it. I truly loved and admired that man.

We drove her on Sundays to Grandma and Grandpa's house. We also took the kids in it to carnivals or to the zoo. Debbie loved animals. Sometimes on Sunday afternoons, we would drive out into the country. The kids always got so excited to see the farm animals in the fields. One particular spring day, there were a bunch of milk cows eating along the fence. Harold pulled over and let the kids watch them for a few minutes.

Junior cocked his head to one side as he watched one cow chew on the grass, and then he said, "Hmm…it's sure got a lot of pee pees on it."

Harold and I couldn't stop laughing.

Junior was a chip off the old block for sure. He had those gorgeous dimples just like his dad; and just like his dad, he could melt me with just one smile.

One afternoon we went to the zoo with Peevine and Lil and their kids. Debbie and Junior were fascinated by a huge red orangutan with long arms who kept scratching himself. Debbie suddenly pointed and cried out, "Look, Mommy! He has red hair all over his body like Daddy!"

Harold choked on his hot dog, and the crowd snickered. His poor face turned as red as his hair. Peevine couldn't stop laughing. The rest of the afternoon, Peevine kept making monkey noises.

That was probably my last enjoyable afternoon for a very, very long time.

Chapter 8

Harold was my prince in shining armor. My husband and my kids were everything to me. I had never known anyone like him or anyone since. We weren't rich in material things, but we were rich in love. We had it hard from time to time trying to make ends meet, but God always provided. And we were thankful.

We had settled into a good like with five kids. Harold worked every day, and I stayed home with the kids and cooked and cleaned. We went out on the weekends for a drive or to visit family. We were happy.

Harold was thirty and I was twenty-three when he started having urinary problems. He had severe pain when he urinated, and then it became difficult for him to urinate. I begged him to go the doctor, but he refused because he said we needed the money for groceries and rent. I think he just didn't want to accept the fact that he might be seriously ill.

One morning as he was getting ready to go to work, he fell over on the bed and curled up into a ball. "Harold!" I screamed. I ran over to him. "Please, Honey! Stay home today! You have to go to the doctor!"

He shook his head miserably. "I can't stay home," he groaned. "I have to make money to support you and the kids." After a few minutes, he got up and stumbled to work.

This went on for about a year. Finally, he made an appointment with the doctor when he couldn't go on anymore. The doctor said he had inflammation of the kidneys, emphysema, and heart disease.

He got so sick that he started missing work. We had to do something to bring in some money. I worked at a dry-cleaning company for a short time, and then I worked as a waitress at the Winchester Café because I could make a little more money waitressing. After I started working at the restaurant, Harold needed blood transfusions to get the poison out of his body, but the hospital had a hard time finding his blood type. The doctor advertised on the radio that the hospital was looking for Harold's blood type, and that's how the owner of the restaurant I worked at found out about our situation. I think he felt sorry for us because he let me bring home any food left over at the end of the night that had to be thrown out.

We prayed together every night that God would heal Harold, but he kept getting worse. The doctor wanted to put Harold in the hospital, but we couldn't afford it. He came to the house to see Harold when he got so sick, he couldn't get out of bed. He was on all kinds of medication for pain, swelling, irregular heartbeat, etc. The blood transfusions helped for a little while, and then his body filled up with poison again, and he needed another transfusion.

I found out later that while I was at work, Harold continued to pray. Debbie told me years later that she watched her father get on his knees in the living room while I was working and ask God that if he wasn't going to heel him to please take him. It broke my heart to hear that.

The kids knew something was wrong. They couldn't understand why Daddy was in bed all the time, and why he wasn't playing with them like he used to. They played quietly and let their father rest while I was at work. Debbie began taking care of the smaller children. She fixed them sandwiches and stood on a stool by the sink and washed the dishes afterward.

As Harold continued to get worse, he was in and out of the hospital for tests or blood transfusions. Then one afternoon after I got home from work, Harold looked up at me and said, "Honey, I think you better call an ambulance."

I felt of his head, and he was burning up. His face was beginning to swell. "I'll take you, Harold."

He shook his head, "No. You stay here with the kids. Please call an ambulance for me."

I did as he asked, then I helped him out of bed. He was too weak to get dressed, but he made it out to the porch in his pajamas with all the kids surrounding him. He bent down and kissed each one and told them, "Daddy loves you."

When the ambulance pulled up outside, he refused to allow them to put him on the stretcher, and he walked out to the ambulance with their help. Then he glanced once more time at me and the kids standing on the porch and smiled and climbed in the back. The ambulance took off with red lights flashing.

I called Mildred, and she came over and stayed with the children while I went to the hospital. He was in intensive care, and when I went into his room, he had all kinds of machines and tubes and wires running all over the place and hooked up to him. He smiled weakly and said, "Now I know how Frankenstein felt."

The whole time he was sick, he never complained. He loved life and his family to the fullest. I learned a lot about life from Harold. When I look back on our marriage now, it seems like we were married a lot longer than just nine years. We lived a lifetime in those nine short years.

He was in the hospital five days. I visited him every day. He refused to allow me to bring any of the children. He didn't want them to see their daddy like that. One evening he took my hand, and he said, "Honey, if I don't make it, please don't let the kids come to my funeral."

I started to cry. "Please don't talk like that, Harold."

"Listen to me," he begged. "Please don't let them come. I don't want any of them to remember me all laid out and stiff and cold in that casket. When they think of me, I want them to always remember their daddy like he used to be." He smiled weakly at me.

I had just gotten home that evening when the phone rang. It was the hospital. They wanted me to come back to the hospital because Harold was having some difficulty. Mildred had already left to go home, and I didn't want to have to ask her to come back. I called Aunt Edna, and she came over with her oldest daughter Pauline who sat with the children while we went back to the hospital.

As we walked down the hall to Harold's room, a nurse came out carrying sheets in her arms. When we went into his room, the bed was empty and the sheets stripped off it. Another nurse came into the room and asked, "Mrs. Clouse?"

I turned to look at her.

"The doctor wants to see you." She escorted Edna and me to a little room at the end of the hall. The room was empty when we first got there, but we were both too nervous to sit down. A few minutes later, a tall young doctor walked in and said all business like and without hesitating, "I'm sorry, Mrs. Clouse. Your husband expired two hours ago."

I glanced over at Edna, and she was crying. I asked, "What does that mean?"

The doctor said, "He's passed away, Mrs. Clouse."

"*No! No! No! Please God!*" I screamed. I couldn't stop. I kept screaming over again. "*No! No! No! It isn't true! This can't be happening. It just can't!*"

The doctor just stood there looking at me like I was a maniac while Edna tried to calm me down. "I want to see him!" I begged. "I have to see him!"

He shook his head. "No. That is not a good idea, Mrs. Clouse. He doesn't look like himself right now. His body is swollen. I don't believe he wanted you to see him like that."

"I have to see him!" I begged.

"No."

I couldn't believe it. "Not Harold!" I cried. "Please, dear God! Not Harold! Please!" I continued to beg, "Not Harold!" I just couldn't stop.

Then I begged God, "Take me! Take me! Take me! Not Harold! Please, dear God, not Harold!" I crumbled to the floor and pounded the carpeted floor with my fists. "Not him! Please, dear Lord, not him!"

I felt as though I were dreaming. This couldn't be happening. It wasn't true. This was not real. I knew that as soon as I woke up, Harold would be sleeping peacefully beside me. But I didn't wake up. It was happening. Harold died when he was thirty-two years old. I was twenty-four with five children to raise.

Aunt Edna refused to let me go home alone. When we got back to the house, I felt like I had died right along with Harold. The children could tell I had been crying. I took one look at all of them, and the tears welled up inside of me again and came spilling down my cheeks. I just couldn't stop crying. Debbie looked at me and asked with the most worried look in an eight-year-old's eyes I had ever seen.

"What's wrong, Mommy?" she asked.

She knew. Dear God, she knew something was so terribly wrong. I tried to calm down, but I cried harder. She became afraid and wrapped her little arms around my waist. I finally managed to whisper hoarsely, "It's Daddy. You're daddy's gone, baby. Daddy's gone."

She burst into tears then. I'm not sure if she really understood at the time.

"When's Daddy coming home?" Junior asked.

Tears continued to flow as I whispered, "He's never coming home." Then I broke down again and fell on the couch and buried my head under one of the sofa pillows and sobbed. The children all gathered around me and tried to comfort me as best as little ones could. Aunt Edna gathered up a few of our belongings and packed them and ushered us all out to her car. When we got to Uncle Eugene and Aunt Edna's house, Uncle Eugene called Mom and Dad, and they drove down as fast as they could. I wasn't mentally able to make any funeral arrangements. Eugene, Edna, Paul, and Clifford made all the arrangements.

They asked where I wanted Harold buried, and I remembered something he told me one Sunday while we were out driving. We had just passed the Winchester Cemetery and Harold said, "What a beautiful view it must be up on that hill beneath that tree there." Then he turned and smiled at me and said, "I wouldn't mind being buried up there." That spot was still available and, that's where we buried him. Later, I learned that Mr. and Mrs. Clouse bought plots next to Harold's lot, so they could be buried with him when they passed away.

Those days were so very difficult for my children and me. I still felt as if I were dreaming, and I would wake up any minute and find that none of it was true. I kept thinking back to the first time I ever laid eyes on him. The sun was in my eyes and I looked up at the sound of his voice. The sun was behind him, and it glowed around his beautiful red hair making it appear that he had a golden halo, and he had stepped right out of heaven and into my heart. And now he's gone. Dear God, it can't be. It just can't be.

The funeral home called and said that they had him all ready, and that I needed to go see him. Aunt Edna and everyone said that I had to go, but I just couldn't go. I just couldn't go see my precious Harold lying there. *Dear God,* I thought, *please don't make me do this. Please don't make me do this.*

I was so wrapped up in my own pain that I couldn't see what my children must have been going through, especially for Debbie and Junior. They were the oldest, and I knew they had to be suffering. I didn't want them to see me. I couldn't stop crying. I could not seem to get a hold of my emotions. I kept thinking, *Dear Lord, how am I going to support these children? What am I going to do? I have no education. All I've ever done is be a mommy and a wife. I don't know how to do anything else."* I did not want my kids to do without like I had as a child.

Uncle Eugene tried to talk to me and get me to stop crying. I just kept on crying. "This isn't true. This just isn't happening," I cried over and over.

Uncle Eugene patted my back as I lay on the bed crying and said, "Donna, you will get his social security and veteran's widow pension for you and the kids."

"I just want my husband back! And my kids' daddy back! Can you do that?" I sobbed.

When it came time to go to the funeral home, Pauline stayed at Uncle Eugene's with the children. Mom was on one side of me and Daddy on the other as we walked in together. It was a very nice funeral home. It was cold and cool with lots of marble floors and beautiful draperies. As we walked in the room where Harold was laid, I saw his beautiful red hair shining brightly under the fancy floor lamps the funeral home had positioned on either side of his casket. His family had laid him to rest in a dark blue suit with a white shirt and blue striped tie. He had on gray socks but no shoes I wondered why they didn't put any shoes on him.

I crumpled down on top of his body and tried to hold him in my arms. I had to hold him again. Just one more time, but his body felt so cold and stiff. Inside I was screaming, *Get up, Harold! Please get up! Tell me this is just another one of your jokes!* But all I could do was sob uncontrollably. *Please don't make me leave you here! Please don't make me leave you here!* Suddenly I knew. It wasn't a dream. It was true. God had taken by prince in shining armor. He was gone forever...

I'm not sure how I got through that evening or the next two. It felt as though I were in a vacuum. I could hear conversations going on around me, but I felt unattached to everything. I know that's a strange thing to say, but it was how I felt. My body was there, but my spirit was gone. I had no feelings. I was dead inside. I kept thinking over and over. This had to end. Let me die too, Lord. Oh God, please don't leave me here alone.

I remember Mom and Dad riding with me in the limousine to the cemetery. I was in such an unbelievable fog. My body was there but my mind was somewhere else and I vaguely remember seeing anyone at all. He got so many flowers from so many people. He was a person that was loved by everyone he met and would be missed by everyone he knew.

Mom and Dad took me home to be with them for a few weeks until I could get myself pulled together again. Ronnie and his wife took Donna Kay, Clifford took Junior, Carmen and her husband took Terry and Eugene, and Edna took care of Cheryl and Debbie for those two weeks. Mom and Dad did their best to pull me out of it. But it was almost useless. I just couldn't make any sense of it. I kept asking God, "Why? Why Harold? Why now? Why, God, why? Show me why! Explain to me why! I just don't understand! He was a wonderful husband! A wonderful father! More than that, he was a good friend, coworker, brother, son. Tell me why? Why him? Tell me, Lord!" I kept praying that over and over again—why?

My thoughts wandered back to a time when we were trying to figure out how to come up with the money for something we needed.

I couldn't remember what it was. Debbie, Junior, and Cheryl were playing on the floor, but Debbie must have been listening. Harold said, "Well, I don't know, Honey. I'll have to put my thinkin' cap on."

Suddenly Debbie asked, "What's that, Daddy?"

"What's what?"

"A think cap?" she replied. "Can I have one?"

It broke the tension in the air and we both burst out laughing.

Her big blue eyes were innocent and beautiful. Her Daddy was everything to her, just as he was to the rest of our kids—and to me. He was our whole world. And now our world was crumbling. What were we going to do now? He was our provider, our confidant, our entertainer, our fixer-upper, our mechanic, our maintenance man, our father, brother, uncle, son, and a husband—all rolled up into one. Not just for the children but for me also. With God's help, Harold did all those things for us. Now what were we going to do?

Mom and Dad tried to talk me into moving back to Ohio. As I think back on it now, that's probably what I should have done. They said they would help me get a job and a place to live, and they would help get Harold's social security and veteran's widow pension started. I refused because the children had just lost their father, and I didn't want to suddenly uproot them from the house where they played and romped with their father. I didn't want them to forget about their dad.

Those were the longest two weeks of my life. I just wanted to get back to my kids and try to make some sense of my life again. I started worrying about the children and what they must be thinking. Their Mommy and Daddy were both gone. It reminded me a little of Marie, my biological mother, who gave all her kids away. But I wasn't Marie. I loved my kids more than life itself. Somehow, we had to go on.

Mom and Dad drove me back home. I gathered up all my children as soon as I got home. After all the Clouse family had left, Mom and Dad were getting ready to leave. They were kissing us all goodbye and told me that if we needed anything to please let them know. I said I would. As I look back on it now, I realize that my problem was that I had to do everything myself. I have always been like that, and I still am today. God has changed me a lot. I now look to Him for advice and support and love and understanding and wisdom.

The kids were all happy to be home again and had about a million questions about their daddy and what we were going to do. I did my best to answer all their questions and put their little minds to rest. I had promised Harold that if anything happened to him that I wouldn't bring the kids to his funeral. That was the last thing he had ever asked of me. I kept that promise against the Clouse family will. Harold and I had never broken a promise to each other in our entire marriage. He had told me he was very close to his Grandpa Clouse; and when he died, he never got over seeing his grandpa in his coffin. "I could not remember all the good things we did," he told me that night. "All I could think of was seeing him lying stiff and cold in that coffin. I do not want my children to remember me like that. Promise me!"

"I promise, Harold."

He had also asked me to have an autopsy performed should anything happen to him. It caused a big turmoil with the Clouse family, but the doctors never did know for sure what was wrong with him, and he hoped that if they found something it might help one of the kids later in life to know what had caused his death. The doctor found so many things wrong with him. The family was amazed when the autopsy report came out. And it has helped several of our children. Later in life Debbie developed lupus, and Cheryl suffers with nerve problems, and Terry suffers with a form of paralysis. Harold's autopsy has helped their doctors with the treatment of our children.

I found out later that the midwife who delivered Harold pronounced him dead and placed him in a bucket under the bed. Mrs. Clouse said, "No. My God is a big God, and He will not let something like this happen to one of my children! She pulled him out from underneath the bed and performed mouth-to-mouth resuscitation and brought him back to life. They told me he was sick a lot and started to come out being sickly when he was about six years old.

After the family saw the autopsy report and saw all the problems he had, they forgave me for having it done. Again, I was only keeping a promise to Harold. I am so glad now that I listened to my husband. It has been a great help to our children.

I remembered one night not long after he had passed away, I was sound asleep in the house where we lived together before the kids and I moved away. I felt the bed sink down like someone had sat down on it next to me—like Harold had done so many times before. I felt frozen. I couldn't open my eyes or move my hands and arms. I felt as though someone was rubbing my back. Then I heard Harold's voice reassure me softly, "Don't worry, Honey. You will get my social security and my VA pension. You and the kids will be all right." He didn't say anything else.

I wanted to put my arms around him and hold him close, and he said, "You can't, Honey. I haven't crossed over yet. You'll be all right. You'll be all right..." His voice faded, and then the mattress went back up like someone had stood up. It wasn't a dream. It was Harold, and the Lord let him appear to me because I was so worried about him and how I was going to support our children.

I started sleeping on the left side of the bed. I felt closer to him somehow. It took me a long time to wash his pillow case. I used to lay my head on it and smell the Brylcreem he used on his hair and his Old Spice aftershave. I took his shirts out of the closet and just held them in my arms smelling him and remembering his caresses. I kept the smell of his body for as long as I could.

Harold died on May 14, 1966. He was gone, but we had to go on in this world without him.

Chapter 9

My children and I fell into a routine. I got a job working at the Parker Seal in Lexington on third shift. It worked out well for us because I was home when the children woke up and be there when they went to bed. I hired the lady next door to come over and sleep at the house with the children while I was at work Monday through Friday. I paid her $35 a week. She was a nice clean lady, and the children liked her.

On my way to work every night, I stopped by the cemetery to visit Harold's grave and every morning on my way home I stopped by again. I never failed to visit him every day. That was the only way I could keep him close. I never let his memory die for our children. I kept him alive for them with stories of when we met and when they were first born. I kept his pictures out on the tables and on the walls. We talked about him. Debbie missed her father so much. I could see it in her face, although I could tell she tried not to worry me. All the children missed him, but I think Debbie and Junior did the most. The children were ages eight, seven, four, three, and eighteen months when their father passed away. Little Donna Kay and Terry were so young, they kept asking for months, "Where's Daddy? Where's Daddy." It broke my heart every time, but they eventually realized that he was never coming home again.

The landlord told me that we could live in the house rent free. He thought a lot of Harold and me and the kids. Thank God for people like him. I wish God had given more people hearts like his; maybe this world wouldn't be in the shape it's in now.

I knew in my heart that the only way to try and make a life without Harold in it was to start over.

I had been working at Parker Seal for about a year when I found a house in Lexington closer to work. I could save on gas and wear and tear on the car. We lived there for about four months when some girls I worked with told me that houses were cheaper in Danville, and we could all carpool together. It sounded like a good idea to me, plus the children and I needed more room.

I met with the realtor my friend had told me to go see, and he asked me, "Why do you want to rent? You can buy a house cheaper than you can rent."

"Where am I going to get a down payment?" I asked.

He shrugged and replied, "You don't need one. You're a widow, your husband was a veteran, you have a job, and you have a widow's pension. You'll be sittin' pretty."

He showed me several houses, which I didn't like for one reason or another. A few weeks later, he called me on a Saturday and said, "Hey, are ya free? I've found a great house for you and the kids. It's got five bedrooms and almost brand new. It has two and a half baths with a large backyard, a fireplace, a large eat-in kitchen, living room, den, and dining room. You'll love it!"

I piled all the kids in the car to go see this "great house" he told us about. I met him at his office and then followed him out to a beautiful big gray stone house. It sat on top of a hill. I could see in my mind the kids riding a sleigh down the hill in the winter. Harold loved to ride a sleigh in the winter. There was a large concrete driveway that went all the way from the road up to a huge two-and-a-half-car carport. It had all hardwood floors and a big kitchen window that I could almost see the whole town from. There was even a dishwasher. I had never had a dishwasher before. The previous owners left their washer and dryer. I thought to myself, *God still knows me and my kids. Thank you, Lord.* We all walked around back, and there was a large swing set with a brick grill to cook outside on. I thought to myself, *Harold would love this.*

I bought the house on a VA loan with nothing down and monthly payment of 525 dollars a month. Harold was still taking care of us with his social security and veteran's pension. It was a beautiful home, and I was grateful to God and my dear departed husband.

A week after the closing, I hired Thelma, a black woman in her fifties who had been watching the children for me in Lexington while I worked, to move in with us and take care of the children, cook, and clean. She was a wonderful live-in housekeeper. I gave her weekends off, and she was happy.

All the kids who were in school enjoyed their new school. I had to buy another car because the Chevy was on its last leg. I bought a red and white '62 T-Bird. It was beautiful. I couldn't fit all the kids in that small car, so I kept the Chevy for when I had to take all the kids with me somewhere.

I took the children to visit Harold's parents as much as I could. Sometimes I let them stay the night with them while I visited with friends of mine and Harold's. Sometimes I visited with girlfriends I had made at the factory, but I really missed the closeness that Harold and I had. We always fell asleep in each other's arms.

About nine months to a year after Harold died, a friend of ours walked up to me at the factory where I worked. Rod and Harold were friends and had worked together at the Blue Grass Manufacturing Company in Winchester. He asked me, "How are you doing?"

"All right," I replied.

"Did you get the flowers we sent to the funeral?"

"Yes. Thank you."

"Let us know if you and the kids need anything."

He reminded me so much of Harold.

I had the house of my dreams, I had a beautiful car, I was making good money for the first in my life, and I had a great housekeeper. But I still had a great void in my life. I longed for the touch of my husband. I missed his kisses on my cheek as he often did when he came home from work or going to work.

The kids and I were happy again. We still missed their father very much, but we were beginning to bounce back into society again.

One night while I was working on the assembly line, Rod came walking back from dinner break and said, "Hey, I just bought a new car. Would you like to take a spin in it after work?"

"I'll think about it," I told him hoping he forgot about it.

Later that night when the whistle blew that the shift was over, I was walking out with my girlfriends, and Rod was standing by the time clock. "Well?" he asked. "Have you thought about it?"

I shook my head and replied, "I don't know, Rod. You're married, you know."

"I'm not asking you to go to a hotel with me." He sounded disgusted. "I'm just asking you to take a drive with me."

He was tall and slim with blue eyes and a big nose. He had thin brown hair. I didn't realize it at the time, but I was sizing him up to my Harold. Harold had big shoulders, a slim waist, and the most magnificent hairy chest that a woman could ever want. He had thick red wavy hair, but Rod's hair was straight and hung to one side. He had big hands; so did Harold. I wanted to slap myself. *He's married,* I told myself. *Don't let anything start here, stupid.* I didn't listen, and I went with him.

As we were driving, we were talking about our families; and the next thing I knew, he pulled into the Frostie Root Beer drive-in. When the waitress brought us our mugs of root beer, I began to cry. "I'm sorry," I cried. "Please take me back to my car."

"What did I do?" Rob asked surprised. "Did I say something?"

"It's not you," I sobbed. "This is where my Harold proposed to me, and I was thinking of that day and that we brought our children here a lot, plus you're married. You shouldn't be here with me, and I shouldn't be here with you." I missed my Harold so much.

He took me back to my car, and I drove home. After that night, I tried to make sure that I was nowhere near the aisle when the whistle blew for break or when break time is over. Rod's department went first because they were further back in the plant, and then our department took a dinner break. The bathrooms were halfway between the front and back of the factory. Weeks and weeks went by, and I managed to avoid him. In the meantime, I was working hard to do what I was supposed to do and take care of my family the best way I knew how.

One night, Rod purposefully came by where I was working and asked, "Can we meet later and just talk? No holding, no responsibility. Just talk?"

I thought, *Why not? Can't hurt, just as long as all he wants to do is talk.* "Okay. Just talk."

When our shift was over, we got in his car, and he drove us to the drive-in theatre for the late movie. We didn't watch the movie. I sat on one side of the car, and he sat on the other. He asked, "How can a redhead like Harold get a girl like you to fall in love with him the way you are?"

"I fell in love with the man inside. Harold had a very big heart, and he was loving and caring and gentle and the most understanding man I had ever known. He was everything that most men like you can never be," I replied softly.

"Well, thanks for the compliment!" he retorted.

I didn't say anything. I just looked calmly at him.

"Well, tell me something?"

"Okay."

"What do you intend to do about sex?"

I shrugged, "Without. Unless I can find myself another Harold. Once you've had the best in a marital partner, nothing else or no one else will do. Understand?"

He nodded. "I do, but how about a substitute till you can find that person?" he inquired hopefully.

I was shocked. "What about your wife, Eve?"

He shook his head, "My wife is growing further and further away from me."

"Maybe it's you, Rod."

"Possible," he replied. Then he turned and looked me straight in the eye. "From the first time I laid eyes on you, Donna, there hasn't been anyone else for me. I can't get you out of my mind!"

"Oh, I see." I snorted. "You thought you could seduce me and put another notch on your belt!" I felt myself getting angry, so I continued, "And you'd go home to Eve feeling all good about yourself because you had helped a little widow get over her poor dead husband! Is that it, Rod?" I was furious by now.

"No! I'm saying my sex life with Eve is little to none, and I think yours is none since Harold passed away! What do you say?"

"I'll say you're right on one score. It's none since Harold passed away. Do I need and miss that time with my husband? You bet I do and more and more each day!" I began to cry then. Oh, how I missed Harold.

Rod scooted closer and said softly, "How about I fill that void for you, and you fill that void for me? No strings attached." Then he took me in his arms and kissed me softly. It wasn't Harold's lips and Harold's arms, but they were better than no lips and no arms; and when it was over, I could go home and forget it until next time.

Rod made hotel arrangements the next time we saw each other in another state about one hundred miles away, and we spent the weekend together. He told his wife that he was going on a fishing trip and took the kids to spend the weekend with their Grandma Clouse.

I enjoyed the ride to the hotel more than anything else. He put the top of his car down, and it reminded me of some of the drives I had in the country with my precious Harold. I soaked in a hot bath while he went out and got some drinks for us. I was still in the tub when I heard him come back. I had been wrestling with my conscience. I liked his wife, and I was guilty for what we were doing behind her back.

I had never drunk whiskey or beer before—I never felt the need to. I thought, *Why not? Maybe it will help get the children, my Harold, his wife, and their kids out of my mind, and I could loosen up and relax and enjoy some great sex no matter who the organ donor was.*

I was a good mom and a decent person. I worked hard taking care of our kids, so I figured I deserved to let my hair down and plant a few wild oats—with protection of course. He made sure of that, and so did I. I did not want another baby. I loved the ones I had, but please no more!

I had several 7 Ups and whiskeys and began to feel a little tipsy. The more I drank, the more interesting Rod began to look. After a few more drinks and some slow dancing to soft music, we began to kiss. The next thing I knew we were all over each other. I couldn't get enough of him—it had been so long—and he couldn't get enough of me. He wasn't my Harold, but I liked it. *What the hell,* I thought, *relax and just go for it, stupid. It's not your fault Eve is not giving him enough.*

The next day, there was a small carnival going on that little town we were in, so we went to see what was going on. We rode all the rides and did a little shopping in the antique shops, and then we went out to eat and back to the hotel and started up where we left off. To make a long story short, I was satisfied and felt a little less stressed.

When I drove up to pick the kids up at Grandma Clouse's on Sunday afternoon, they all came running out to meet me. That was the best part of the whole weekend. The drive back to Danville was such a scenic view. We had to drive through and around the mountains and by the river. It was just beautiful. The children were gawking at the farm animals and the countryside. It reminded them of our Sunday drives with Harold. They loved it. I took them to our favorite place before we hit Danville, the Frostie Root Beer drive-in. We ordered our food and drinks to go and had a picnic before we got home.

The kids told me everything they had done that weekend, and they asked me what I did. I told them that I mostly thought of them and how much I missed them. They all told me how much they missed me.

All was great for a while. I had my babies and a sort of substitute for Harold with no strings attached. Or so I thought at the time. It was good to just unwind with the opposite sex for a change. It wasn't like it was with my Harold, but it was better than nothing.

Rod and I continued to see each other whenever we felt the need, and we dated sometimes. Looking back on it now, that must have been the game we were playing. He was just a stand-in for Harold, whom I really wanted. One afternoon after sex, and we were lying there being lazy, he looked over at me and said, "I'm going to divorce Eve, and you can give up your kids." Then he shrugged lazily and continued, "We're young enough to where we can have our own kids."

If looks could kill, that man would be dead. I felt anger boil out of me like I had never known before. I jumped out of the bed like someone had thrown scalding water on me, and I pointed a trembling finger at him and screamed, "*I will never! But never, ever leave my children! For no one! Absolutely no one! Not ever! You got that?*" Then I dressed as quickly as I could and peeled out of the motel parking lot sideways.

Rod never mentioned anything like that again, and we continued to see each other for sex only. After a while, Rod rented a small apartment just outside of town for us to meet. Whenever we were together sexually, I always thought of Harold. He was the man I really wanted but I never told Rod.

Late one evening, while we were in the middle of the throes of passion, and the moment of sexual release had come for me, I called out, "Harold."

Rod stopped moving, and a look of pure hatred flashed across his face. He jumped out of bed like I had thrown a glass of cold water on him and screamed at me, "Donna! I can't compete with a dead man!"

I shook my head sadly and said very softly, "No, you can't." I sighed because I was glad he knew. "Nor can anyone else for that matter. I will always love *him*. Harold will always be number one with me. Always." I started to cry then. "Do you understand? I did not pursue this '*arrangement*.'" I couldn't bear to call it a relationship. "You did, remember?"

This time, he dressed and stormed out of the room and out of my life. I didn't care. Deep down, I was glad it was over. I buried myself in my children, my home, and my job. I was lacking the contact with a man that a young woman of twenty-five needed, but I put it in the back of my mind. I decided to put myself on *temporary hold* until the kids were a little older.

Every so often, Rod made a point to walk by my workstation and whisper, "Still thinking of a dead man?"

I looked him square in the eye with my head held high and say with as much venom as I could, "Is there any other kind?"

By the way, he stomped off. I don't think he appreciated my sense of humor.

Chapter 10

The Holidays were especially hard for the children and me. Harold was like a big kid at Christmastime—he loved Christmas and always made us feel special during those times. From Thanksgiving through New Year's, I smiled a lot on the outside, but on the inside I was falling apart. I tried very hard not to make it show. I put up a front for my kids, my family, Harold's family, coworkers, and friends.

It kept getting harder and harder to go on. I just didn't want to live anymore. I kept praying over and over, *God, forgive me for what I am thinking, but I just want to be with Harold. Please, Lord, he was the only one who ever loved me unconditionally with all my faults. He accepted me for who I was, the good and the bad. He loved me for what I was, not what I could do for him but for what he could do for me.* I kept thinking there had to be another man out there somewhere like my Harold.

As the holidays grew closer and closer, I could feel myself sinking further and further down into despair. No matter how hard I tried not to think like that, the more I missed Harold. I was so alone and lonely. Sometimes my gut wrenched like I was hidden in that black hole in the wall again, and I often cried into my pillow at night.

To try and pick myself up one afternoon, I went to a hairdresser. After I had my hair done, I still wasn't ready to go home yet because the kids had been asking me about putting up a Christmas tree. I drove over to my girlfriend's house, and we sat and talked for a while. I went to the bathroom and looked in her medicine cabinet and saw a bottle of sleeping pills sitting there on the shelf. Without hesitating or even thinking about what I was doing, I swallowed the entire bottle and flushed it down with water from the sink.

I recall walking back into the kitchen and sitting down at the table where we were drinking coffee and talking. After a few minutes, I started to feel as though I was in a numbing fog. Rita kept saying, "Donna? Donna? Donna?"

I just looked at her; I couldn't respond. Her face started to go far away from me. I could hear her voice, but it sounded like it was far away and off in a tunnel somewhere.

"Donna!" she cried, "Donna! What did you take?!" When I didn't answer, she picked up my purse and dumped everything out on the table. When she couldn't find anything, she called the police.

I remember there was a commotion all around me, but I couldn't make out what was happening. The last thing I remember before I lost consciousness was a policeman's hat because it had a huge badge on it. Then everything went black.

After I was in the emergency room, I must have regained some partial level of consciousness because I heard lots of frantic voices all around me, but one voice stood out in all the commotion. It was a lady's voice, and I felt a cool hand stroke my forehead, and she whispered very softly, "She is so beautiful. Look at all that black hair and that beautiful skin. Why would someone who looks like her want to end her life?"

Another voice, "Look at her figure! And she's a mother of five!"

I lost consciousness again. Next thing I remember, I could hear noises and voices, but they seemed very, very far away. I felt my body being lifted up, and it felt as though I melted through the ceiling, and the ceiling turned into clouds and blue sky. I looked back, and I could see nurses and doctors and uniformed people all around the table I was lying on. I could see my body still on the table, and I thought, *That's strange. I'm way up here?* Then whoosh! I was gone and far away from that scene.

I entered a tunnel, and I was standing upright. My hair was blowing behind me, and there was a light in the tunnel that kept getting closer and closer. I heard the most beautiful music like I had never heard before. The closer I got to the light, I began to see a figure far away walking toward me. As they got closer and closer to me, I began to see their beautiful copper red hair glowing in the sunlight. It was Harold! I felt my heart begin to pound, and I started to run to him, but he held up his hands to stop me and shook his head sadly. "You must go back, Honey. You must go back and take care of our children. It's not your time yet."

I stopped in my tracks, and I screamed, "*No, Harold! No! Don't make me go back!*" The fear and dread of living a life without him consumed me. "I want to be with you! Don't you see? I must be with you!"

"It's not your time, my Sweet Thing. Take care of our children. I'll be waiting for you when it's time."

Suddenly, I was picked up and put back into the tunnel, and I felt my body moving backward, and my hair went from blowing behind me to blowing in front of my face. I reached out to him, but he kept getting farther and farther away, and my body was moving faster and faster, and the music faded away. I felt a sudden intake of air as I reentered my body. I heard a woman's voice calling my name, "Donna, Donna, Donna." She slapped my face and shook me. My arms and legs felt as though they weighed a thousand pounds each.

"She's back!" a man's voice called.

Then there were people everywhere plugging me up to machines. "My…my…my kids!" I finally managed to squeak out.

"Your kids are fine," a young nurse told me as she patted my hand. "They're with relatives."

Later, they told me that I was clinically dead for thirty seconds.

I lost consciousness again, and I stayed in a coma for three weeks.

When I finally gained consciousness, I was in a hospital room, and my mom was holding my hand and rubbing my face and hair, crying softly. Dad stood behind her with tears in his eyes, and he said, "You scared us to death, Honey. We thought we had lost you."

Mom hugged me and asked, "Why, Donna? Why did you do such a thing? Why didn't you call us and let us know you were so upset?"

All I could do was shake my head and cry. How was I going to make them understand? "My kids?" I cried between tears.

"It's all right," Dad reassured me. "We are with the kids, and we'll stay with them. You don't have to handle the burden all by yourself, Donna. We are here for you. We'll help you raise the kids."

The doctors told me that I was very lucky, but that I may have repercussions later in life because of my attempted suicide. I had several weeks of therapy (mental and physical) before I was finally released. I was in the hospital for six weeks.

The children were split up while I was in the hospital recuperating, like they were right after Harold died, and I was in Ohio with Mom and Dad those two weeks. All I could think about was getting back to my children. I didn't want them to think that I had abandoned them like my mother had me.

Whenever I think of Harold now, I can still see him in that tunnel with all that light and beautiful music. He was so happy and at peace without any pain. Deep down, I long for the day when I will be with him once again.

Chapter 11

When I was better and able to go home, Mom and Dad were there to take me home with all my children. Dad helped me sell the house in Danville and moved me and the kids to Columbus, Ohio. We stayed with them for a short time while I looked for a house. We saw several, but none of them really appealed to us. We finally found a house about four blocks from Mom and Dad that was a lease option. It needed some work, but I knew I could make it look good—after all, I had a lot of experience in that regard. It pleases me to take something that doesn't look like much and turn it into something beautiful. It gives me a sense of achievement. Later in life, the kids still laugh and call me "Sanford" and sing the song *Sanford and Son*. I love to pick up somebody else's trash on the side of the road and fix it up. When the kids laugh at me, I just smile and say, "You'll see." And they were always amazed at what I can do with it.

The outside of the house was a light brick. The inside had been treated rough, and we had to paint it and install a new carpet. The house was a trilevel and plenty big enough for all of us. It wasn't near as nice as our house in Danville, but it was nice. I had enough money coming in to make the payments and pay all the bills

After we got the house and yard in shape, I started looking for work. Western Electric hired me for a position on the assembly line working second shift. Rose, my niece, came over and babysat the children until I could find a housekeeper. I hired and fired about ten different housekeepers before I finally found Julie. She was sixties old and a widow who was living with her daughter and son-in-law at the time. I hired her as a live-in housekeeper with the weekends off for one hundred dollars per week, plus room and board. Julie was great with the kids and great with the house and an excellent cook. We loved her. I was a little worried about her Pomeranian, Mickey, because we had never had a dog that lived in the house with us, but he was well trained and very clean.

Julie turned out to be a dream come true. She was more like a grandma to all of us, and we truly enjoyed her being with us. The kids learned to love Julie, and they showed her respect. She was stern with them and didn't let them get away with anything.

We were all very happy with each other. I think Julie needed us, and we needed her. Strange how God puts people together. He always works it out to help you meet someone who needs you as much as you need them. Everything was falling into place for us. We had a nice house. I had a good job, and we had a wonderful house-keeper. I was beginning to feel satisfied with life once more, although I still missed Harold.

I worked second shift, which meant that I got off around 11:00 p.m. Once some of my coworkers discovered that I was a widow, they asked me every Friday to go out with them. Most of the time I refused because it made me miss Harold more if I went out. Harold was a superb dancer, and we were made for each other's arms. After a while, I said yes just to shut them up about it, but I didn't stay very long.

One hot night, they took me to place on Fifth Street that had go-go dancers in between the band's breaks. The girls I was with kept buying rounds, and I had a little too much to drink. As we sat there watching the girls dance, I sputtered out, "Hell, let me show them how to dance!"

My girlfriends giggled and rolled their eyes. They knew I was feeling pretty good and was probably just mouthing off. They stopped giggling when I stood up and made my way over the stage. I looked up at one of the dancers and said, "Hey! Is it all right if come up there on stage and try one?"

She grinned and waved me up, "Sure! Come on up!"

I climbed up on the stage and danced the song my way. The entire place went nuts, including the bartenders, the owner, and the guys in the band. When the band's break was over, I got off the stage with the other girls and sat back down with my girlfriends. Before I had a chance to say anything, the owner of the lounge came rushing over to our table and asked, "How would you like to come to work for me as a dancer?"

"I don't know. I'll have to think about it."

My girlfriends kept taking me back to the Sahara on Fridays and Saturdays, and every time I showed up, the owner, Nick, gave us a free round of drinks, although all I ever drank was 7 Up. He kept offering me more money to come to work for him. Eventually, he offered me more money to dance a few hours a night and make more money than I was making at the factory. I finally took him up on his offer and started the following weekend.

I wanted to make my act more than just getting up on stage and dancing in a bathing suit like the other girls were doing. I made my first costume by taking a white bathing suit, and between sewing and gluing on various colors, I had a costume that dazzled. I picked a pair of silver-glittered high heels to dance in, and I finished my costume off with black fishnet stockings.

My first night, the crowd loved me. It was more of an act than just dancing on a stage. By the second week, the Sahara's business doubled, and Nick had increased my pay from 150 dollars a week to 250 dollars a week. After that first couple of weeks, I started to have shows at 9:00 p.m., 11:00 p.m., and 1:00 a.m., and I always went home after my last show. The other girls danced before I came in, and between my shows while the crowd waited for me to come back on again. I kept making my own costumes, always coming up with different ideas. Eventually, I started adding fringe and wearing a see-through scarf wrapped around my hips when I first went on stage. Between each show, I changed costumes. I didn't want the crowd to see the same one the same night.

As it turned out, I loved dancing. I was paid well for my time, my looks, and my talent. It helped fill the void of losing Harold. I missed him so much. The money was a blessing. I was able to keep food in the house, clothes for the children to wear, toys, and enough money left over for my costumes. Because of the late hours I worked,

I was able to be home to help Julie get the kids to school and to be home when they got out of school.

After a couple of months at the Sahara, I started to become well-known and began stealing business from some of the other lounges all over Columbus. I was getting so popular that Nick, the owner of the Sahara, built me a stage with flashing lights and plain white lights when I wanted them. It was my choice. I introduced a new act to my dancing. I first came out on stage wearing a sexy evening gown and told a few jokes. Then I sang a few songs. For my second show, I changed into my dancing costume and performed. My costumes were all sparkly, and I always wore a different one. Some of them had fringe along the top part, and the bottom had fringe along the middle and around to the behind. I did three forty-five-minute shows, one at 9:00 p.m., one at 11:00 p.m., and the last one at 1:00 a.m. The crowd always hung around for my next show.

After about three months, I noticed a new guy in my audience every night for a week. He looked to be in his late forties with salt-and-pepper gray hair. He was tall with a big nose and the bushiest eyebrows I had ever seen. Occasionally, he came in with another guy who was shorter and probably around the same age.

One night, just as my first show ended, the two men approached me as I came down off the stage, and the taller of the two said, "Hi, I'm Joe Bananas, and this here is Mike Morretti."

I didn't reply but only looked at them curiously.

"We want to talk business with you." I noticed Nick, the owner of the Sahara, come running over.

"Donna," he interrupted, "You need to go and get ready for your second show."

Since he was paying for my time, I shrugged. "Sure." I glanced up at the other two gentlemen and said sweetly, "Excuse me."

When I came back on stage for my second show, Bananas and Mike and some of their friends, who looked like bodyguards, were sitting right up front. I also noticed a man standing by the back exit and another one by the front exit, and they were watching the crowd closely.

I went through my typical routine, and they loved it. They were all smiles and clapping and whistling right along with everyone else. I could tell that Nick was getting nervous. He kept watching Joe Bananas and Mike Morretti and pacing back and forth shaking his head.

When my show was over, Bananas approached me and handed me a business card and asked, "Can you meet me after your last show?"

I shook my head. "No. I go straight home when I get off."

"But why?" he asked.

"Because I give it all I have when I'm on stage. I'm tired, and I want to go home to my kids."

"You have kids?"

I simply nodded and replied, "Yes. Now get out of my way." I shoved past him because Nick was motioning me to follow him into the kitchen.

When I walked into the kitchen, Nick was wringing his hands. He softly touched my arm and said worriedly, "Donna, they're here to take you away from me. I can't compete with their money. They are big money, and I can't afford to pay you what they will offer you. I'll pay you as much as I can. I'm asking that you please don't leave."

As I walked back to my dressing room, I was walking on air because I realized that I could go to work anywhere I wanted to and name my own price.

Bananas and Mike came back several times after that, sometimes bringing their other friends with them. They always wore suits with overcoats and looked like mobsters. They sat in front of my stage and whistled and clapped as hard as everyone else. They never left without asking me to work for them and offering more and more money.

Finally, one night after my last show, Bananas caught me coming off the stage and said, "We will make it worth your while to talk to us before you leave. Trust me."

I shook my head and said, "No, but I will call you tomorrow and meet you and Mike for lunch somewhere. By the way, I will bring someone with me for protection."

"No. We don't want to wait until tomorrow it has to be tonight."

"I didn't come here to see you," I reminded him. "You came here to see me. I'm holding the cards. What do you think?"

He smiled and snorted, "You're pretty tough for such a little girl."

Bananas was a cross between Humphrey Bogart and Dean Martin. I discovered later that everyone who knew Bananas liked him—it might have been because they were afraid not to. He handed me a white business card, and I promised him that I would call them tomorrow.

Nick was so afraid that Mike and Bananas was going to steal me. He knew that I always put my kids first. He also knew that if I could better myself to better provide for my children, I would. Nick had been very good to me, and he knew I was all business and hands off. When I got through with my last show, they knew to stay out of my way because all I had on my mind was going straight home. I was never late for work. I don't believe in being late—no matter what you do for a living—and always give it your best.

I didn't know it at the time, but Bananas and Mike had me followed for a couple of months to make sure I was telling the truth about having five kids. When they found out that I was all business and went from home straight to work and back home again, they wanted me to work for them. They couldn't believe that a woman of looks and talent was that dedicated to her children.

The next morning was Sunday, and when I got up and had my coffee, I dug the card Bananas gave me out of my purse and looked at it. The card had a drawing of a banana and inside the banana was the initials JBC. I called Mom and Dad and told them about a business lunch and if could they go with me for the meeting just to make sure that everything was on the up and up. Once they agreed to go with me, I called Bananas and made a 2:00 p.m. appointment at the China Jade downtown Columbus. Dad said that he and Mom would get a table off to the side and keep an eye on us.

I took my shower, fixed my hair, put on my makeup, and dressed in a nice white two-piece outfit. I walked into the restaurant promptly at 2:00 p.m. Bananas met me at the door and said, "Hi, beautiful." He took my arm and escorted me over to the table where Mike was waiting. Mom and Dad came in a minute later and sat in a booth across from us. After he had seated me, Bananas asked, "I thought you said you were going to bring someone with you?"

I smiled sweetly and said, "They're here."

Both men glanced around but didn't see anyone suspicious. Whether or not they suspected Mom and Dad, I never knew.

We ordered our meal, and while we were waiting for our food, Bananas said, "We want to offer you a contract to perform at the A-Lounge downtown or the Sun Lounge on the west side of town. Three shows a night at 9:00 p.m., 11:00 p.m., and 1:00 a.m. for forty-five minutes each show, same as the Sahara but for a whole lot more money."

I took a sip of the hot tea that they always serve in Chinese restaurants and said, "I'll have to think it over, but no contracts. I want to keep myself free. If something should happen that I don't like, I'm free to just walk away. And if I agree to come work for you, I want the A-Lounge because it's closer to home."

On my drive home, I thought about their offer. I hated to quit the Sahara. Nick had been so good to me, plus they respected me. One night before I had given Mike and Bananas my answer, they came in to catch my last show. The crowd was wild that night and kept clapping. Just as I walked down the stairs to get off the stage, Bananas walked up and said, "Okay, I know when I'm being held up. Why don't you just carry a mask?"

I laughed at him.

"Look, here's our final offer." He ran his fingers through his hair, and said, "We'll give you five hundred dollars a week plus two percent of the nightly take each week." He shook his head like he couldn't believe what he was saying. "No contract."

I paused for a few minutes as though I was contemplating his offer. I had already made my mind that I would take it. He was holding his breath as he waited for my answer. "Okay, you got a deal."

His eyes sparkled in triumph. He glanced over at Mike and slightly nodded and a huge grin spread across Mike's face.

Now for the hard part—I had to tell Nick. He had been good to me, and I considered him a friend. I made them money, and they paid me well. When I told Nick the next night, his face fell, and he shook his head. "Donna," he groaned, "I've sunk everything I had into this place. I can't compete with those two. You know that."

I nodded. "I know. I understand." I touched his shoulder gently as though I were comforting one of my children. "I have to do what's best for me and my kids. I hope you understand."

Nick looked up at me with sadness and said, "If they don't treat you right or if you ever want to come back for any reason, all you have to do is call. You know that, don't you?"

"Yeah, I know." I finished out the week at the Sahara and said goodbye to everyone.

On Sunday afternoon the next day, I drove out to the A-Lounge to look around. As soon as I walked in the place Bananas's face lit up, and he ran over to me. Several patrons looked up, but no one interrupted us. He showed me around the place. It was a nice stage complete with strobe lights, and they were setting up my sound equipment. I looked up at him and said, "I want a dressing room all to myself."

He snapped his fingers. "As luck would have it, we have one downstairs. It was used by Gypsy Rose when she performed here in the thirties and forties." They had been using it to store whiskey in; but other than that, it worked out fine. It had a dressing table and a wardrobe rack with lights all around the mirror, so I could see while I put on my makeup. It just needed a little cleaning up.

"Get the whiskey out and have it cleaned up for me by tomorrow night." I was all business.

Bananas grinned and jokingly replied, "Do you always call all the shots?"

I repeated what I told him that first time, "You came looking for me. I did not come looking for you. So I hold the upper hand, don't you think?"

He smiled and said, "I've been robbed before but not by such a beauty as you."

I cocked my head to one side. "Huh, life sure teaches us a lot, doesn't it?"

Then I left and went home to my family.

I didn't know it at the time, but my new career as a dancer and entertainer was about to take off—as well as my new life married to a mobster.

Chapter 12

A few weeks later, it was my and Harold's anniversary. I had a hard time all night trying to get through the evening. There were tears behind my eyes, but I tried not to show it. I finished my last show and got off stage like I always did and spoke to a few people. Whenever I got off stage, I was always soaking wet with sweat because I always gave it everything I had when I performed. After I was in my dressing room, Bananas came in a few minutes later and said, "Don't leave. There's a lot of important people out there that I want you to meet."

I looked up at him and growled, "I'm tired. Do you understand that?"

"Donna, all you have to do is walk out there and let them see you. If they can see you, they won't leave."

"You and Mike pay me from nine to two, and it's two twenty. Now get out of my way!" I spat.

"Now, come on and change your clothes and just mingle with the patrons!" he snarled back at me.

I leaned back and spit in his face. I must admit, I had a temper. Still do. It's a miracle he didn't pull out his gun and blow my head off that night.

"Okay," he said calmly as he wiped his face off. "You're mine now."

"What do you mean by that?"

"Any woman who's got the nerve to do that to me is going to be my wife. That's what I mean!"

"Oh, is that right?" I parried back.

"You just sealed your fate, my little Angel Dust." He always called me Angel Dust because silver and gold flakes floated through the air and down to the floor when I performed because I shook them off my costumes.

I noticed a man coming in and sitting in front. He had dark blonde hair and resembled Harold. He started talking to me when I made my way by the tables after my show. He stopped me as I began to walk by, and he asked me if I could talk to him for a few minutes. I sat down at the table and talked to him. He introduced himself as John and told me he was a doctor. The more he talked, the more I could tell I wasn't interested in him. Bananas kept watching us, and his eyes were smoldering. Mike walked up to him and glanced over at me and nudged him in the ribs laughing. Bananas ignored Mike and stayed focused on us. John kept coming back every night and tried to talk to me. I spoke with him occasionally because he was a regular. Every night Bananas watched him.

Several weeks later, I noticed that John wasn't coming to the club anymore. I didn't know it at the time, but Bananas had the police pull him over. Then Bananas pulled up in a black limo and told him, "Leave Donna alone or I'll break every bone in both your hands, and you'll never operate again. Donna doesn't know it yet, but she's going to be my wife."

Bananas was nice-looking for his age, and there was something about him that intrigued me. It wasn't long that afternoon that he called me, and he asked, "Hey, what are you doing this evening?"

"Relaxing with my kids."

"How about all of you go with me to the carnival that's in town?"

"No. I really got to get ready for tomorrow night."

He laughed and said, "Honey, you don't have to do anything but walk in and the whole place lights up."

"I'm really not interested," I tried to let him down easy.

"Okay," he said thoughtfully. "How 'bout I pick the kids up and take them to the carnival, and I'll take them to dinner?"

I was a little nervous about it, but he seemed genuinely interested in my kids, and I said, "Okay."

Bananas picked them up around 5:00 p.m. and had them all home promptly at 9:00 p.m. It was a school night, and I didn't want them out any later than that. The kids came home raving about how nice he was and how crazy he was about me. *So that's his game,* I thought. This went on for several weeks. He picked the kids up on Sunday afternoons and took them some place and bought them things and took them out to eat.

One Sunday afternoon around noon, he called me and said, "Hey, I'm going to Buckeye Lake, and I'd like to take you and the kids with me."

"The kids can go."

When he arrived at the house, he said, "Why don't you get ready and go with us?"

The kids joined in and jumped up and down and begged me, "Yes, Mommy, please go with us! Come on, Mom!"

I glared at Bananas, but he smiled smugly and shrugged his broad shoulders. I sighed and caved in. "Okay." And we all went. It was nice being around someone who enjoyed being with my children. It meant a lot to me.

He even had Julie on his side. "You'd better get to know this man," she told me one morning when I walked into the kitchen to get my coffee. "He can do a lot for you and your kids. He's the kind of man that will love, respect, and take care of you and those kids."

For my first show, I came out in a sexy evening gown and sang some Brenda Lee, Connie Francis, and Tammy Wynette songs. After singing, I told a few jokes. My second show, I told jokes and danced. I added tassels to the tops of my costumes, and I practiced at home being able to twirl them around by shaking my chest. Eventually, I could spin them in the same direction, then change direction, and then have one spin clockwise and other one counterclockwise. The crowd always went wild.

In a few short months, I turned the A-Lounge around. Our clientele changed from the usual bar crowd to lawyers, judges, detectives, and doctors with their wives or girlfriends to catch my act. Mike couldn't believe the difference I had made in his place. We went from selling a lot of beer to mix drinks, which he could make a lot more money on.

I was making good money, and the kids were happy and liked Bananas. I had known him about six months. Bananas was fifty with dark brown eyes and wavy dark hair that was graying at the temples. He was good with my children. In many ways, he reminded me of my Harold. We all had so much fun together. After a while, the kids and I came to look forward to Sunday afternoons.

My job was extremely demanding because the crowd screamed for more. I had to constantly come up with new jokes, new songs to sing, and a new dance routine. I practiced at home as much as possible. An audience wants more and more of you every night. I loved what I did, but the more I gave them, the more they expected. An entertainer needs to be careful to keep your job separate from your homelife. That's how a lot of entertainers get into trouble and get caught up in drugs or drinking. I know because I almost went down that road, but my kids meant more to me than my audience.

Bananas had his own box at the racetrack—both harness racing and horse racing. The track knew Bananas, and as soon as we walked in escorted us to the front and our private box. Everyone knew Bananas no matter where we went. We never had to wait in line for dinner anywhere we went. After a while, I was recognized wherever I went. I couldn't go grocery shopping unless it was late at night or I disguised myself with a blonde wig or a large hat and sunglasses.

One morning around 11:00 a.m., Julie woke me up and said that a truck was parked outside our house, and two men were at the door asking for Mrs. Harold Clouse, and that they had come to get the furniture I owed them for or to get paid. I pulled on a pair of slacks and a T-shirt and went to the door. "Yes?"

"Ma'am, I'm from the Winchester Furniture Store, and you owe $450 on some furniture."

"I don't owe you a dime," I snorted.

The man who did the talking motioned at the other guy and said, "Pick up that chair."

It was Saturday morning, and all the kids were home. I looked at Junior and said, "Junior, sit on that chair." He grinned and jumped up on it.

"Cheryl," I called, "go sit on the other chair." Then I glanced over at my eldest and instructed, "Debbie, go sit on the sofa. And do not get off."

I went upstairs and got Harold's shotgun and cocked it as I calmly walked down the stairs. Just then, Bananas pulled into the driveway. I didn't know it at the time, but Julie had called him.

"Hey! What's going on here?" he shouted at the two men.

One of the men from the furniture store turned around to look at Bananas, and the other kept his eye on me and the shotgun. The first man said, "She owes $450 for this furniture."

I shook my head and pointed the gun at him, "No, I don't. I paid them for all my furniture."

Bananas reached into his pocket and pulled out five one-hundred-dollar bills and handed him the money. "Now get the hell out of here before she kills us all."

"But Bananas!" I screamed. "I don't owe this—"

"It's okay, Honey. We don't need this kind of steam." Bananas looked at the men menacingly and said, "Now get the hell out of here."

The two men ran and jumped into the truck and peeled out of there trying to get as far away from us as possible. He turned back to me and said, "I'll always be here for you, Baby. You don't have to do everything by yourself anymore, okay? Do you understand me?"

He was talking to me as though he were trying to calm a rabid dog down from biting him. When I realized what I had done, I started to laugh. Then he laughed and took me in his arms and whispered in my ear, "You have to stop getting so uptight about everything." He squeezed me. "I have to teach you to relax."

I tried to kiss him on the cheek to show my appreciation, but he turned his head, and I caught his lips instead. That was the first time we had kissed. I felt like I had my protector again.

There was a circus in town, and Bananas took the kids and me to see it. We enjoyed watching the children's eyes light up watching the circus. It felt wonderful seeing the kids so happy again. The children were exhausted when we got them home. Julie and I got them their baths and ready for bed while Bananas went home to get cleaned up. He came back about an hour later and took me out to Gloria Dinner Lounge for dining and dancing. While we were waiting for dessert, he asked me, "Would you like to dance?"

I was a little nervous, but I was hoping he asked me. It was the first time I had danced with anyone since Harold. When he held me while we danced, I realized that I fit in his arms almost as perfectly as Harold and I fit together. While we danced, I felt as though I were dreaming. I thought stupidly, *Maybe I can find love again. Maybe it's not too late for me and him.* He had told me before that he was divorced with three grown children. Vonna, his daughter, was twenty-five; then there was Joe, eighteen; and Phillip, who was sixteen. Bananas had gotten custody of the children in the divorce twelve years before I met him. He was over his wife, so I knew I wouldn't have to fight that battle. He had a lot to offer me—companionship, love—if I just let it happen.

While we danced, he taught me some new steps. He was quite a dancer. He was smooth and gentle. He whispered in my ear, "Do you know how long I have waited to hold you like this? You are a very hard person to get to know."

I didn't know what to say, so I just didn't say anything.

"You can let down your guard now, Donna," he continued as he turned and looked deep into my eyes. "I will never hurt you or your family. Ever."

We stopped dancing and stared at each other for a moment. He said, "I have been in love with you ever since I laid eyes on you. Can't you just love me a little back?"

"Oh, Bananas," I said breathlessly, "I'm not sure…I respect and admire you, but I don't know if I love you."

He smiled. "Okay, that will do for now." Then he pulled me into his embrace and our lips touched in a long passionate kiss. Everyone else in the lounge stopped dancing and watched us and then applauded. We laughed and continued dancing. It was like a scene out of an old Betty Davis movie. I knew he was beginning to steal my heart away from Harold, and I felt pangs of guilt, but at the same time I was happy all at once.

The following Sunday, Bananas had invited me and my family to his mother's house for dinner after church. Julie's daughter picked her up for the day. I told Bananas that the kids and I would meet him over there because she lived on the West Side of

Columbus, and we lived on the East Side; but he said, "I'll pick you and the kids up."

As soon as we pulled into the driveway, I could smell all that great Italian cooking—all those spices and garlic and sauce. My mouth began to water as the delicious aroma wafted through the air to my tantalized nostrils. She had a nice brick home, and it had been well taken care of inside and out. As soon as we walked in, there were people everywhere. It reminded me of the gatherings we used to have with Harold's family, except they were all dark-skinned and speaking Italian—not because they couldn't speak English, but the rule was when everyone was together, you spoke Italian. Bananas explained that it helped them not to lose their Italian heritage.

He pulled me up to a very small woman wearing an apron over her dark blue church dress. He said to her in Italian, "Ma, this is Donna. She's one in a million. And these are her children." And then he introduced each one of the children. "Donna, this is my mother, Theresa."

She turned to me and said something in Italian as she took my hand and hugged me. Then she turned to Bananas and said a few more words, and Bananas translated: "We have been waiting to meet you. Bananas told us so much about you. All good. We're glad you and your children are here. Sit, eat, and enjoy."

One by one, each of his family members came up to me and the kids and introduced themselves. As we sat down to eat, they began to introduce all the different Italian dishes that she and the other ladies had prepared. There was no way that I could ever remember all those Italian names. Everything that was said in Italian, Bananas interpreted for me and the children. Such as, "She's beautiful, and the children are beautiful and well-mannered too."

His mother kept saying over and over, *"Mangiare, mangiare, mangiare!"* Bananas told me that meant eat, eat, eat!

We had a wonderful time. The kids played with the other little Italian children there. We pitched some horseshoes and played ball. The kids and I learned a few new Italian words. I think we made a great impression on his mother and family. I didn't know it at the time, but Bananas had told his mother he was going to marry me. She asked him, "Have you asked her yet?"

"No. But you'll see."

Bananas's father was killed while driving bootleg whiskey in Youngstown, Ohio. He was twelve years old when his father died, and he went to work before and after school to help his mother take care of the rest of his brothers and sisters. He finished high school with highest honors. I found out later that Bananas was born on the way over to America from Italy. His mother named him after the president of Italy, Venanzio, and the first president of America, George. Venanzio George Casasanta was his full name. When his brothers and sisters were very young, they had a hard time pronouncing Venanzio, and it came out Bananas, and that's how he got his nickname.

His mother felt a close bond with me, being a widow herself. She was widowed when Bananas was twelve, and he was her oldest. Her children ranged from twelve, ten, eight, six, three, and one when her husband passed away. She remarried when Bananas was twenty years old. She was a very nice lady, and I learned to love her very much in the few years that I knew her. I loved his sisters too. They were all very kind to me. His entire family was very respectful, and we spent the day getting to know each other.

They set up a dance floor in the backyard complete with colored lanterns. The kids played games, and everyone enjoyed each other's company. It was so reminiscent of the Clouse gatherings, except Italian style, and I thought to myself, *My children and I really needed this.*

When we got ready to leave, I invited everyone over to our house the following Sunday. Bananas was so pleased that I had done that. He had the food catered in from Gloria's because they had the best Italian food in town. We had an aboveground pool in the backyard, and everyone brought their swimsuits. There were wet towels everywhere, and food sprawled from one end of the house to the other, but everyone had a wonderful time. Everyone slowly began to leave around 10:00 p.m. By the time everyone had left, it was around 10:00 p.m. The caterers began to clean up the mess, and Bananas pulled the main caterer to the side and handed him one hundred dollars and said, "Make sure everything is in place before you leave."

The kids were in bed, and Julie had retired for the night. Bananas had packed a suitcase for me and had one for himself in his car. As soon as the caterers had left, he grabbed me by the hand and said, "Come with me." He drove us to a swank hotel in Columbus, where he had already registered us that morning.

"What are you up to?"

He turned and looked at me with blazing black eyes, "Don't you think we had better find out if I can please you, and you can please me?"

I laughed a little nervously. "Maybe so."

He had registered us in the honeymoon suite. He had me lie down on the bed, and he gave me the most magnificent massage I had ever had. Then he prepared me a hot bubble bath that was full of bubbles and rose petals and two glasses of champagne on the edge of the tub. He picked me up ever so gently and lowered me into the tub. Then he slipped off his robe and joined me in the tub. His strong hands began to rub my feet, legs, and toes. Then he put one of my toes in his mouth and said, "This little piggy goes to the market," then he pulled it out and nibbled at another toe. "This little piggy stayed home, and this little piggy had roast beef, and this little piggy had none." Then he put my big toe in his mouth. "And this little piggy belongs to me."

I laughed, and we made love right there in the tub. There were bubbles all over the marble floor. I hadn't been able to let myself go like that since Harold. I think that if there had been fireworks in my hair, my head would have exploded. I began to wonder why I had waited so long before I let him get this close to me before.

We made love until we were both exhausted. My knees were so weak that I could hardly stand up. "You think you're in bad shape," Bananas retorted, "how about this old man? You killed me, girl."

We fell back on the bed laughing. It was 2:00 a.m., and I knew I had to get home before the kids woke up. "I have to go," I told him. "I don't want the kids to wake up and I'm not there. They'll worry."

He just raised his bushy left eyebrow at me and frowned.

"Now, you know that if I stay here, we will not get any sleep!" I admonished him. "Besides, I have to get ready for tomorrow night's show."

He didn't want to, but he drove me home. Deep down I wanted to stay with him, but I did not want my kids to lose their respect for me, and I always tried to put them before myself. Bananas drove me home and came inside and stood by the door. I took one look at that man, and I smiled. I took his hand in mine and began walking toward the stairs, leading him behind him. He pulled back and groaned, "Wait! You mean you're going to let me stay?"

I glanced back at him and whispered, "Yeah."

"But what about the kids?"

"They will understand. They like you, Bananas." Then I looked at him hotly and said, "Besides, I'm not done with you yet!"

He snorted. "I don't think I can do anymore tonight."

"Oh, I think you can." And I led him up the stairs and into my bedroom.

That was the first time he had ever been upstairs in my house. There was a picture of Harold in uniform on the chest of drawers. Bananas asked me softly, "Can I turn that picture around to face the wall? I feel funny him seeing me in bed with you."

I giggled and placed it tenderly in the drawer. "I'll find another place for it tomorrow." And we fell asleep with my head on his shoulder.

Sometime around 6:00 a.m., I heard my bedroom door open, and it was Terry and Donna Kay. Terry came over to my side of the bed and whispered, "Mommy, is that Bananas?"

"Yes, Honey."

Terry's eyes lit up, and she whispered happily, "Oh boy! I like him, Mommy. Is he going to be our new Daddy?"

I shrugged my shoulders and smiled at them. They both jumped in the bed between us.

Chapter 13

All the children were happy about Bananas being with us, and everyone, including Julie and Mickie, welcomed him to the family. Most of all, I knew that he would protect and take care of me and my family. Bananas kept trying to get me to marry him, but I kept putting him off. We let everyone think that we had eloped and got married, but we really didn't. He was just not going to be happy until I became Mrs. Bananas, and he put his ring on my finger. My children and I had welcomed him into our family, and we enjoyed his company, and he was very special to us. He made our life complete.

Although the kids and I had never discussed it, they had been missing that father figure that all children need growing up. They craved the security that only a man can give them, and I needed that extra support that only a father and husband can give when raising children. Bananas filled in a lot of those empty gaps we had in our lives after Harold died.

Finally, Bananas just wouldn't take no for an answer, and I couldn't put him off any longer. We took a week off and went to Vegas to get married. As far as everyone else knew, we went out there on vacation. Bananas had already decided that I was going to marry him. That's why he bought the rings before we left—he just didn't tell me. I cried all the way through the ceremony. The pastor of the little church asked me, "Are you sure you are not being forced to do this?"

I shook my head. "No, it's a long story." I felt somehow that if I married him that I would lose him.

After the ceremony, I took Harold's ring and wore it on my other hand for a long time.

On our wedding night, we had fallen fast asleep in the honeymoon suite. Suddenly I was woken up by Harold's voice. I shot a look at the TV screen, and Harold's face was on the blank screen just as clear as day, and he was smiling at me. "It's okay, Honey," he said. "He'll take care of you and the kids." And just as quickly, he vanished. Deep down I felt as though I were letting Harold down, and this was his way of letting me know that everything was okay.

We had a wonderful time in Vegas. We saw Frank Sinatra, Dean Martin, and Tom Jones. During Tom Jones's show, he called for anyone who was in the entertainment industry to come up on stage and help him sing "She's a Lady." Bananas threw a fit because I wouldn't get up on stage. It was never my desire to be discovered and become famous. My only interest was to be able to raise my family and provide for them the best way that I knew how. I feel like I had succeeded in that regard. Of course, I couldn't have done it without the wisdom, good looks, and talent that God has given me.

I knew the kids were being taken care of back in Columbus, but I missed them terribly. I was so happy when we were on our way home. I never tried to let my children down in any way like my biological parents had done to me.

I loved being an entertainer, and I was getting a lot of publicity. Bananas used to tell me that when I walked in the back door of the lounge, I entered as a wife and mother. But when I came out on stage, I was a woman who when she went out on stage set it on fire. He said that I could hold the audience spellbound for hours. He always told me that I had so much more to give, and the world was a stage built for people like me. He wanted so much for me than I wanted for myself.

Bananas got me a spot on the TV show *Here Comes the Judge*. I had to play a person who was practicing their songs on a car tape player while driving, and I had run into the back of another car. It was only about a fifteen-minute spot, but every time it aired, I received a check in the mail.

Our club grew in popularity too. Our clientele consisted of lawyers, judges, doctors, school teachers, public officials, narcotics squad, detectives, and even the underworld and high-class call girls. I was there to do a job and go home; I didn't care about anything that didn't concern me. We got a lot of well-dressed married couples who loved my act and kept coming back to see me week after week.

I had worked on this one act for a long time where I had tassels hanging from my top, and I could twirl them by shaking by breasts. I could make them spin clockwise, counterclockwise, and one going one way and one going another. The crowed loved it. Bananas and Mike Joseph had my picture on the outside of the Lounge; the caption over my picture read, "Donna, Queen of the Go-Go."

One night while I was performing my tassel trick, a young cop trying to make a name for himself accused me of letting my breasts fall out and put them back in again without touching my breasts or my costume. The cops busted me that night and took me to jail. The cops closed the A-Lounge for the rest of the night. Bananas had the lounge's attorney meet me at the station. I was booked, finger-printed, and released within the hour.

My picture hit the front page with the story that I had exposed my breasts. It wasn't just the local paper either. Several other states ran the story as well. The next day, the kids got into some fights at school defending my honor. Debbie came home crying, and Junior was furious over the things the kids had said about me. Of course, they were just repeating what they heard their parents say. I was extremely hurt because they were suffering. I personally didn't care what other people thought; I knew that I hadn't done anything wrong. But they were kids, and it hurt them that other kids were saying terrible things about their mother.

That night, Bananas had one of our bodyguards pick them up in a limousine and bring them to my first show because he wanted my kids to see for themselves what I did on stage. The cocktail waitress served the girls Shirley Temples and Junior a Roy Rogers. Bananas didn't want them to be ashamed of me, and he wanted them to see what I did on stage. After my first show, I got off stage and introduced my children to the audience, and the audience applauded them. Their ages at the time were ten, nine, eight, six, and four. They loved watching my show and talked about that night for years.

I had to go to court and before the liquor board since I was part owner. There were nine judges on the liquor board, and I had to put on the costume that I was arrested in and perform my act in front of them, dancing to the same song that was playing that night, which just happened to be "Drums A Go-Go." After the act, all the judges just looked at one another, and one of them banged his gavel and said, "Case dismissed." One down, one to go.

For the actual criminal offense of lewd and lascivious exposure, the courtroom was packed with reporters and spectators. Once again, our lawyer had me put on my costume, and I had to do my act in front of the criminal judge. After the act, the judge banged his gavel and said, "Not enough evidence! Case dismissed!"

As we left the courtroom the reporters were going crazy trying to take my picture, and Bananas lifted my white coat up over my face to protect me from the cameras. My face was plastered all over the front page again, only this time the headlines read, "Queen of the Go-Go Proved Innocent." I started wearing a tiara in my hair when I performed.

The A-Lounge was known as a place where mobsters hung out, but it was also known as the place to go for fun and entertainment. I came to find out later that it was all politics. There were the new people running for office, and then there were the people already in office trying to stay there by putting a lot of heat on the night spots. Some of the politicians had a vendetta against Bananas and Mike. They knew Mike and Bananas had the underworld in their back pockets, including a lot of the police department. They were always trying to bust us. In the long run, all it did was make us more popular. After a while, the politicians left us alone.

Bananas got me gigs all over Ohio. Pretty soon, I was doing shows in Toledo, Cincinnati, and Cleveland. I usually performed out of town on Sunday nights and then back to our place for Monday through Saturday. I tried to train the other girls how to keep my audience happy while I was gone, but they couldn't do it, and after a while I just gave up trying to teach them. We changed our plans to where I performed only on Sundays at other clubs.

In the meantime, Bananas wanted me to get pregnant. He wanted a baby in the worst way. He told me, "I'll help you raise your children, but you must have one of ours together."

"How am I going to have a baby when you've got me all over the place doing shows and then at our place six nights a week, huh?" I asked him. "You know if I get pregnant, I will lose my figure and it will take time to get it back again. And we'll be out of commission in the meantime."

I had costumes of all shades and colors, and my high heels matched every one of my costumes. On the nights when I had hecklers, Mike and Bananas always held their breaths because they never knew what I might say or do—funny thing is, I wasn't so sure myself. Bananas and Mike came up with a signal for me. Whenever vice squad was in the audience, Bananas brought me a drink with a red band around the glass, which meant be careful and don't say anything you shouldn't. When the coast was clear, Bananas threw a white towel for me to wipe the sweat off, which meant give them a show they won't forget—and I always did.

One evening we were being cased big time, and when the vice got up to leave, I was in one of those "I don't give a damn" attitudes, and I hollered out, "Hey! What's the matter fellas? Is that a rod your packing, or are you just excited to see me?"

Mike and Bananas turned pale. The vice just smiled and said, "Catch you later."

I knew I was going to have to listen to thirty minutes of "don't do or say things like that when they are in here." I wouldn't for a while, and then I figured it was time to cut up on them just for old time's sake.

Reporters were in the audience almost every night. They were trying to get a scoop on the place or me and Bananas. One night, a woman reporter hollered out, "Hey, Donna! I heard you have five children. Doesn't it bother you to make your living the way you do?"

"Yeah," I parried back, "it bothers me so bad that I laugh all the way to the bank every day!" Then I looked right at her. "I'm here for the kids. They love and respect me. I'm here to entertain, and it must be working. Look around you. You're here, aren't you? And it's because you heard about me and wanted to see me in person."

I was really beginning to get worked up by now. What she said about my kids pissed me off royal and I continued, "I think I got something no one else has. It's the guts and the freedom to entertain to the fullest that the law will allow. If you are unhappy with my performance, pull your pants up and go home. If you're happy, order another drink and shut the hell up!"

The crowd went wild! The more personal I got with people in the audience, the more they loved it. Sometimes I felt like I was running out of ammunition, then suddenly something would pop into my head. It's hard to entertain people with hecklers in the crowd. It was much easier to keep them spellbound with dancing and singing. I had to constantly be on my toes for hecklers in the crowd. I could usually come back on them. I got so good at it that a lot of my audience thought we planted them in the audience, but we really didn't. We had enemies, and they were always trying to discredit us.

We were running two households at the time—mine that we shared and his that his older children lived in. Plus, we had about five houses that we used for high stakes poker games for the underworld, and Bananas ran a bookie business betting on ball games and horse races. Financially, we were doing very well, and I'll have to admit it felt good not having to worry about money. We bought a bigger home in Reynoldsburg, and we all loved it. Julie moved with us too, and I bought all new furniture for it. I decorated the entire house and had new carpeting put in throughout and custom-made drapes. We both bought new Oldsmobiles at the same time.

He loved sports. I enjoyed football once I understood the game—I enjoyed watching it with him. I hated baseball because it was too slow for me, and basketball was too fast for me. Bananas was a very intelligent man. Like me, he knew what he wanted, and he went after it. I'm still like that today.

It was getting more difficult for Bananas's bookie business. The politicians were coming down hard on him and all his friends again. They were continuously under the microscope. Bananas had a photographic memory. He hardly ever had to write anything down. If he did, all he had to do was take one look at it and throw it away because the number was forever etched on his brain. He amazed me how he could do that.

He had a code for each bet, and only he knew what the code was and how much. When we went to the racetrack, people were always coming up to him and asking, "Which horse do you like?" He always had a code for which one and how much. The FBI followed him, but they couldn't get anything on him. They knew he was behind the business, but they couldn't prove it. The reason big shots placed bets with him was because his odds were better than anyone else's.

Sometimes I felt like I was falling apart, and I didn't know why. We were on top of the world financially, and our place of business was the number one club in Columbus. When I went to work, I sometimes cried all the way. After I went into my dressing room, Bananas would hold me in his arms and tell me, "It's okay, Donna. Just let out all the anger, hurt, and pain out on me." Thinking back on it now, he loved me enough for both of us. As soon as the music started and I stepped out onto the stage, I gave the audience all I had. I went into the entertainment business because it was more money and less work hours. Not only could I provide better for my family, I could also spend more time with them.

Bananas told me once, "Honey, you walk in this place as a mom of five, but when you step out into those lights, your face lights up and you turn into the best entertainer in the business. And when you get off the stage, you're that gorgeous mom again."

Bananas taught me how to laugh again, how to love again, and most of all, how to want to be loved again. Many, many times when I got off the stage after my last show, the crowd applauded, but inside my heart was breaking. My eyes were so full of tears that I could hardly see my way through the crowd. Bananas always ran up to my side and helped me through them to my dressing room, and he held me and just let me cry myself out. He was patient and loving and caring. He was a great friend, my confidant, my manager, my lover, my husband, and father to my children. He was always there for me, just like Harold was.

I used to worry about Bananas because of the difference in our ages. He always told me, "Yeah, I'll be there when the smoke clears."

One afternoon, Mike went to the horse races and was placing a bet and suddenly dropped dead of a massive heart attack. We didn't know what was going to happen to the club then. I had three shows to do that night. Knowing Mike like we did, he wouldn't have wanted us to close, so we didn't. It was very hard for Bananas and me.

Mike also owned the Sands on the north side of town and a couple of other places that his sons ran, but he loved the one downtown where we were. He told everyone that my dancing is what bought his new Cadillac. Mike said that he was running in the red until I came along and pulled him and Bananas out of the hole they were in. He told me that I had changed the name of go-go and turned it into something respectful.

He had a large Italian funeral. His wife dressed him in an expensive suit and tie and put the gold cuff links and tie clip I had bought for him for Christmas that had his initials MJ engraved on them. He always wore them. They had been married for forty years. She was a wonderful person, and she respected Bananas and me.

After Mike's death, his oldest son came in to run the business. That didn't sit very well with Bananas and me. We shut the business down for some remodeling and to clean up the place. One afternoon while we were remodeling the club, I was standing on a ladder putting up mirrors over the stage. Suddenly, I lost my footing, and I fell on one of the tables landing on my back. The table broke when I fell, and I was lying on my back. Bananas ran over to me and asked, "Honey! Are you okay?"

All I could say was, "Please don't touch me!" I hit it so hard, I think I almost knocked myself out. After lying there a few minutes, I tried to get up. Bananas helped me, but I was extremely weak and shaking all over. I felt a painful numbness down my back and legs, but I didn't think too much of it at the time. We continued working on the place waiting on the carpet men to come by and install the new carpeting.

Bananas came up behind me and said, "You know what my greatest wish is?"

I smiled, "No. What?"

"I've always wanted to make love to you right here on this stage."

"Are you nuts?" I snorted.

"No, come on," he begged.

I shook my head, "I don't have my cream here."

"Aw, you can use that next time."

"What if I get pregnant?!"

He smiled, "Great!"

I gave up, and we made love several times on the stage where I performed. The minute I got up, I just knew I was pregnant. "You asshole!" I yelled at him. "You got me pregnant!"

"How do you know?"

"Trust me. I know."

When we got home that evening, Bananas got on the phone to take bets for that weekend's ball game, and I got into the shower. After he finished taking the bets, he took the phone off the hook and got into the shower with me. I heard him suck his breath in, and he exclaimed, "Honey! Did you see your back?"

I glanced over my shoulder at him and said, "No. Why?"

"It's all black and blue! Maybe we should take you over to the hospital and get it checked out."

I shook my head, "No. It's been a long day. I just want to get some dinner and see what the kids are doing."

We got out of the shower just as the kids were coming home from school. As always, we shared our day together. They told me about their day at school, and we told them about our day (at least as much of it as we could.)

When Mike's son Sonny took over the club, he had a completely different view of the partnership with Bananas. It got into a heated discussion, and Bananas told Sonny, "We're out of here!"

"Not with Donna you're not!"

Bananas glared at Sonny and said menacingly, "You want to bet? Donna goes where I go." He waved his hand at me and growled at Sonny, "We are a partnership. You get one of your other girls to keep the crowd happy." Then he poked Sonny in the chest. "Now, you pay me our part of the business, and we're out of here."

Sonny didn't have the power to mess with Bananas. He wrote him out a check and handed it to him. Bananas grabbed the check in one hand and my arm in the other, and we turned our backs on the A-Lounge. We started looking for a new place to open. I was glad to get a little break. But Bananas got me gigs all over the country and for more money than I was making before.

One night when he came home, I noticed the dark circles under his eyes, and he didn't have the pep he used to. I consoled him that night and encouraged him. He was depressed because the age of computers was coming in, and it was getting harder and harder for him to do his bookie business. We had a long discussion that night. I said, "I'm tired, Bananas, and I don't want to run all over the country anymore." I sighed and admitted, "I think I'm pregnant."

His black eyes lit up, "That's great, Honey! That's a dream come true for me!" He took my hand and said, "It will be a boy, and he's going to look just like you, and you're going to name him Venanzio after me."

"We'll see. I really don't want to saddle him with such a long name."

He smiled and said, "Well, we can discuss that later."

We found a large cocktail lounge / dinner club for sale in Columbus formerly known as the Bottoms Up. The location and price were what we were looking for, and we put an offer on it, which was accepted by the owner. We sank a lot of money into it, remodeling and cleaning it up, and put in a new sound system. We also built a firm stage and a dressing room for me. Bananas changed the name to the Climax. I didn't care for the name, but I knew Bananas knew what he was doing since he had been in this kind of business a long time.

After a night of dancing up on stage again, the next morning I couldn't get out of bed. I began experiencing a burning, painful, shooting pain down my right leg and lower back. Bananas always massaged me and put liniment on my muscles; and after going to the chiropractor, I got better. Then I turned the wrong way, and my back went out again.

In the meantime, I was pretty sure I was pregnant. We went to see Dr. Price, who confirmed that I was twelve weeks pregnant. We agreed that I should stop dancing until after the baby was born, and I got my figure back; but I continued to sing and tell jokes. We completed all our signed contracts on other gigs I had and didn't sign any more until after I gave birth.

Our lounge was a success, and we stole business from all the other lounges in town, including the A-Lounge. We had the whole state in our back pocket, and we were enjoying the ride. Getting even with Sonny was a feather in Bananas's cap. Mike was a wonderful friend and partner who treated everyone with respect and honesty, but his sons were nothing like him. They were selfish backstabbers.

As I began to show, I stayed home because I didn't want the audience to see me until I got my figure back. Bananas's bookie business wasn't going as good as it used to. He had an apartment down town that he ran the operation from. The FBI set up surveillance across the street from Bananas's apartment.

On one of my appointments with Dr. Price, I told him, "There's something terribly wrong because I'm in pain all the time. Sometimes worse than others."

He patted me on the shoulder and replied, "You're a little older now, and it's been a while since you gave birth."

My baby was eight years old and I was twenty-eight. It didn't make sense to me, but I trusted him. After all, he was a medical doctor, wasn't he?

As the baby grew inside of me, it put more and more pressure on my spine. I stayed home most of the time because of all the pain I was experiencing. It became more and more difficult for me to walk up and down the stairs. Since we had a three-level house, getting around the house became extremely difficult. Bananas kept telling me, "It's okay, Honey. It won't be much longer, and we'll be back in the swing of things. You'll see."

One night he came home after working at the club and woke me up and said, "Honey, I don't feel well. Will you get up and make me some coffee?"

I glanced at the clock on the nightstand and asked, "Coffee at this time of morning?"

He nodded, "Yeah."

I crawled out of bed and slipped into my housecoat and made my way down to the kitchen. He went into the living room and turned on the TV. The entire wall behind the dining room table was mirrored, and I could see him in the mirror sitting there on the sofa. Suddenly he gasped and grabbed his chest and fell toward the coffee table. I dropped the pot of water I had in my hand and ran over to him and picked his head up into my lap. "Don't leave me, Bananas!" I cried. "Please don't leave me!"

He didn't respond. I screamed, "*Julie! Julie!*"

Our housekeeper ran down the stairs and saw me holding Bananas on the floor and called 911. The ambulance came and took him to East Mercy Hospital where he died a few hours later. "*Oh no!*" I screamed, "*not again, God!*"

Chapter 14

I was twenty-nine years old and seven and a half months pregnant with our son and with a business that I couldn't run by myself and had a lot of money sunk into it. I let his family plan the funeral. I was in a fog again, and I signed whatever they needed. I didn't know what I was going to do, and I knew I couldn't do anything until after the birth of our child.

Bananas knew so many people that his funeral was the largest I had ever seen. He had four limousines just to carry all the flowers and six motorcycle cops to lead the way to the Catholic cemetery where he was laid to rest. There were at least four hundred people at the funeral. Mom and Dad and all my children rode with me in the limousine. There was a doctor with me all during the service and at the cemetery.

During the viewing, I stood in front of his casket, and I felt my heart breaking again. It was being torn wide open, and I stared blankly down at his face. The man that Bananas was partners with at the new club was also a client of ours at the A-Lounge. He came up beside me and said, "You know, Bananas didn't have anything in the lounge."

I knew that we had both worked on remodeling it and getting it ready for opening night. I thought to myself, *How can this guy stand here over my husband's body, not even cold yet, and say that to me!* I gave him the coldest look I could and muttered, "Whatever." I stared back down at my husband, and the tears came again. I tried to hold him in my arms and stroke his beautiful salt and pepper wavy hair.

Mom and Dad came up and pulled me away. My Bananas was gone forever! Now what? My baby began to move inside of me as though to tell me, *I'm here. I'm a part of him. You have me and my brother and sisters.* The movement of that tiny baby helped me to go on.

After the funeral, there were all kinds of food all over the kitchen and dining room. I looked up at Julie and asked, "Why did you make so much?"

She shook her head. "I didn't. People have been bringing it and dropping it all off all day."

By 10:00 p.m., everyone was gone except for Mom and Dad. They were still there for me and the kids. I was still in shock. I couldn't believe that God took another husband away from me. I had no idea what I was going to do. I knew I had to concentrate on having the baby, and then plan on what I was going to do for the rest of my life.

A few months later, I found out that the Climax club went out of business. I thought it might be because without Bananas and me there to run it, Bob ran it into the ground. I guess I was right. I didn't feel sorry for him. The biggest thing that hurt was that all of my and Bananas's hard work went right down the drain.

"What are you going to do now?" Mom asked.

"I'm going to concentrate on my kids and having this baby, and then I'll go from there," I reassured them.

I was in terrible pain carrying my sixth child. I asked Dr. Price to please do something because I couldn't stand the pain any longer. He only shook his head and told me that there was nothing he could do. Mom called the doctor one day and told him, "There is something seriously wrong with Donna. She is in pain all the time. You have to do something!"

He told Mom, "I think Donna is having a nervous breakdown from losing two husbands within five years."

Mom replied, "If Donna says the pain is unbearable, then it is! It's all in her back. Donna has always been a strong a person. You must believe her and help her!"

"My hands are tied until she gives birth," he replied quietly.

Eventually, everything started getting back to normal for the children, and I tried to keep myself as busy as I could. Then on Friday, October 4th, 1973, Dr. Price said that I should have my baby.

I didn't go into labor, and he had to put me in labor. I was lying on the delivery table, and Dr. Price was at my feet on a stool, and I began screaming, "It's in my back! It's in my back! Dear God, it's in my back!" Suddenly I went into convulsions during labor, and the baby went into convulsions.

When I started to come out of it, I looked down at the doctor, and his face was white as he snarled, "I can't deliver the baby this way!"

I don't know if I passed out or they put me out. When I woke up, the baby wasn't crying, and he looked so blue. "Let me see him! Let me see him!" I screamed. They wouldn't let me see him, and the nurse rushed him out of the room. I think they must have given me something to knock me out because I didn't wake up until six hours later.

When I woke up, Bananas's family and my Mom and Dad were surrounding the bed. Mom told me that the baby and I had a hard time, but he was fine. He weighed ten pounds three ounces and was twenty-one and a half inches long. He had a full head of dark black hair and an olive complexion. He had the longest eyelashes and darkest eyes I had ever seen on a newborn. The doctor said they had to keep him in the incubator because he wasn't breathing well on his own.

They finally wheeled me down in a wheelchair to see him after I insisted. He was lying spread eagle, and his arms and legs touched the sides of the incubator. He was so beautiful. He was lying there with his eyes wide open looking around. What should have been the whites of his eyes were solid bloodshot red. When I asked about it, the nurse reassured me that it would go away after a while.

Before I came home from the hospital, they did an X-ray of my spine, and the doctor said he couldn't find anything wrong. I didn't believe him, but I couldn't argue with him. We stayed in the hospital six days because of the hard time we had during delivery. I named my beautiful baby boy Venanzio Christopher Casasanta. I promised Bananas that I would, except I changed the middle name George to Christopher, and we call him by his middle name. I didn't want him to be a Junior since we already had a Junior.

When we finally got to go home, the kids were all excited to see me and their new baby brother. Donna Kay thought he was her own little doll to play with. Cheryl, Debbie, and Terry took him to heart like he was their very own. Junior was ecstatic that he finally had a baby brother. Christopher never lacked for attention.

I continued to have back pains and could hardly stand. Two days after we had come home from the hospital, I woke up screaming in terrible pain. I called for Julie because I couldn't move from the waist down; and every time I tried to move my legs, the pain was unbearable. The children had already left for school, and they were spared seeing me in so much pain.

Julie called 911, and the paramedics showed up to take me to the hospital. I pleaded with them, "Please don't move me! Dear God, please don't move me!"

One of the paramedics told me, "If you can stand it long enough for us to get a board under you, it will relieve some of the pain by keeping your spine straight."

He was right. Once they got the board under me, I did feel some relief. I told them I had to relieve myself, but they told me I had to wait until I got to the hospital. Once we got to the hospital, I was rolled into the hallway because there were no beds available. I kept begging everyone that walked by me, "Please, please, please, I'm in pain. My bladder needs emptying." I tried to relieve myself, but my kidneys were not functioning, and I began to swell up.

After a few hours, a doctor passed. "What's wrong with this patient? Who's her doctor? Get him here now!" he demanded.

He glanced down at me and his eyes softened. "Don't worry. This is not my field, but I'll get you some help."

In the meantime, my body was filling up with poison. I turned nauseas, and I tried to turn my head to keep from swallowing the vomit, but it spilled out into my hair. I began to cry, and I wondered, *Dear Lord, how much longer do I have to suffer?*

Suddenly Apple's wife appeared beside me. Norma and Apple were friends of Bananas and mine. "How did you know where I was?" I whispered.

"I called your house to check up on you, and the baby and Julie told me what happened."

She stroked my hair and noticed the vomit. As a nurse scurried by, she grabbed her arm and demanded, "Get me some clean water and a clean hospital gown for her, and I'll clean her up since none of you seem to have the time!"

The nurse shook her head and said, "You cannot touch her until a doctor has been assigned to her."

Norma's blue eyes turned to ice and she growled, "You get me some clean water, and I'll clean this woman up and you catheterize her, so her bladder can empty itself, and I mean now!"

Several other nurses glanced up from their busy work, and the nurse Norma was shouting at just stood there dumbfounded. "If you don't move," Norma screamed, "I'll bring this hospital down! You cannot let her suffer like this!"

A tall doctor about mid forty with black hair that was graying at the temples walked up to us and said calmly, "I'm Dr. Harding, an orthopedic surgeon, and I'm going to try and get you as comfortable as possible. I will also transfer you to Mount Carmel Hospital." He signed the order for me to be catheterized, and Norma cleaned me up and put a fresh hospital gown on me. She washed my long black hair and rode with me in the ambulance to Mount Carmel.

As soon as I got to the hospital, they had a room ready for me. When they rolled me into the room on the stretcher, I suddenly got frightened, and I begged, "Please don't take me off the board!"

The ambulance driver said, "We have to."

"Leave the damn thing!" Norma snapped. "I'll bring it to you personally or just let me buy it! How much do you want for it?!"

The paramedic shook his head and left the room.

The hospital immediately started doing X-rays and various tests to try and figure out what was wrong with my back. Around 8:00 p.m., Dr. Harding walked in and said, "We'll have to do a spinal."

I looked at him stupidly. He smiled and explained, "That's where we insert red die into the spine, which will show what is causing you so much pain." His kind brown eyes softened. "We'll have to give you two sets of injections in the spine to help with the pain as much as possible. I'll have to warn you that it will hurt because I have to put you in a fetal position."

I cried, and I wondered, *Dear Lord, how much more?*

"Are you ready?" he asked.

I nodded.

He gave me the injections, but I couldn't tell if they worked. He waited a few minutes more and then gave me another set of injections. "That should do it," he said. "We'll wait fifteen minutes more for them to start working."

To this day, I don't know if the injections worked. Before I realized what was happening, a nurse pushed on my head while an orderly pushed on my legs to try and put my head between my knees. I felt pain shoot up my spine, and I screamed in agony, "Stop! Stop! Oh, please stop!"

"I am sorry, Mrs. Casasanta," the doctor said, "we have no choice." He injected the die into my spine and ran me through the machine, which gave him the images he needed to see.

When they finally had me stretched back out again, the pain subsided somewhat, but there was still tremendous pain. I was taken back to my room and put on a morphine drip.

A few hours later, Dr. Harding walked into my room with my chart and said, "Mrs. Casasanta, you have three ruptured disks and a pinched nerve. Unfortunately, the nerve that is pinched controls your bladder and kidneys. We will have to perform emergency surgery."

I barely had time to digest all this information at once, and the tears began to slide down my cheeks. "Your body is very weak from just giving birth, but we cannot wait. We have to perform surgery to correct the problem immediately."

Dr. Harding didn't tell me, but I found out later that he told Mom and Dad that the possibility of my survival through the surgery was less than forty percent due to the weakness and strain my body had been through the last nine months and the baby pressing on my spine. But God got me through. I guess He still had plans for me.

After surgery, the doctor came into my room and said, "You may never walk again, and there is a possibility that you could be paralyzed from the waist down on the right side."

I felt the tears well up again.

He patted my hand and continued, "I have to tell you, Mrs. Casasanta, that you may have to wear a bag on the outside of your body for the rest of your life to empty your bladder. Only time will tell."

The tears began to fall. *Oh my God,* I thought, *how much more? How much more? Am I being punished?*

After the doctor left my room, I began to pray, *Dear God, I'm thirty years old and a widow for the second time in my life with six children to raise. Please give me my bladder and kidneys back before I leave here. I will work on the rest of me when I get home to my children because they will help me to get better. With your strength, dear Lord, I know you can make me well again because I need to be able to support my family. In Jesus's name I pray. Amen.*

After my back surgery, I pleaded with the nurses every time they came into my room to take the catheter out and let me try it on my own. Sometimes I could talk them into it, which was usually the late-night shift. After about an hour, they would take the catheter out and let me sit on a bedside potty-chair after I drank a lot of liquids. As I sat on the bedside commode, I prayed over and over, *Dear Lord, please. Please, dear Lord. I believe in You. I trust in You. I know you hear my prayers.*

On the morning that I was being released from the hospital, I begged the doctor, "Please, Dr. Harding, please let me try it one more time. Please don't make me go home like this."

He shook his head sadly and said, "It's no use, Donna. You must accept this."

"Please let me try it one more time. Please take the catheter out and let me pray while I sit on the toilet."

"I don't believe in prayer."

"It doesn't matter what you believe. It's what I believe that counts!"

He finally gave up and let the nurse take the catheter out. After she removed the catheter, she helped me to the bathroom.

"Please leave me alone in here. I'll call you if I need you," I told her. Then I began to pray with all my heart. I sat on the toilet a long time praying over and over. Suddenly I felt this warm tingling sensation, which started at the top of my head and began to flow down through my body. I could see a glowing light all around me in the bathroom, and I knew that God was going to answer my prayer.

I began to cry and praise my Lord. I whispered over and over, "Thank you, Lord. Thank you, Lord. Thank you, Lord. How wonderful and merciful you are." As the light started to disperse, I heard water tinkling in the toilet, and I could tell that I was finally urinating on my own.

I cried harder and rang the bell for the nurse. Several nurses ran into my room and jerked open the bathroom door. They all told me that they could see a warm light around me, and there was no window in the bathroom. I smiled up at them with tears of joy flowing down my cheeks and cried, "Do you hear that? Do you hear that?"

They laughed. The head nurse said, "Yes, Donna, we hear it!"

I smiled at her in triumph. "You tell Dr. Harding that my God is a great God, and He does answer prayer!"

Chapter 15

I was in and out of the hospital for nine weeks for therapy to learn how to use a walker. Everything Bananas and I had saved was consumed in hospital and doctor bills. When I was finally released to come home, I had to face my children in a wheelchair and a walker like an old woman. Yeah, an old woman of thirty! The kids had grown so much in those nine weeks! Debbie and Junior had taken charge of their younger siblings, and Cheryl was glued to Christopher.

While I tried to get better, the children jumped in and took care of their baby brother, cleaned the house, and cooked the meals. I was so proud of them. God had sent me good kids. Cheryl and Debbie worried about Chris so much that he hardly ever had a chance to take a full nap. Every time he was quiet or very still, one of them would walk up to the baby bed and shake him to make sure he was all right.

It was hard for us. I lost the lounge and all the money we had put into it. I also lost a lot of my friends when Bananas died. I guess I couldn't do anything for them anymore, and very few of them called to check up on me to see if I or the kids needed anything.

Gradually, I went from a walker to a back and leg brace. I was in constant pain and had to use my walker when the pain was unbearable. We moved the baby crib down to the third level of the house, and I stayed in the den. We moved a bed down there as well. My sister Delores came to stay with me to help, and she had a three-year-old of her own.

One afternoon while the kids were in school, it was chilly downstairs, and I tried to start a fire in the fireplace. I was having trouble getting it to light. There was a gas can in the laundry room by the den, and I picked it up and sprinkled some gas on the news-paper I had laid over the wood. When I lit the match to throw in to the fireplace, it ignited the gas that had sprinkled on my hand. It scared me so bad that I threw the match into the fireplace along with the gas can. Suddenly, flames shot out of the fireplace and climbed up the wall and ignited the curtains and carpeting. I screamed, "*Oh My God!*"

I grabbed up Chris from his crib, and I struggled to get up the few steps to the second floor where the front entrance was. I yanked open the door and saw some teenagers just getting off their bus. I yelled at them, "*Come get my baby. Please come get my baby!*"

One of the boys ran over and took Chris. I yelled at him, "*Call the fire department! My house is on fire!*"

The boy wanted to come down to help me, but I stopped him because I didn't want him to get hurt. Billy Ray was asleep in the bed-room down the stairs, and I struggled to get him up and out of the house also. Another girl picked him up and ran him across the street to her house. I struggled back down the stairs and filled a bucket with water that was in the laundry room, and I started dousing out the fire. I kept lugging buckets of water over to the fireplace and throw-ing the water on the fire until I heard the firetrucks coming. One of the firemen helped me out of the house while two more dragged the hose down to the den and put out the fire.

When it was all over, my den was a wet, scorched mess. I cried for a few minutes, shaking my head and wondering, *What else, Lord? What else?* Then God reminded me. He saved me and the two children.

One of the firemen told me before they left that it was a miracle the gas can didn't explode, and that I was very fortunate because some-one upstairs was looking after me. I nodded and said, "Thank you."

I wasn't happy in that house anymore. It reminded me of Bananas, and the fire was like the last push to make me want to leave. I also hated looking like a cripple when I once had been on top of the world. All the neighbors knew who I once was, and I didn't like being a cripple in front of them. I wanted to move away from there and live where no one knew me.

The kids and I looked after each other as best we could. With all the doctor and hospital bills, money was even tighter, and it became apparent that I was not going to be able to keep that house. On top of the usual house payment, utility bills, and groceries for six kids, Debbie loved horses, and before Bananas died, we bought her a horse for her fourteenth birthday. The stable bill was eighty dollars per month, which included feed. Junior loved cross-country bike racing, and we had bought him a dirt bike. I wanted my kids to be able to keep the things that they loved, so I looked at buying a house in the country.

While driving back and forth to my therapy sessions, I had to pass a huge old country house. It looked to be one hundred years old with a huge red barn and a fenced-in area for horses. Something about that house drew me to it. There were huge trees in the large front yard that provided shade year-round. Every time I passed this house, my eyes kept wondering over to it and admiring it, and I thought, *What a nice, peaceful place this is to live.*

A couple of months later, there was a for sale sign in the front yard. I pulled over on the side of the road and wrote down the number. I called it after I got home and made an appointment to see it. I didn't tell the children about it until after I had seen it and put a down payment on it.

The next day, I met the realtor at the house. The driveway was crushed shell, but once you got up to the three-car garage, it turned into concrete. You had to walk up these concrete steps to the side entrance of the house, and I had a hard time climbing them. I was hopeful that as I got better, I could climb them easily.

As soon as I stepped on the porch and the realtor unlocked the door, which led into the kitchen, this sense of belonging just washed all over me. There were three bedrooms upstairs and another one downstairs. There was only one bath, and it was upstairs with an old-fashioned clawfoot tub. Off the kitchen was a den with another door that led into another smaller room, which could be used for storage or another bedroom. As I walked through the house, I saw a lot of things I could do with this house to make it a home for me and the children.

The door to the basement was off the kitchen. The realtor said that I was welcome to go down there, but that she was going to stay in the kitchen while I looked around. I didn't think too much of it at the time. The basement was huge, and the walls were damp with moisture running down the walls. It was cooler down there than the rest of the house. I noticed the washer and dryer hookup was in the basement also. I knew that the kids and I had to go down there a lot doing the laundry. With seven of us, we had our fair share of laundry. At the very back of the basement, there were shelves that looked like they use to hold canning jars of food and other items to keep cool. The hairs on the back of my neck stood up on end, but I figured it was just because it was so much cooler.

There were four stalls in the barn with a loft. I knew Debbie could keep her horse with her at the farm, and we wouldn't have to board any more. There was a huge field to the left of the house that I could have fenced in for horses, and there was plenty of woods a little farther away from the house for Junior to ride his minibike. I just had this feeling that the kids and I could be happy there.

One evening, I sat on the couch with the kids around me, and they watched me quietly. They knew I had been gone a lot, and they worried about what I was going to do, especially the older ones who remember when I attempted suicide. I looked at each of them, and my heart broke at the worry I saw in the depths of their eyes. I knew deep down they wanted to know what we were going to do.

Debbie was the first to speak up, "Mom, what are we going to do? Can we still afford to live here?" Debbie was always the worry-wart and more resourceful of the children.

Junior piped up next, "Where are we going to go, Mom?"

"Why do we have to go anywhere?" Terry asked innocently.

Cheryl stomped her foot and cried, "I don't care what you guys say! I'm staying here with my baby brother!"

We all laughed. It felt good to laugh again. Oh, how much I loved my children!

I shook my head and whispered, "Well, we're going to move from here out to the country. I love all of you very, very much, and we'll have to work together to get through this. It's not as nice a house as we live in now, but if we work together, we'll make it into a nice house that we can all love.

Debbie was ecstatic when she found out that we could have her horse there. Junior couldn't wait to check out the woods on his minibike.

I hugged each one of them and said, "I will need your help."

Everyone nodded in agreement.

I smiled. "Working together, we'll get through this with God's help no matter what lies ahead for us."

I felt pride swell up inside of me for me and my children, and I continued, "We are not quitters! We are strong! And we are doubly strong together! Our daddies did not live and die for nothing! They made us strong when they were here with us, and we will stand strong for them together!"

A couple of months later, we moved into that old farmhouse; and, well, let's just say that a lot of strange things happened there, but that's another story...

9 781645 310730